An Introduction to
General American Phonetics

An Introduction to
General American
Phonetics Third Edition

Charles G. Van Riper

Dorothy E. Smith

Western Michigan University

HARPER & ROW, PUBLISHERS

New York Hagerstown Philadelphia San Francisco London

Sponsoring Editor: Alan Spiegel
Project Editor: Brigitte Pelner
Designer: Helen Iranyi
Production Manager: Marion A. Palen
Compositor: Syntax International Pte. Ltd.
Printer and Binder: The Murray Printing Company
Art Studio: Danmark & Michaels, Inc.

An Introduction to General American Phonetics, Third Edition

Copyright © 1979   by Charles G. Van Riper and Dorothy E. Smith

Library of Congress Cataloging in Publication Data

Van Riper, Charles Gage, Date—
   An introduction to general American phonetics.

  Includes index.
  1. English language—Phonetics. I. Smith,
Dorothy Edna, joint author. II. Title.
PE1135.V35   1979   421′.54   78-15339
ISBN 0-06-046779-7

Contents

Preface to the Third Edition

Since 1954 when this text was first published, we have sought to find ways of improving its usefulness to students and instructors. In this, the third edition, we feel we have created a better tool than the ones offered before. We have incorporated linguistic principles that are coming to play a major role in modern speech pathology. New chapters dealing with the transcription of on-going speech and narrow transcription are included. The application of phonemics and phonetics to the understanding of the problems of deviant speech and language, foreign accent, and dialect should prove more useful. We have tried throughout to use reading passages and transcription material that are attractive to students and will facilitate their mastery of both without pain or boredom. And, finally, as in the other editions, we have sought to minimize the chore work of the instructor. We hope you will like this revision.

CHARLES G. VAN RIPER
DOROTHY E. SMITH

An Introduction to
General American
Phonetics

1 The Phonetic Alphabet as a Tool

So you've set out to master a new tool—the phonetic alphabet. Why? Because you may plan to be a newscaster who must handle a fascinating diversity of strange names and places? Because the world has grown smaller and closer together and you may need to be able to pronounce your Korean neighbor's name, or the name of the town you will visit in the Ural mountains of Russia? Because you may have to work with an aphasic whose speech sounds have become confused? Or help a child with an articulation disorder? You cannot correct such a child's errors unless your own knowledge of how standard sounds are produced is accurate. Because you are an actor who must assume the dialectical utterances of your character so that it sounds genuine? Because you are a student majoring in English, linguistics, speech pathology or audiology, and you need to know the phonology of our language? Or for a hundred other reasons. No matter; we welcome you to the study of the phonetics of the English language.

If the Romans had been as wise as the Greeks, there would be less need for this book, which has as its prime purpose the teaching of the International Phonetic Alphabet. As it is, our English alphabet as a tool for indicating the pronunciation of the spoken word is woefully inadequate, as any foreigner will be quick to tell you. We, of course, take it for granted. The haze of forgetfulness that covers the unpleasant experiences of childhood has fortunately wiped out, for most of us at least, the suffering and struggling of our early efforts to master spelling and reading. It is only when we have to master unfamiliar words or a dialect, or when we have to teach correct pronunciation to speech-defective children or to foreigners that we realize vividly how inadequate an alphabet we really have.

HOW IT GREW

Most scholars feel that the first form of our alphabet originated about 4000 years ago when the Phoenicians modified some of the script symbols of the Egyptians to fit their Semitic language. This grandparent of alphabets had many symbols for the Phoenician consonants but none for the vowels. You might think it impossible to use such an alphabet, but the following sentence will probably be intelligible without any vowel symbols: gd mrnng stdnts; th clss wll plz km t rdr. The Greeks who stole their alphabet from the Phoenicians took as many letters as they needed to fit the spoken consonants of their own language. They were very wise in their modification, however, since they chose only one symbol to represent each consonant sound. In a sense they had a remarkably phonetic alphabet. But the Phoenicians used many more consonants

| Phoenician | Greek | Roman | English |

FIGURE 1

than the Greeks, so the latter took some of the symbols left over and employed them to represent their six vowel sounds. This was a tremendous improvement in providing a written representation of spoken speech, and the Roman and English alphabets still employ them, though not in their original form. Many of us were taught—and very incorrectly—that the only vowels in English are *A, E, I, O, U*, and sometimes *Y*. Actually, we have a total of at least 18 vowels used in English speech today, and yet we represent them by the same 6 vowel symbols used by the ancient Greeks. Figure 1 represents the changes in these symbols down to the present time.

Five or six vowels should be enough for any language, but unfortunately languages precede alphabets, and when the Romans conquered the Greeks and adopted many of their civilized tools, they took over their alphabet without adding any symbols to represent the five additional vowel sounds they themselves possessed. Unwisely, they used the same five letters for their ten vowels, so that each symbol came to represent two sounds. Written Latin therefore became less phonetic and unable to represent clearly the pronunciation of the spoken language. The Romans did what they could to remedy this early error: they wrote the letters twice to indicate the long form, so we get words like *weed* to distinguish its pronunciation from *wed*. They also used little accent marks above the top of the letter to indicate a different vowel, and thus began the system of diacritical marking which cursed dictionary exploration in our schooldays. If the Romans had followed the Greeks in inventing a new symbol for each sound, and if our modern languages had followed suit, no text such as this would have been required. But unfortunately we followed the Romans rather than the Greeks, and our present written language represents our spoken speech with only meager accuracy.

THOSE CONFUSING DIACRITICAL MARKINGS

Up until a few years ago dictionaries used a complicated, imprecise assortment of diacritical markings to indicate pronunciation. Even in the most modern of dictionaries today, you might have difficulty deciding how to say *är* and *âr*. The first is the word *are*, and the second word is *air*. There are six different ways to indicate the letter *a*: āble, dâre, ärt, Amé, əlone, act.

2

A thoroughly phonetic language should have exactly as many letters in its alphabet as it has different sounds. In English we have at least 44 different sounds, but only 23 letters to symbolize them. Twenty-three? Are there not 26 letters in our alphabet? Yes, but some are unnecessary. Do we really need our letters *c*, *q*, and *x?* The sounds represented by *c* are usually *k* or *s; q* is unnecessary since a *k* or a *kw* would handle almost all *q* words, and the *x* could be replaced much more conveniently and phonetically by *ks* or *gz*, as in *six* (sicks) or *exit* (egg-zit). So we have 23 letters to symbolize 44 sounds, and millions of little children learning to read have been forced to suffer because of the confusion built into our language.

Many attempts have been made to simplify our spelling and make it less confusing. President Theodore Roosevelt did his utmost and failed; so did George Bernard Shaw. For years the Chicago Tribune valiantly spelled *freight* as *frate* before it surrendered. One of the most enduring attempts has been the initial teaching alphabet (ITA) which some schools in England and America use to teach children beginning reading. It is a compromise between how our words look in traditional orthography and how our words sound. Since it helps some children and confuses others, it has been going in and out of fashion pretty regularly during the last 50 years. But too much has been written in the regular alphabet, and too many people have been taught it for any of these attempts to gain widespread acceptance.

THE QUEEN'S ENGLISH

The English language once did have, however, a wonderful chance to improve itself, and might possibly have succeeded had Queen Elizabeth I been less fickle. English spelling during the reign of that great queen was still fairly unstable. Even Shakespeare spelled his own name three different ways, and as long as the Elizabethan came pretty close to representing the Queen's English, his spelling was entirely acceptable. There lived at that time a remarkable scholar, Charles Butler, who devised a system of spelling and wrote several texts and grammars using it. It seemed for a time that his new system of spelling would come to dominate the entire publication field. But he was a protégé of Lord Essex, and when the Queen turned her affections elsewhere, Charles Butler lost favor, and his beautiful system of phonetic English was forgotten. Many generations of school children have cause to regret love's labor lost.

The Roman alphabet came to England, probably by way of Ireland, and the Irish monasteries in the British Isles served as nuclei for its adoption by the clergy and the educated leaders of the Anglo-Saxons. King Alfred encouraged his people to use this Roman alphabet and, long before the Norman conquest, its symbols were being used and abused in the representation of Old English speech. The Celts gave us few words except *curse* (*cursian*); but the Nordic invasions and settlements left behind many new words with new sounds to be represented by too meager a set of Latin letters. When the Normans came to England in 1066, they caused even greater linguistic havoc. The governing classes in both church and state for a long time were made up of Normans, and they used their own variety of the Old French language which, though based on Latin, was itself a strange conglomeration of tongues. But by the end of the thirteenth century Englishmen were speaking not French, but English. The French influence, however, had a great impact on English spelling, and although the pronunciation of the words changed, the letters used to represent them immortalized the Norman influence. In Old French, for instance, the diphthong was gradually lost, but we still have the words *fruit* and *suit* spelled in the old way. In some cases the spelling of the common people's English word was changed to look like a word used by the nobility.

Thus, *tough*, coming from the Anglo-Saxon *toh*, acquired the *ou* of French words like *touch* (*toucher*). The spelling of the word *house* has a similar history.

In 1476 William Caxton introduced England to the process of printing. Since many of the early printers were Dutch, they sometimes added letters or changed the spelling to conform to their own notions of how words which were similar in the two languages should be spelled. The English word *ghastly* probably got its unpronounced *h* from the Dutch printers in this way. At any rate, the invention of printing helped to fix forever many of the peculiar conbinations of letters and to render our written language even more unphonetic and, to a foreigner, unpronounceable.

THE GREAT VOWEL SHIFT

Throughout this period many changes in pronunciation of familiar words were occurring. As Old English passed into Middle English, many long vowels became shortened. Old English *axian*, with a long *a*, became *asken* in Middle English, much like our word *ask* today. The letter designating the vowel did not change with its pronunciation, however, The converse also occurred; the Old English word *bacan* became Middle English *baken*, much like our derived word *bake*. But the major change in English pronunciation took place in the time between Chaucer and Shakespeare. This is known among linguists as the Great Vowel Shift. No one knows why such a profound change occurred, but most of the long vowels gradually came to be pronounced with higher tongue positions and smaller mouth openings, and those which could not be raised were made into diphthongs. Thus the number 5, pronounced *feef* by Chaucer, had become *five* by Shakespeare's day. The word *root* was first pronounced *rota*, then as *rute* with a long *oo*. *Down*, similarly, has descended from a word pronounced, as it is in Scotland today, as *doon*.

In certain words in the English of Chaucer's time, people pronounced letters which now are silent. *Sword* had five sounds in it; *folk* had four; the number 2 had three. Although the sounds were dropped out of spoken language, the letters remained in the written form. In this way, too, modern English was made unphonetic. Some sounds have been lost forever, for example, the two velar fricatives [y] and [x], but we also have gained two others; the *zh* [ʒ] sound as in *measure*, and the *j* [dʒ] sound, as in *judge*. Only in a few words has the spelling been changed to fit the changing pronunciation. *Mill* was once spelled and pronounced as *miln*, but we still have the silent endings of *column* and *autumn*.

No change in spelling occurred to parallel the Great Vowel Shift. Pronunciation changed but spelling did not. The resulting distortion leaves us with vowel symbols which often have no correspondence to the sounds they are supposed to represent. In 1755 Dr. Samuel Johnson published his *Dictionary of the English Language* in two folio volumes, and the spelling of English has changed in only minor ways since his time. So we have a language in which one letter may represent as many as eight different sounds and in which one sound may be spelled in 15 different ways. Our orthography bears little relation to our pronunciation, and it is for this reason that we must have a phonetic alphabet when our occupations require us to transcribe and reproduce exact pronunciation. Diacritical markings have never been adequate tools.

WHO NEEDS THE IPA?

One of these occupations requiring phonetics is speech pathology. The speech therapist in England, in order to receive official certification, must have at least three years of phonetics. In this country the phonetic requirements are not so stringent, yet all professional speech pathologists must master the use of the phonetic alphabet in the course of their training. They use it to record and to analyze articulation errors, to diagnose the speech of children who speak a jargon, to train foreign-speaking individuals to talk English without obvious accent, to teach the deaf and hard of hearing a usable speech pattern, to identify the defective vowels in disorders of phonation, and in countless other ways.

In the theater, radio, and television, training in phonetics is part of the general speech improvement process which all participants must undergo. The use of authentic dialect can best be taught phonetically. The pronunciation of foreign place names and names of people in the news can best be presented in the phonetic alphabet.

Anyone involved in the study of linguistics must have a system for recording speech sounds. No one can understand the history of the English language, nor the differences in speech patterns among people, without a thoroughgoing mastery of phonetic principles. Without phonetics, any person in the field of general speech is considered illiterate.

Even in the field of music, phonetic symbols are widely used. Singers are trained in these skills to enable them to analyze the sounds on which poor tonal quality occurs and to help them sing the foreign words of many musical masterpieces.

To sum it up, then, our English alphabet, because of its history, is too cumbersome and inaccurate a tool for your present use. First you must master a new alphabet, and it may not be as easy as you think. Most of us have been reading so long that when we think of a word we think of the way it looks. We are eye-minded rather than ear-minded—even those of us who are poor spellers. We think of the letters that make up a word rather than the sounds which compose it. The word *whose*, for example, has only three sounds in it; an *h*, an *u* (oo), and a *z*, and the word *daughter* has four. Over half of the words in a standard American dictionary have silent letters in them. You will find difficulty at first in analyzing words into their component sounds and even more difficulty in synthesizing them, but we will try to make the learning process as easy and pleasant as possible.

In learning to master any new tool, especially a complicated one, we must expect to make some mistakes, and to be clumsy in its use at first. Moreover, although we need someone to teach us, to show us how to use the tool, we also need some opportunity to manipulate it privately and without penalty so we can learn from the mistakes we are certain to make. This workbook has been designed expressly to provide such an opportunity. Self-correction of errors can be accomplished more easily in the safety of your room. Both in the reading and writing of the phonetic symbols you will find opportunities for the immediate discovery of errors, models of correct responses, and extra practice material. We have offered many hints and helps, and have anticipated some of your troubles. Any student can work largely at his own pace. We have also provided an occasional quiz to keep you on your toes, and programmed the material so that previously mastered symbols are continually reviewed, while the new symbols are introduced gradually. The reading material is designed so that it is always a bit ahead of the transcription, so far as difficulty is concerned, but this should aid rather than hinder your progress. Phonetics can be fun. This is your challenge; how soon can you learn to read and write in this new alphabet without error? [ðoz læst tu wɝdz ɑr ðə most ɪmpɔrtnt‖]

Name _____ Date _____ Score _____

Test Your Understanding

1. Why are you going to learn the IPA?

2. We have six vowel symbols, but how many vowel sounds?

3. Why did the Romans start the system of diacritical markings?

4. What three alphabet symbols can we certainly do without? Why?

5. What happened to English pronunciation during the Great Vowel Shift?

6. What is meant by being eye-minded rather than ear-minded?

2 The Sounds of American English

It has been many years since you learned your ABCs and you have probably forgotten some of the difficulties you had acquiring them. Now you must master another alphabet and we want to make the process as painless as possible. Some instructors just give their students the list of new symbols and key words that you will find on the inside front and back covers of this book, and tell them to memorize the whole batch. We will do it differently. In this chapter we will present only a few sounds at a time and use them to point out the features by which they can be recognized and classified. There is much that you do not know about the speech you have used for so many years. [ɪn fækt most əv ʌs ɑr prɪtɪ ɪgnərənt əbaut hau wi tɔk‖]

We shall seek to dispel that ignorance as we discuss the characteristics which distinguish one sound or set of sounds from another. We will be introducing the phonetic symbols of the International Phonetic Alphabet (IPA) so gradually that you will probably learn them without ever trying to do so.

CONSONANT OR VOWEL

If you were an anthropologist from Kuppa Kapi, or some other exotic island in the south seas, and trying to learn the strange language called American English, you would probably try to record phonetically a corpus (a core vocabulary) of words as spoken by the American natives, and then you would try to sort out the vowels from the consonants before trying to master their pronunciation. But how does one tell the consonants from the vowels? The vowels are always voiced; they are the cores of syllables; they are longer and stronger; they are tonal, not noisy, and they are oral (the airflow through the mouth meets no obstruction by the tongue or lips).

Were the anthropologist from such an island to come to this country and try to learn to speak our language the hard way, he would finally recognize that these strange American natives have at least 18 different vowels or vowel combinations in their speech. And, if he knew the IPA he would put them down as follows: [a] [ɑ] [ɔ] [e] [ɛ] [æ] [i] [ɪ] [o] [u] [ʊ] [ʌ] [ə] [ɝ] [ɚ] [aɪ] [aʊ] [ɔɪ].

But, how would he sort out the consonant sounds from the vowels? He would listen hard and watch our mouths for the sounds that begin syllabic pulses, or that end them. He would know that a speech sound is consonantal when the airflow meets some obstruction or constriction along the midline of the airway. He would try to identify the little noisy sounds made by lip and tongue movements as they impede the outflow of voice or air. And, perhaps he would be skillful enough to list at least the following 25 of them: [p] [b] [w] [hw] [m] [n] [ŋ] [f] [v] [θ] [ð] [s] [z] [ʃ] [ʒ] [h] [k] [g] [r] [l] [tʃ] [dʒ] [j] [d] [t].

But, listening to what must seem like gibberish, how could our native anthropologist from Kuppa Kapi tell one vowel from another vowel, or distinguish one consonant from another? He probably would first use the concept of *minimal pairs* and hunt for words, for example, which are identical except for their final sounds; pairs of words such as *cup* and *cub*, which mean entirely different things. He would then know that [p] and [b] are different consonants and, listening hard to find out in what way they differ, he would conclude that the [p] is unvoiced and the [b] is phonated (voiced). Both are made with the lips in the same way, but it is the voicing of the [b] which makes it different. In much the same fashion, our anthropologist would examine all the words he could collect, hunting for other minimal pairs such as *nose* and *rose*, in which the beginning sounds are the ones that differ, or pairs such as *shut* and *shoot*, where the vowel-like middle sounds provide the only contrasting features. By such procedures he could perhaps identify the basic sounds in our strange language and, being a professional, he would call these basic sounds *phonemes*.

SOME WORDS YOU WILL NEED TO KNOW

Throughout this book you will constantly be confronted with words whose precise meanings you will need to know. For instance, the combining form *phon* or *phone* crops up over and over again. *Phon* means sound or, more usually, speech sound. A *phoneme* is the smallest unit of speech sound capable of making a difference in meaning. As we mentioned above, *p* and *b* are two different phonemes because *cup* and *cub* are two different words.

However, each *phoneme* is comprised of several slightly different sounds, the differences between which are *not* meaningful. The way you say *k* and someone else says *k* will be slightly different, but both *k*'s belong to the same phoneme, or sound family. All of us pronounce the same sound differently when it, for example, begins a syllable, from the way we say it when it ends that syllable, and, in fact, no one says the same sound in the same word in exactly the same way every time the word is uttered.

In English, the *t* that we use in a syllable such as "too" is accompanied by a little rush of air, that is, it is *aspirated*. When the *t* ends a syllable, such as in the word *at*, we do not hear that same kind of airflow. But these *phonetic* differences are nondistinctive in English because we have no two words in our language where the aspiration or lack of it make a difference in meaning. There are other languages where there are such contrasting pairs, and in them the two kinds of *t* sounds (the aspirated and the nonaspirated) are different *phonemes*. The nonsignificant variants of a sound are called *allophones*. In English both the aspirated and unaspirated [t]'s are different allophones of the phoneme [t]; they belong to the same phonemic family. In this text we shall first be using what is called *broad* (or phonemic) *transcription*, using a unique symbol for each unique phoneme and generally ignoring the allophones until you have mastered the alphabet. Then we shall shift to *narrow transcription*, showing you how to record the little phonetic differences, the allophones, which represent precisely the way we really speak and the way a person speaks who has a speech disorder or a dialect.[1]

---

[1] Early in this text we shall often be speaking of phonetic symbols and phonetic transcription when we are really referring to phonemic symbols and transcription. Don't worry. The differences will become clear as we proceed.

phone	a speech sound
phoneme	a family of allophones meaningfully different from any other sounds
allophone	a phonetically different variant of a phoneme
phonetics	the study of all perceptibly different speech sounds, whether meaningful or not
phonemics	the study of meaningfully distinctive speech sounds

Exercise 2.1.   In order to conceptualize these word meanings, see if you can complete these statements.

1. If you want to record exactly the speech of a certain person, you would listen for _____ .

     allophones/phonemes

2. The difference between the first sounds in the words *bad* and *pad* is _____ .

     phonetic/phonemic

3. The difference between the way we say the *p* in *pan* and the *p* in *nap* is _____ .

     phonetic/phonemic

To get back to our discussion of how we produce our speech sounds, let us begin by introducing the three nasal phonemes of general American speech.

ORAL AND NASAL SOUNDS

Through what doors do our speech sounds depart when they leave us? Most of them come out of the mouth outlet, but there are three sounds that use the nose; the *m* as in *map* [mæp], the *n* as in *nose* [noz], and the [ŋ] as in *gong* [gɔŋ]. All of our speech sounds, then, can be classified as being either *oral* or *nasal*. You possess many more oral sounds than nasal sounds, and here are just a few of them written in the phonemic alphabet:

ORAL: [p b t d k g f v l r a e i o u]
NASAL: [m n ŋ]

The only unfamiliar one of the whole lot is the third nasal [ŋ], the symbol that looks like a sketch of an elephant's head and trunk. (Be sure to curl the trunk.) This is the final sound of *bang* [bæŋ]. Note that *bang* has no *g* in it at all. You do not say ban-g; you say [bæŋ]. The [ŋ] ends up in the nose, with the sound reverberating around in the nasal cavities.

All three nasal sounds get their distinctive feature of nasality by being produced with the soft palate (velum) lowered, thus opening up the back door to the nasal passageway above. Moreover, each of them plugs the oral airway in a different way, as shown in Figure 2. The [m] seals the oral airway shut with the lips, the [n] closes it off by using the front of the tongue against the upper gum, and the [ŋ] builds a barrier by humping up the back of the tongue against the lowered soft palate. The airborne sound in all these phonemes must detour to the upstairs outlet when the lower oral passageway is blocked. Prolong the last sound of each of these words and notice how you produce them: *hummmmm, pennnnnn,* and [rɪŋŋŋŋ].

Consonant Chart

MANNER OF ARTICULATION

PLACE OF ARTICULATION	Stop-Plosive		Fricative		Affricate		Nasal		Glide		Lateral	
	*UNV	V	UNV	V	UNV	V	UNV	V	UNV	V	UNV	V
Bilabial	p	b						m	hw	w		
Labio-dental			f	v								
Lingua-dental			θ	ð								
Lingua-alveolar	t	d	s	z				n		j		l
Lingua-palatal			ʃ	ʒ	tʃ	dʒ				r		
Velar	k	g						ŋ				
Glottal			h									

* UNV means Unvoiced, and V means Voiced.

FIGURE 2

It is interesting that people think we talk nasally when we have a cold. The reverse is actually true; our nasal passages are plugged up, and our speech is *denasal.* You can prove this to yourself by holding your nose as you say "My nose is numb."

Because the [ŋ] sound is usually spelled *ng,* it may give you some trouble. Remember that there is no [n] sound in [ŋ], and no [g] either; [ŋ] is a separate sound in itself. You can hum a tune with it. Say the word *tongue* [tʌŋ] and then add a [g] to it. It will not sound at all like *tongue,* a word that has only three sounds, not four. Observe how that word *tongue* is spelled as compared with how it is sounded. Phonetically, only the *t* is valid. There's no [o], or [n], or [g], or [u], or [e]. The three sounds are [t], the vowel [ʌ], and the nasal [ŋ].

Well, you have three symbols already. Let's see if you can recognize them in this short reading passage. Try to translate it without looking up a single symbol. We bet you can.

[lɛts sɪŋ aʊr sɔŋ naʊ| sɛd mɛrɪ pæntɪŋlɪ| æz ðə mun kem ovɚ ðə maʊntɪn|| o| nʌts tu sɪŋɪŋ| sɛd ðə mæn| aɪm hʌŋgrɪ|| lɛts go gɛt ə hæmbɚgɚ ɪnstɛd|| dæmɪt| frɛd| mɛrɪ kraɪd| kænt ju ɛvɚ bi romæntɪk|| nɑt hwɛn maɪ bɛliz rʌmblɪŋ| hi ænsɚd||]

SONANT OR SURD

These terms refer to another basic way that we distinguish one speech sound from another. *Sonant* means that the sound is *voiced;* that the vocal folds are vibrating. *Surd* means that it is *unvoiced,* almost whispered. Prolong the *z* sound and notice that your vocal folds are vibrating; that the *z* is *sonant.* Then, prolong the *s,* and notice that it is unvoiced, or *surd.* Plug up your ears with your fingers, and then *prolong* for a second or two the last sounds of the following words to see if they are sonant or surd: *fish, thing, filth, through, enough.* Two of them are sonant, and three are surd. Are the three nasal sounds [m], [n], and [ŋ] voiced or voiceless? We hope you said that they are all sonant.

Now use the same procedure as you say the following nonsense words to determine whether or not the *middle* consonant is sonant or surd. If you hear a break in the phonation, the middle consonant is voiceless (surd); if not, it is voiced (sonant.) Try to say them very slowly: *ulu, utu, ono, ava, ofo*. Now try to find which of the following sounds are surd: [m s p d b l k z].

From these exercises you have begun to recognize the distinctive feature of voicing and unvoicing of our speech sounds. In learning the phonetic alphabet you may have some difficulty choosing the correct symbols unless you examine the words you are writing to hear if this distinction exists. For example, one very common student error is the use of incorrect phonemic symbols for the two *th* sounds our language possesses. The symbol for the voiced, or sonant *th* is [ð], as in *then* [ðɛn]; the one for the surd *th* is [θ], as in *thin* [θɪn].

Exercise 2.2. Fill in the gaps in our phonemic transcription of the following words with the appropriate symbol.

1. think   __ɪŋk   2. thine   __aɪn
3. brother brʌ__ɚ   4. three   __ri
5. the   __ə   6. south saʊ__

INTERRUPTED OR CONTINUANT

A third distinctive feature which characterizes certain sounds of English, but not other sounds, is reflected in the word *continuant*. Most of our sounds are uttered with a continuous flow of voiced or unvoiced air through the oral or nasal cavities. Most of them can be prolonged without distorting their nature, and so they are called *continuants*. But there are some others, such as [k] or [b], in which the airflow is interrupted or stopped for a fraction of a second. These are called *stops* or *obstruents*. If you can prolong a speech sound without sounding like a machine gun, the sound is a continuant; mmmmmmm, ffffff, llllll. If you attempt to prolong a [p] sound, you find yourself saying puh, puh, puh [pʌpʌpʌ], so, [p] is a stop or obstruent sound. Let's explore this feature by examining the middle sounds of these words to see if they are continuant or stop consonants: (1) eager [igɚ]; (2) other [ʌðɚ]; (3) any [ɛnɪ]; (4) easy [izɪ]; (5) old [old]. Only one of the middle sounds is a stop consonant. Did you choose the first word? You should have.

Exercise 2.3. Underline the words below whose *final* sound you can prolong for at least two seconds.

1. fish [fɪʃ]   2. sieve [sɪv]   3. sick [sɪk]
4. peel [pil]   5. cooed [kud]   6. whose [huz]

We have six stop consonants in English, and they occur in three pairs, depending on the place in the vocal tract where the interruption or blockage to airflow occurs. One sound in each pair is sonant and the other is surd. Here are the three twin pairs: (1) [p] and [b]; (2) [t] and [d]; (3) [k] and [g].

Exercise 2.4. Use this key: L   lip closure
                        TTUG   tongue-tip upper gum ridge
                        BTV   back of the tongue against the velum (soft palate)

Where in the airway is the airflow blocked when uttering:

1. [b] _____   2. [k] _____   3. [t] _____
4. [p] _____   5. [g] _____   6. [d] _____

THE AFFRICATES

There is also another pair of voiced or unvoiced sounds, called *affricates*, in which the airflow is momentarily interrupted. They are the *ch* [tʃ] as in *cheap* [tʃip] and the [dʒ] as in *joke* [dʒok]. They are single sounds, but the affricates have two components: an initial stoppage and then a subsequent continuous constricted airflow. This is why the phonetic symbols for these two affricate phonemes are not single, but double. Thus the IPA symbol for *ch* begins with the stop consonant [t] and then is followed immediately with the continuant consonant *sh* [ʃ] to make [tʃ], and the words *cheek, beach*, and *chew*, are written [tʃik], [bitʃ], and [tʃu].

The other affricate [dʒ], as in *judge* [dʒʌdʒ], is articulated just like the *ch* [tʃ], and you might think of it as its voiced twin since the major difference between them is due to the presence or absence of vocal fold vibration. The [dʒ]'s first component is the sonant stop consonant [d] (the twin of [t]) and its second is the continuant consonant [ʒ] (the twin or cognate[2] of [ʃ]). If you try to say these two affricate sounds in slow motion you will note that neither the [t] in [tʃ] nor the [d] in [dʒ] are exploded suddenly after the closure, as they are in such syllables as [du] or [tu]. Instead of ending with a sudden puff of voiced or unvoiced air, they are released gradually into the voiced [ʒ] or the unvoiced [ʃ] sounds. An affricate, then, contains both a stop and a continuant sound blended sequentially together.

Exercise 2.5.   Write these words in phonetics and then underline all symbols in which an interruption of airflow occurs. We have provided the vowels. You put in the consonants.

1. jeep ___i___   2. hootch ___u___   3. sheep ___i___
4. cheap ___i___   5. badge ___æ___   6. church ___ɝ___

Reading passage

[dʒæk ænd dʒɪl wɛnt ʌp ðə hɪl tu fɛtʃ ə pel əv wɔtɚ‖ ɔr so ðe sɛd‖ juv hɝd tɛl əv ðə mæn ænd ðə farmɚz dɔtɚ‖]

[sɪŋ ə sɔŋ əv sɪkspɛns‖ ə bɛlɪ fʊl əv raɪ‖ ɔr bɪr ɔr waɪn ɔr kʌtɪ sɑrk wɪl lup ju tu ðə skaɪ‖]

[piz pɔrɪdʒ hat‖ piz pɔrɪdʒ kold‖ hwɛn juv stɑpt jʊr oglɪŋ‖ juv ʃʊr gatn̩ old‖]

THE STRIDENT CONSONANTS: THE FRICATIVES

We have a set of consonants, called *fricatives*, whose basic distinguishing characteristic lies in their noisiness, or *stridency*. Vowels are not strident; they are "mellow." We tell one vowel sound from another by listening to the complex tones that are their distinguishing features. But in continuant consonants we mainly find noises, not mellow

---

[2] Cognates are pairs of sounds produced in the same way with the only difference being that one is voiced and the other is unvoiced.

tones. If you will prolong the first sounds of the words *fat* [fæt], *think* [θɪŋk], *soon* [sun], and *show* [ʃo] you will discover that each consonantal noise differs from the others.

These sounds—the [f], [θ], [s], and [ʃ]—are called fricatives because their noises are produced by the friction caused by the rush of air through a constricted opening. In the [f] sound the airflow is squeezed between the teeth and the lower lip, so we call it a *labio-dental* fricative. In [θ] as in *thank* [θæŋk] the compressed air is forced through a narrowed opening between the tongue and the teeth. We call it a *lingua-dental* fricative. The hiss of the [s] sound is created by blowing air through the narrow channel made by grooving the tongue. And, the slushy noise of [ʃ] as in *shoot* [ʃut] comes from the rush of air through a broader groove of the tongue.

All of these sounds are voiceless (surd) fricatives. But, as we saw in our discussion of the sonant and surd classification, many consonants have twins or cognates, produced in the same way except that one is phonated and the other is not. Here are the twins of the unvoiced fricatives described above: When [f] is voiced it becomes [v]; when [θ] is voiced it becomes [ð] as in *father* [faðɚ]; when [s] is voiced it becomes [z]; when [ʃ] is voiced it becomes [ʒ] as in rouge [ruʒ]. The voiced, or sonant, fricatives then are [v] [ð] [z] and [ʒ].

There is also another fricative sound which may surprise you. Unlike the [f] [v] [θ] [ð] [s] [z] [ʃ] and [ʒ] phonemes which get their friction noises by squeezing the airflow through narrowed openings in the mouth or lips, this one is produced in the larynx itself. It is the [h] sound as in *hello* [hɛlo], *who* [hu], or *hotel* [hotɛl]. The [h] sound is called the *glottal fricative* because its friction noise is caused by air rushing through the constricted glottis, the space between the vocal folds. It is unvoiced.

So now you have a whole covey of symbols and we have inserted most of them in the following reading passage. Please write out the translation.

Exercise 2.6.

[aɪ ʃur lʌv ðoz æʒur aɪz əv jurz| hi sɛd æz hi briðd pæʃənətlɪ daun hɚ blaus|| ʃi slʌgd hɪm θri taɪmz ɪn ðə fes|| jur θɪŋkɪŋ əv sʌm ʌðɚ gɚl| maɪ aɪz ɑr braun ænd jurz ɑr blæk||

THE VOWELS

Many of us were taught in grade school that the English language has only five or six vowels: *A,E,I,O,U* and sometimes *Y*. This statement is completely false. We have at least twelve or thirteen. For example, we have the five *front vowels*, whose tongue positions are illustrated in Figure 3. Consider just the highest of these, the *ee* [i] as in *beet* [bit], and contrast it with the lowest one, the [æ] as in *bat* [bæt]. If you will rest your chin on your hand with your elbow on the arm of your chair as you say these

Front Vowels

TONGUE POSITION		MOUTH OPENING
High	i	Narrow
	ɪ	
to	e	to
	ɛ	
Low	æ	Wide

FIGURE 3

two vowels in sequence, you will discover that your tongue tends to flatten out as your jaw drops. When you say *ee* [i] the front of your tongue is humped up as high as it ever goes for any English vowel, and each of your other four front vowels is produced by a lessened humping. Thus, the [ɪ] (as in *bit*, *hit*, *mitt*) is held slightly lower than [i], while the [e] (as in *hay* or *hey!* [he]) shows, in turn, a slightly lower position. Then, in descending order, come [ɛ] (as in *met*, *set*, *fret*), and, finally, the lowest of all these front vowels, the [æ] vowel, as in *cat* [kæt]. Let's try some transcription, using these symbols.

Exercise 2.7.   Transcribe the following words into phonetic script:

1. meat _____   2. mitt _____   3. mate _____
4. met _____   5. mat

Note that these words contain the front vowels in terms of descending tongue position. Now transcribe the following five, which are in ascending order.

6. rat _____   7. red _____   8. rate _____
9. rid _____   10. reed

Reading passage

[i]   [wi it mit ænd tʃiz‖ mʌŋkiz it fliz‖]
[ɪ]   [ɪt ɪzn̩ izɪ tu pɪk fliz‖ ju nid tu bi kwɪk‖]
[e]   [ðe se et fliz mek ə mil fɔr ə mʌŋkɪ‖]
[ɛ]   [sɛvn̩ əv ðɛm krɛpt ʌp ðə mʌŋkiz hɛd ænd hɪd ɪn hɪz hɛr]
[æ]   [ræts hæv fliz tu bʌt ðe kænt kætʃ ðɛm‖]
      [ænd ðæts ɪnʌf tu se əbaʊt fliz ɪf ju pliz‖]

Back vowels

As you have seen, the manner in which the vowels are produced makes a big difference in terms of which vowel is heard. So far, we have shown that the height of the tongue is a very important factor. But there is another factor, too: the location of the elevated tongue in the mouth. You have already learned that we have five *front* vowels: [i], [ɪ], [e], [ɛ], and [æ]. We also have some *back* vowels. In these it is the rear of the tongue which is elevated, rather than the front. Figure 4 portrays them. As you can see, the vowel [u], as in *do* [du], *shoe* [ʃu], *flu* [flu], has the highest elevation, while the [ɔ] as in *ought* [ɔt] or *law* [lɔ] or *sauce* [sɔs] has the lowest, with the [ʊ], as in *cook* [kʊk], and the [o] as in *hope* [hop], coming in between. All of these sounds are made in the back part of the mouth, and their sequence, *in terms of descending elevation*, is as follows: [u] [ʊ] [o] [ɔ]. Say that sequence (the vowel sounds in "True cooks know

Back Vowels

TONGUE POSITION		MOUTH OPENING
High	u	Narrow
	ʊ	
to	o	to
	ɔ	
Low	ɒ	Wide

FIGURE 4

14

sauce") several times as you try to fix in memory the symbols for these back vowels. If you followed our suggestion, you probably noticed that your lower jaw descended along with the tongue and also that the rounding of your lips changed. This rounding does not make much difference in the production of the front vowels, but it sure does for the back vowels. Try watching yourself in a mirror as you prolong each of these sounds: [u] [ɔ] [u] [o] [ɔ] [ʊ].

Reading passage

[u]   [du ju no ðə gus ɪz lus|| ɛvrɪ gus ɪz lus||]
[ʊ]   [æz ðə bʊk sɛz| ju kʊd kʊk æn old gus tu dez ænd ɪt stɪl wʊdn̩t test gʊd||]
[o]   [ɪf ju go hwɛr ðə waɪld gus goz jul wɪʃ ju hæd sted hom ɪn jʊr on bɛd mopɪŋ
        ovɚ ə gʊd bʊk||]
[ɔ]   [no lɔ kɔlz fɔr ɔl gus hʌntɚz tu gɛt kɔt ɪn ə fɔg||]

Exercise 2.8.   Transcribe these words and rearrange them in sequence, so that the vowels in them range from a high tongue placement to a low one. Make one list for the front vowels, and the other for the back vowels. The first word in each list should contain the highest vowel.

soap, set, caught, mate, through, fish, reach, shook, badge.

FRONT VOWELS   BACK VOWELS

Middle vowels

We have a third set of vowels in which the placement of the tongue is a crucial feature. These are the middle vowels [ɑ] as in *father* [fɑðɚ], [ə] and [ʌ] as in *above* [əbʌv], and [ɝ] or [ɚ] as in *murder* [mɝdɚ]. In producing these five vowels it is the middle, not the front or back of the tongue, which is raised or tensed, as can be seen in Figure 5. Note that in the production of the unstressed middle vowel [ə] (the schwa vowel) the tongue is hardly humped at all, but tends to lie almost flat in the mouth. It is therefore the lowest of all the five middle vowels, while the [ɝ] is the highest. Also note that the shape of the upper surface of the tongue in [ɝ] has a double hump like a camel, with the forward hump usually being higher than the rear one.

You probably noticed that although we have presented five different symbols for the middle vowels, there seem to be two pairs and one single sound [ɑ] among them. One pair, the [ʌ] and [ə], seem to represent very similar, if not identical, sounds. Both sound like *uh*. And we also have two different symbols, the [ɝ] and [ɚ], for a vowel

Middle Vowels

TONGUE POSITION			MOUTH OPENING
High			Narrow
to		ɝ	to
	ə	ʌ ɚ	
Low		ɑ	Wide

FIGURE 5

that seems to have the same *rrrr* quality. Why two symbols for the same sound? Why have to learn four symbols when only two should be enough?

In this general overview we will not go into a detailed explanation, although we will do so later on. Let us just say for now that you should use the [ʌ] and the [ɝ] in stressed syllables, that is, in those which are accented, and use the [ə] and [ɚ] in unaccented, or unstressed, syllables. The [ʌ] and [ɝ] are *tense* vowels, the [ə] and [ɚ] are *lax*. You will have to check whether the syllable of the word is accented or unaccented to know which one to use. To help you we will list some words in which we use the ['] marker before the syllable which has the *primary* accent. Use [ʌ] and [ɝ] only in such syllables. If the syllable is not accented at all, or has only a secondary accent [ˌ], you should always use the [ə] and the [ɚ] symbols: church [tʃɝtʃ]; anger ['æŋgɚ]; cup [kʌp]; alone [ə'lon]; another [ə'nʌðɚ]; murder ['mɝdɚ]; further ['fɝðɚ]; among [ə'mʌŋ]; above [ə'bʌv]; murmuring ['mɝmɚɪŋ].

Essentially, it is in transcribing the polysyllabic words that you will have to decide whether to use [ʌ] or [ə] and [ɝ] or [ɚ]. But, please remember that all four of these plus the [ɑ] are middle vowels.

Reading passage

[hiz æn 'ʌtɚ 'ɪdɪət| ðə gɝl 'mʌtɚd|| hi θɪŋks 'vɝdʒɪnz kʌm frʌm vɚ'dʒɪnjə|| pliz 'notɪs ðæt ðə dʒɪn ɪn vɚ'dʒɪnjə ɪz ðə 'sɪləbl̩ wɪθ ðə 'praɪmɛrɪ 'æksɛnt|| ðə fɝst 'sɪləbl̩ hæz sʌm 'æksɛnt| bʌt ɪt ɪz 'sɛkəndɛrɪ| æz 'ɪndɪketɪd baɪ ðə [ˌ] 'markɚ|| so wi juz [ɚ] ɪn vɚ'dʒɪnjə| ænd [ɝ] ɪn 'vɝdʒɪn||]

Exercise 2.9. Here are some terms used to describe all these vowels. Write the phonetic symbol for the vowel that best fits the description.

1. Low back rounded _____
2. Highest mid central _____
3. Lower high back rounded _____
4. Highest front _____
5. Lowest central _____
6. Higher mid front _____
7. Lower mid front _____
8. Lower high front _____
9. Highest back rounded _____
10. Lowest front _____
11. Mid back rounded _____
12. The central vowel with the widest mouth opening _____

Diphthongs

A diphthong is the smooth joining together of two adjacent vowels in the same syllable. The tongue moves without interruption from one tongue or lip position to another. Thus, in the word *height* [haɪt], we find that the vowel starts with the [a] and then smoothly shifts to [ɪ]; the combination producing the diphthong [aɪ]. There are three standard diphthongs commonly used in general American speech: the [aɪ] as in *buy* [baɪ] or *lie* [laɪ], the [aʊ] as in *ouch* [aʊtʃ] or cow [kaʊ], and the third is [ɔɪ] as in *boy* [bɔɪ] or *toy* [tɔɪ]. Other diphthongal combinations are to be found, but we shall reserve our discussion of them for a later time. For now we will concentrate on [aɪ], [aʊ], and [ɔɪ].

Exercise 2.10 Transcribe only the words which contain the above diphthongs, and place them in the appropriate column.

16

[most əv ju ɑr prɑbəblɪ ridɪŋ ðɪs fənɛtɪk skrɪpt prɪtɪ izɪlɪ bɑɪ nau‖ wi hæv
gɪvn̩ ju æn ɔful lɑt əv ɪnfɚmeʃn̩| pɚhæps tu mʌtʃ‖ bʌt sʌmhau juv kʌm tu mæstɚ|ɔr
æt list tu rɛkəgnaɪz| most əv ðə sɪmbl̩z əv ðɪs nu ælfəbɛt‖ so lɛt ʌs stɑrt lɝnɪŋ hau
tu raɪt æz wɛl æz hau tu rid fənɛtɪklɪ‖ hau mɛnɪ sɪmbl̩z dɪd ju hæv tu luk ʌp‖ æt
list juv gɑt ə gud stɑrt‖]

We have been describing the speech sounds of our language in terms of their
manner and place of articulation. Each of these phonemes consists of a set of distinctive
features, a set that differs from the collection of features which characterizes any other
phoneme. Some of the component features of one phoneme are to be found in other
phonemes, as we have seen in the cognate sounds, such as [s] and [z], which are distinguished primarily by being either voiced or unvoiced. But there is always at least
one distinctive feature that makes the difference; a feature that gives a particular sound
its unique identity. These features include the *manner* of articulation and the *place* of
articulation; the *manner* identifies *how* the phoneme is produced by the tongue, lips,
etc. The *place* tells *where* it is produced (front, center, back, high, low, etc.). Figure 6
shows the speech organs.

Throughout this chapter we have sought to give you an overview, a catalog of
the phonemes of our language. You will not remember the details of how they look
and sound and are produced, but when you meet them again you will recognize their
features.

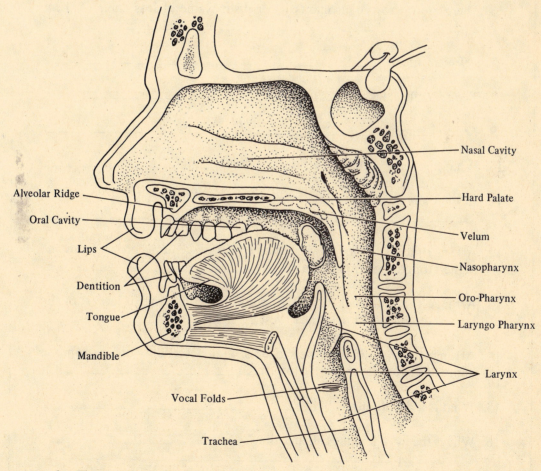

FIGURE 6. The speech mechanism. Samuel R. Faircloth and Marjorie A. Faircloth, *Phonetic
Science: A Program of Instruction*, © 1973. Reprinted by permission of Prentice-Hall, Inc.,
Englewood Cliffs, N.J.

This has been a mighty meaty chapter, and you have been exposed to many things which we will reintroduce later. This self-checking test will help you grasp the rudiments of speech production which, in turn, will make future chapters much easier to understand.

1. You can tell that a speech sound is a consonant rather than a vowel because _____

2. An allophone is _____

3. The three nasal speech sounds are _____

4. "Sonant" means _____

5. "Surd" means _____

6. There are six stop consonants in English. Name at least four of them _____

7. *Affricate* means _____

8. The two affricates are _____

9. *Fricative* means _____

10. What phoneme is called a glottal fricative? _____

11. In what way do front, middle, and back vowels differ? _____

12. Arrange the five front vowels [æ ɛ i e ɪ] in descending order, from the highest tongue position to the lowest _____

13. Arrange the four back vowels [o ʊ u ɔ] in descending order, from the highest tongue position to the lowest _____

14. Arrange the five middle vowels [ɑ ʌ ə ɝ ɚ] in descending order, from the highest tongue position to the lowest _____

15. What is a diphthong? _____

16. Why is the [w] phoneme called a glide? _____

17. What two consonants can also become semivowels? _____

Do whatever rereading you have to do, in order to get every one of these questions right.

CLUES

1. Remember the guy from Kuppa Kapi?

2. A phoneme is a group of allophones.

3. The opposite is de-nasal.

4. Your vocal folds vibrate.

5. You fold back your vocal folds.

6. There are really 3 pairs (cognates); one of each pair is sonant and the other, surd.

8. Think of Judge Church. [dʒʌdʒ tʃɝtʃ]

10. The glottis is the space between the vocal folds.

12. See Figure 3. Also, sing them, starting with a high note and going lower for each succeeding phoneme.

13. [sɪŋ ðiz| tu]

ANSWERS

1. The airflow meets some obstruction.

2. The exact reproduction of a speech sound.

3. [m n ŋ]

4. voiced

5. unvoiced

6. [p b t d k g]

7. Two sounds produced simultaneously in which the airflow is momentarily interrupted.

8. [tʒ dʒ]

9. The friction of air rushing through a constricted opening.

10. [h]

11. They differ in what part of the tongue is humped up.

12. [i ɪ e ɛ æ]

13. [u ʊ o ɔ]

CLUES	ANSWERS
14. [wʌns mɔr]	14. [ɝ ʌ ɑ ɚ ə]
	15. The smooth joining of two vowels in the same syllable. The three diphthongs you learned were [aɪ aʊ ɔɪ].
	16. Because it is transitional; the sound comes out as the following vowel is being produced.
17. They get a liquid, vowel-like sound in such words as handle [hændl̩] and murmur [mɝmɚ].	17. l r

Go over these one more time before you take the examination.

Name _____ *Date* _____ *Score* _____

Hand this in to your instructor.

MATCH GAME

1. Classify these sounds by putting each in the appropriate column(s). A symbol can belong to more than one column. For instance, [z] is both an oral sound and a continuant.

   [z]   [ŋ]   [f]   [p]   [b]   [n]   [m]

NASAL	ORAL	SONANT	SURD	STOP	CONTINUANT

2. Put these vowels in the appropriate column.

   [ɑ]   [æ]   [ɛ]   [ɝ]   [u]   [o]

FRONT	MIDDLE	BACK

3. Put these phonemes in the appropriate column.

   [tʃ]   [aɪ]   [j]   [dʒ]   [w]   [ɔɪ]   [r]

DIPHTHONGS	AFFRICATES	GLIDES

MATCH GAME

4. Put these words in the appropriate column, according to whether the *l* and *r* are consonants or semivowels.

lost   erase   angle   belie   butter

CONSONANT	SEMIVOWEL

5. Describe what happens to the mouth and tongue when you say the word *we*.

3 The International Phonetic Alphabet

Although many alphabets have been designed to represent more exactly the sounds used in speaking, the one which has come to dominate the field of phonetics is the IPA, which was designed in 1888 by a committee of European scholars. We must remember that the symbols they chose were symbols which had to be familiar not only to English speakers but also to those who spoke French, Swedish, German, Italian, and other continental languages.

Accordingly, a symbol such as [i] was assigned to represent the sound of our English *ee*, as in the word *machine*, since in most European languages the letter *i* does signify a sound similar to our English *ee*. The French use the letter *i* for this sound in *chic* (sheek); the Norwegians use it in *ski*, though pronounce it *shee*. The Italians say *vino*; the Spaniards say *sí, sí*. Although an English scholar, Henry Sweet, helped to formulate the IPA, he too felt it wiser to use [i] rather than [e] as the phonetic symbol for this sound. As a result, you must expect that this, as well as other symbols, may seem expressly designed to confuse rather than to clarify. Fortunately, there are not too many of these exchanges of symbols and sounds, and you will soon get them straight.

In the last chapter we presented most of the IPA symbols, along with their method of production; the entire list can be found on the front and back covers of this book. But we reproduce them here in script form, so that you may learn how to write the symbols as you associate them with their sounds.

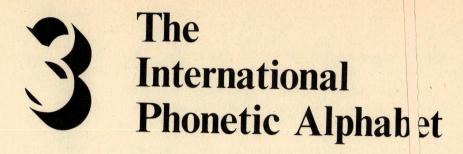

3 The International Phonetic Alphabet

Although many alphabets have been designed to represent more exactly the sounds used in speaking, the one which has come to dominate the field of phonetics is the IPA, which was designed in 1888 by a committee of European scholars. We must remember that the symbols they chose were symbols which had to be familiar not only to English speakers but also to those who spoke French, Swedish, German, Italian, and other continental languages.

Accordingly, a symbol such as [i] was assigned to represent the sound of our English *ee*, as in the word *machine*, since in most European languages the letter *i* does signify a sound similar to our English *ee*. The French use the letter *i* for this sound in *chic* (sheek); the Norwegians use it in *ski*, though pronounce it *she*. The Italians say *vino*; the Spaniards say *si*, *sí*. Although an English scholar, Henry Sweet, helped to formulate the IPA, he too felt it wiser to use [i] rather than [e] as the phonetic symbol for this sound. As a result, you must expect that this, as well as other symbols, may seem expressly designed to confuse rather than to clarify. Fortunately, there are not too many of these exchanges of symbols and sounds, and you will soon get them straight.

In the last chapter we presented most of the IPA symbols, along with their method of production; the entire list can be found on the front and back covers of this book. But we reproduce them here in script form, so that you may learn how to write the symbols as you associate them with their sounds.

In order that phonetic script may be written swiftly, the written symbols are slightly different from the printed ones. They are never joined as in ordinary writing; instead manuscript writing is used. To familiarize yourself with both printed and script symbols we suggest that you fill in the blanks in the following exercise, using the script forms.

	SCRIPT		PRINTED	SCRIPT	PRINTED	SCRIPT
b	b	as in beg or tub	bɛg	bɛg	and tʌb	_____
d	d	as in do or and	du	du	and ænd	_____
f	f	as in fan or scarf	fæn	fæn	and skɑrf	_____
g	g	as in grow or bag	gro	gro	and bæg	_____
dʒ	dʒ	as in judge or enjoy	dʒʌdʒ	dʒʌdʒ	and ɪndʒɔɪ	_____
h	h	as in hem or inhale	hɛm	hɛm	and ɪnhel	_____
k	k	as in kick or uncle	kɪk	kɪk	and ʌŋkḷ	_____
l	l	as in let or pal	lɛt	lɛt	and pæl	_____
ḷ	ḷ	as in apple or turtle	æpḷ	æpḷ	and tɝtḷ	_____
m	m	as in men and arm	mɛn	mɛn	and ɑrm	_____
m̩	m̩	as in spasm or wisdom	spæzm̩	spæzm̩	and wɪzdm̩	_____
n	n	as in nose or gain	noz	noz	and gen	_____
ṇ	ṇ	as in sudden or curtain	sʌdṇ	sʌdṇ	and kɝtṇ	_____
ŋ	ŋ	as in wrong or anger	rɔŋ	rɔŋ	and æŋgɚ	_____
p	p	as in paper or damper	pepɚ	pepɚ	and dæmpɚ	_____
r	r	as in run or far	rʌn	rʌn	and fɑr	_____
s	s	as in send or us	sɛnd	sɛnd	and ʌs	_____
t	t	as in toe or ant	to	to	and ænt	_____
ʃ	ʃ	as in shed or ash	ʃɛd	ʃɛd	and æʃ	_____
tʃ	tʃ	as in cheap or each	tʃip	tʃip	and itʃ	_____
θ	θ	as in thin or tooth	θɪn	θɪn	and tuθ	_____
ð	ð	as in then or breathe	ðɛn	ðɛn	and brið	_____
v	v	as in vow or have	vɑu	vɑu	and hæv	_____
w	w	as in wet or twin	wɛt	wɛt	and twɪn	_____
hw	hw	as in when or white	hwɛn	hwɛn	and hwaɪt	_____
j	j	as in you or yet	ju	ju	and jɛt	_____
ʒ	ʒ	as in pleasure or vision	plɛʒɚ	plɛʒɚ	and vɪʒən	_____
z	z	as in zoo or ooze	zu	zu	and uz	_____
a*	a	as in ask or rather	ask	ask	and rɑðɚ	_____
ɑ	a	as in father or odd	fɑðɚ	fɑðɚ	and ɑd	_____
e	e	as in make or eight	mek	mek	and et	_____
æ	æ	as in sat or act	sæt	sæt	and ækt	_____
i	i	as in fatigue or east	fətig	fətig	and ist	_____
ɛ	ɛ	as in red or end	rɛd	rɛd	and ɛnd	_____
ɪ	ɪ	as in it or since	ɪt	ɪt	and sɪns	_____
o	o	as in hope or old	hop	hop	and old	_____
ɔ	ɔ	as in sauce or off	sɔs	sɔs	and ɔf	_____

26

SCRIPT			PRINTED	SCRIPT	PRINTED	SCRIPT
ɒ*	ɒ	as in log or toss	lɒg	lɒg	and tɒs	_____
ɝ	ɝ	as in earn or fur	ɝn	ɝn	and fɝ	_____
ɜ*	ɜ	as in earn or fur	ɜn	ɜn	and fɜ	_____
ɚ	ɚ	as in never or percale	nɛvɚ	nɛvɚ	and pɚkel	_____
u	u	as in truth or blue	truθ	truθ	and blu	_____
ʊ	ʊ	as in put or nook	pʊt	pʊt	and nʊk	_____
ʌ	ʌ	as in under or love	ʌndɚ	ʌndɚ	and lʌv	_____
ə	ə	as in about or second	əbaut	əbaut	and sɛkənd	_____
aɪ	aɪ	as in sigh or aisle	saɪ	saɪ	and aɪl	_____
au	au	as in now or owl	nau	nau	and aul	_____
ɔɪ	ɔɪ	as in coy or oil	kɔɪ	kɔɪ	and ɔɪl	_____
ɛr	ɛr	as in share or air	ʃɛr	ʃɛr	and ɛr	_____
ɑr	ɑr	as in car or are	kɑr	kɑr	and ɑr	_____
ʊr	ʊr	as in sure or poor	ʃʊr	ʃʊr	and pʊr	_____
ɔr	ɔr	as in oar or tore	ɔr	ɔr	and tɔr	_____
ɪr	ɪr	as in here or ear	hɪr	hɪr	and ɪr	_____
aɪr	aɪr	as in fire or liar	faɪr	faɪr	and laɪr	_____
aʊr	aʊr	as in tower or our	taʊr	taʊr	and aʊr	_____

* Regional pronunciations most commonly heard in eastern and southern United States.

Exercise 3.1.   Write in phonetic script only the first sound in each of the following words.

1. put _____   8. England _____   10. need _____
2. reach _____   9. zest _____   11. end _____
3. after _____   12. sin _____
4. cod _____   13. above _____
5. toil _____   14. sting _____
6. ink _____   15. error _____
7. psalm _____   16. idiotic _____

If you will read down the list of what you have written, it should spell out [præktɪs ɪz nɛsəsɛrɪ]. Practice is indeed necessary.

Exercise 3.2.   Now try to write the whole words in the list above. Refer to the IPA whenever you are in doubt. Write the words on the lines provided above.

Exercise 3.3.   Write the following sentence in phonetic script:

My script looks like this. _____

Exercise 3.4.   Read this aloud, then write it in English.

ðɛr ɑr tɛn strɔŋ θɪŋz‖ aɪrn ɪz strɔŋ bʌt faɪr mɛlts ɪt‖ faɪr ɪz strɔŋ bʌt wɔtɚ kwɛntʃəz ɪt‖ wɔtɚ ɪz strɔŋ bʌt ðə klaʊdz ɪvæpɚet ɪt‖ klaʊdz ɑr strɔŋ bʌt wɪnd draɪvz ðɛm əwe‖ mæn ɪz strɔŋ bʌt fɪrz kæst hɪm daʊn‖ fɪr ɪz strɔŋ bʌt slip ovɚkʌmz ɪt‖ slip ɪz strɔŋ jɛt dɛθ ɪz strɔŋgɚ‖ bʌt lʌvɪŋ kaɪndnəs sɚvaɪvz dɛθ‖

frʌm ðə talmud

PROBLEMS TO OVERCOME

There are four main difficulties that students encounter when learning the phonetic alphabet. They are as follows:

1. Freeing oneself from the visual alphabet; we must listen to sounds and stop seeing letters.
2. Analyzing words into their component sounds.
3. Combining sounds into words, and words into speech.
4. Establishing a strong and immediate association between a sound and its phonetic symbol.

Freeing oneself from the visual alphabet

Few of us realize the strength of past associations. This is especially true in reading. For years we have been translating visual symbols into inner speech. The letters in the word [hut] have been translated so often as a small dwelling that we find it hard to realize that phonetically it spells *hoot*. If we are to read phonetics easily, we must replace these old associations. We must free ourselves from the visual alphabet when we read or write our new symbols.

Our new task is to use a new tool, the phonetic alphabet, so that we can always be sure of how a word is pronounced. We need this in many areas—in speech therapy, in TV newscasts, in the theater, in the study of linguistics.

We think of our alphabet as being adequate, but as soon as we have to spell an unfamiliar word we have just heard, we flounder. Spelling in our language is a poor guide to pronunciation. If a strange word has an *o* in it we [du nɑt no] if it is a *short o* or a *long o*, or if it even sounds like an *o*. Look at the words *boot*, *bomb*, and *tough*. Let's [si] what happens when we can see just the beginning of a word, Ro___. How [ʃʊd] it be pronounced? Will it be spoken as in the word *row* (or *roe*)? If so, what about the words *rot*, *roar*, *rough*, *rowdy*, *rouge*? Now we have six different ways of saying *ro*. Our old alphabet is just not good enough.

Exercise 3.5. Suppose you take [ənʌðɚ] pair of letters: *b* and *e*. Fill in each blank in the following list with one or more letters and you will have seven ways of pronouncing the syllable. Notice how the *be* changes with each word.

1. be_ , a wager
2. be_ , a stinging insect
3. be__ , past participle of the verb "to be"
4. be__ , boyfriend
5. be____ , comeliness, fair to look upon
6. be___ , bed on a train

And that gives us six different pronunciations of *be*, with [sʌm] of the words having no *e* quality at all. The word *beau* sounds [ɪgzæktlɪ] like the word *bow*. "That's all very well," some people will say, "but that is the way the French pronounce that sound. It is taken [frʌm] the French and should be pronounced that way." If that is [tru], what should be [dʌn] with the word *beauty?* It has the same derivation as *beau*, [bʌt] it is pronounced *byooty* [bjutɪ]. English is a twisted tongue.

Even the [nemz] of our alphabet letters have little relationship to the sounds they represent.

Exercise 3.6. Here are some letters of the alphabet written as their names are pronounced. Print the letter after its name. *Example:* [waɪ] ___Y___

[waɪ _____   ɛs _____   ɑr _____
etʃ _____   ɛks _____   dʒi] _____
dʌbļju _____   kju _____

Now that we have spelled out the letter names, we could teach a child to "recite the alphabet." But it would do him little good if he had to sound out a word. When we see the word *he*, we don't say it *aitchee*. [ɪt wɪl nɑt hɛlp] a foreigner trying to say the word *wow* to know that it is spelled *double-you, short oh, double-you*.

You must break free from the limits of our visual alphabet. Just consider the vowels. In our language they contribute more than their share to the difficulties of pronunciation. The English language has many more vowel sounds than the five we were taught. Actually, vowels are like rainbow colors: [wʌn slaɪdz ɪntu ðə nɛkst wɪð no ril dɪvaɪdɪŋ laɪn bɪtwin ðɛm‖]. However, just as there are 16 principal colors in the spectrum, there are 17 distinguishable vowel sounds most commonly in use in this country: [a ɑ e æ i ɛ ɪ o ɔ ɒ ɝ ɜ ɚ u ʊ ʌ ə‖]. The vowels *A, E, I, O, U* that we learned as children are perfectly good vowels sounds (or diphthongs at least), but any of the others would have been just as valid. The vowel letters in the following sentence *look* like *A,E,I,O,* and *U*, but they sound altogether different: *After Every hIll DOn pUffs*. Try saying that sentence using the common letter names for the vowels.

Exercise 3.7.   Here is a poem in English. Read it aloud, making all the final words of the lines rhyme with the final word of the first line. Then read it through, pronouncing all words as they should be spoken.

> There was an old woman so *tough*
> She hung all her clothes on a *bough*
> And swam even *though*
> There was ice on the *slough*
> Yet didn't develop a *cough*

The preceding verse is an "eye-rhyme." From the way the written words look, the poem should rhyme exactly, but nothing could be farther from the truth. Two of the words end with a *f* sound, where no *f* is indicated by spelling, and all the vowels differ.

We must learn to ignore the looks of a word; we must listen to it instead. Our ordinary alphabet is inadequate. If our numerals were as inexact as our letter symbols, what effect would this have on our arithmetic? If 2 could mean 2, or 3, or even 7, just as *a* means *ah*, or *ay*, or even *uh*, every addition problem could have an infinite number of correct answers. Fortunately we have the IPA symbols which have set values to approximate the exactness of our numerals. Once the IPA is learned it will be possible to pronounce a difficult polysyllabic technical word with as much ease as the authority who knows its meaning. Modern dictionaries are now using the IPA in some instances. For example, the pronunciation of *appose* is indicated in this way: [əpoz], and *control* in this way: [kəntrol].

Analyzing words into their component sounds

Another difficulty experienced by beginning students of phonetics is due to *hearing* words as wholes, as chunks of sound. The word *through*, for example, is heard as a unit, almost as a [sɪŋḷ] sound. Actually it consists of a sequence or series of three sounds, beginning with a prolonged *th* [θ], followed by an *r* and ending with an *oo*, or [u]. When in a hurry many of us often write it as *thru*, thus indicating our desire to write phonetically and our impatience with unnecessary complexities of English spelling. In phonetics we would spell it similarly as [θru]. Words have heads, tails, and middles. They [ɑr] little melodies of sound. The difficulty new students experience is that, like a poor singer, they can easily [tɛl] that the tune is "Home on the Range," but they cannot sing the individual notes in their proper order. The word *six* both begins and ends with an *s* sound but there are two sounds in between. In the word *few*, it is easy to hear the *f* which begins the sequence and the *u* which ends it, but the middle sound causes many students some trouble. (It is the same as the first sound of the words *you*, *usually*, and *yellow*.) In phonetics we must be able to hear each of the notes that make up the tune; we must be able to recognize the individual sounds that follow each other to make a word. The word *few*, written phonetically, is [fju]. Without the [j] it would be *foo*.

In speech therapy a great many articulatory cases—those who mispronounce their speech sounds—are unable to correct their own errors because they cannot break down these word-wholes into their component [pɑrts]. They often know that they have trouble saying certain words, but they cannot tell exactly what is wrong. In the ear-training we [gɪv] these cases, "vocal phonics" is stressed. We try to get [gɛt] these individuals to isolate the defective sounds, to understand where their errors are located. Little children, in learning to talk, commonly go through a stage in speech development in which they play with words, exchanging the sounds within them. They say, "Hello, Daddy, ole maddy, ole faddy," and find the game hilarious. Somehow, they seem to know that, if they are ever to "outgrow" their baby talk, they must learn to analyze words into their parts. How else can a child exchange the wrong *w* for the correct *r* in the word *wabbit* unless he does some of this analyzing? His fascination with rhymes is another illustration of the same need.

In order to convince yourself of your own need to perfect your ability to break down words into their component parts, try analyzing the simple word *for*. There are three sounds within it. The first is, of course, the *fff* sound and the last is the *r*, but can you tell what the middle sound is? Most students would say that it is an *o*, but few of them actually pronounce the word in that way. The middle sound is generally [ɔ], a vowel which you can easily hear in the word *ought*. The distinction is even more easily seen in the words *mower* and *more*. If such a simple and familiar word gives you trouble, how much more difficulty will you have when you are required to transcribe foreign speech, a dialect, [ɔr] the jargon of a child with defective speech.

Throughout this book we shall return again and again to this problem, but on the following pages are some preliminary exercises which you can use to improve your vocal phonics.

Exercise 3.8. Underline the word in the test group that has the same vowel sound as the model word. Say the words aloud, holding the vowel sound for at least a second. Watch that your eye does not delude your ear.

MODEL	TEST WORDS		
1. though	through	sewed	cough
2. said	braid	sex	laid
3. break	crate	bread	creak
4. psalm	salmon	odd	storm
5. aisles	wait	height	hail
6. tough	out	ought	hut
7. cook	should	junk	tooth
8. breath	friend	near	heard
9. sues	would	group	quest
10. says	flays	eyes	guest

Exercise 3.9. Do you remember when you were a child, you would try to say words backwards? *Stop* became *pots*, *kneel* became *lean*. We want you to try to say these backwards, to form other meaningful words. Ignore the spelling and think only of the sounds. Caution: one of these becomes a nonsense word. Write the reversed words in English in the spaces provided.

1. tile _____   2. soon _____   3. face _____
4. pass _____   5. zone _____   6. sauce _____
7. laugh _____   8. church _____ 9. Dick's _____
10. mock _____   11. tax _____   12. dough _____
13. stun _____   14. damn _____   15. less _____

[ðə wʌn nɑnsɛns wɝd ɪz ðə sɛvənθ‖ ðɪ ʌðɚ wɝdz ɪn rɪvɝs ɔrdɚ ɑr sɛl mæd nʌts od skæt kɑm skɪd tʃɝtʃ sɔs noz sæp sef nus laɪt]

31

To read or write in the phonetic alphabet you must learn to analyze words into their component parts. Many English words have many more letters than sounds. One of the best methods for beginning this analyzing process is to count how many separate sounds a word contains. At first you may have to use a sort of slow motion speech to do this. Try it out on the test below. Read the hints first.

HINTS	HOW MANY SOUNDS?
ache has two sounds	1. caught _____
six hæz fɔr saundz: sɪks	2. quick _____
whom hæz θri saundz: hum	3. shoot _____
thought hæz θri saundz: θɔt	4. throw _____
feather hæz fɔr saundz: fɛðɚ	5. buy _____
should hæz θri saundz: ʃud	6. cough _____
wrong hæz no dʌbḷju: rɔŋ	7. though _____
calf hæz θri saundz: kæf	8. rough _____
four hæz θri saundz: fɔr	9. who _____
taught hæz θri saundz: tɔt	10. own _____
show hæz tu saundz: ʃo	11. laugh _____
gnu hæz tu saundz: nu	12. gnaw _____
Philadelphia hæz tɛn: fɪlədɛlfɪə	13. clams _____
Xerxes hæz sɪks saundz: zɝksiz	14. foreign _____
x has three sounds	15. reached _____
	16. half _____
	17. box _____
	18. church _____
	19. know _____
	20. thought _____

Now, look at the next page for the answers.

The phonetic transcription below will help you understand why your count was wrong—if it was. Be sure to read the left-hand explanation whenever you made an error. You'll learn what your error was, and besides, it's good practice.

		ANSWERS
1.	k æz ɪn kæt|ɔ æz ɪn ɔf|t æz ɪn bɪt||	1. θri
2.	ðɪs wɝd ɪz rɪtn̩ kwɪk||	2. fɔr
3.	ðə fɝst tu lɛtɚz rɛprɪzɛnt ðə ʃ||	3. θri
4.	θro kɔʃən tu ðə wɪndz||	4. θri
5.	aɪ ɪz ə dɪfθɔŋ|| kaʊnt ɪt æz wʌn saʊnd||	5. tu
6.	ɪt ɛndz wɪð ə f saʊnd||	6. θri
7.	bɛt wi fuld ju an ðɪs wʌn||	7. tu
8.	ɑr ju faɪndɪŋ ðɪs stʌf rʌf||	8. θri
9.	hu ɑr ju tə du sʌtʃ laʊzi wɝk||	9. tu
10.	dʒʌst tu|| on ʌp|| ju guft||	10. tu
11.	læf klaʊn læf||	11. θri
12.	no ðɛrz no dʒi||	12. tu
13.	ɪn ðɪs wɝd jul faɪnd klæmz||	13. faɪv
14.	ə tʌf wʌn ðɪs|| prɪtɪ fɔrɪn tu ju||	14. faɪv
15.	ðə tʃ ɪz kənsɪdɚd e sɪŋgl̩ saʊnd||	15. fɔr
16.	wɝ ju hæf raɪt||	16. θri
17.	ðə wɝd ɪz bɑks||	17. fɔr
18.	tʃ plʌs ɚ plʌs tʃ ikwəlz θri||	18. θri
19.	aɪ no ju no ðɪs wʌn||	19. tu
20.	æt list ju ʃud no ɪt||	20. θri

Combining sounds into words

Just as analysis is very important in writing phonetics, synthesis is vital in the [rɪdɪŋ] of phonetic script. You must be able to integrate a series of sounds to form a word-whole. In order to read the word [væljueʃən], even [æftɚ] you know the sounds represented by the symbols, you will still have to sound it out symbol by [sɪmbl̩], carrying all preceding sounds in your head, until you arrive at its final n sound. Only [ðɛn] will you be sure that the word will [bi] actually pronounced as *valuation*. Some students never acquire this [skɪl], and they have a bad time reading phonetics with accuracy.

Two factors [sim] to be basic in this skill. First of all, it requires some training in auditory memory span. As you read along the sequence of symbols in an unknown word, you [mʌst] carry in your head all those which have gone before. This process is called *scanning*. At first, it may [sim] unnecessary. In simple words, the [ɪntaɪr] sequence may be synthesized at a [glæns]. Reading the phonetic word [sut] is easy, once [ju no] that u equals *oo*. But in a more complex word, or in a strange or mispronounced word, you must [skæn] it carefully if you are to pronounce it in the same way as it is written. You will [faɪnd] yourself reading the phonetic word [but] as a conjunction [ɪnstɛd] of the name of a foot covering. What is another name for the [ərɔrəbɔrɪælɪs]? In order to pronounce [ðɪs] word, you will have to combine each new sound with all preceding ones. In the sentence [ðɪs stʌf nɔsɪets mi], you probably found that on the third word you had to go through some such process as this: [nɔs . . . nɔsɪ . . . nɔsɪe . . . nɔsɪets] before you were sure that the word actually meant *nauseates*. If you protest that this [præktɪs] will never help you get any speed in phonetic reading, you are [rɔŋ]. We soon learn to scan with incredible speed, even as we learn to recognize [hol] words on the printed page or notice immediately those which are misspelled. But if you slight this scanning process, you handicap yourself unwisely.

The [sɛkənd] basic factor may be called *blending*. Not [onlɪ] must you [rɪmɛmbɚ] the sounds you [hæv] been scanning, [bʌt] you must [ɔlso] be able to blend [itʃ] new [wʌn] with the one which preceded [ɪt]. You [mʌst] be alert [ɪn] order [tʊ] combine little subgroups of symbols into syllables. You must be careful to accent and [strɛs] the proper part of the word. Blending requires that you recognize a syllable in a word, and that you can tell which syllable in that word receives the stress.

SYLLABICATION, STRESS, AND ACCENT

Syllabication

Unless you know what constitutes a syllable you cannot know where to place the stress in a word. Most people were not given enough practice in their early school days in separating words into syllables. If you think you are a little hazy on the subject, read on. If not, skip down to the exercises, and prove to yourself that you understand syllabication.

A syllable is a segment of speech produced with a single puff of air pressure from the lungs. Every syllable contains a single vowel sound, or vowel diphthong. If you have two different vowel sounds together, you know that you have two syllables; the word *chaos* has two syllables. So does the word *caper*.

The vowel sound in a syllable may be accompanied by one or more consonants, or none. The word *a* is a syllable. So is *up*, and *pup*. The word *screams* is a single syllable, because there is only one vowel sound, even though there are five consonants [skrimz].

Take the word *scrimps*. How many vowel sounds? One, of course. How many consonants? [skrɪmps]. Six.

Exercise 3.10.   Listen to yourself say these words. Decide how many syllables each of them contains.

1. midnight	_____	2. worst	_____
3. vowel	_____	4. fix	_____
5. program	_____	6. parliament	_____

We have said that many of our vowels are diphthongized; the sounds are said so close together that they are considered to be one sound. The *oy* sound in *noise* is a diphthong. You are saying an *aw* [ɔ] sound, immediately followed by an *ee* sound. We will be discussing this in more detail later. There are some double vowel sounds in words which are *not* diphthongs. The word *truant* is divided syllabically between the two vowel sounds [tru ənt] The thing that will help you the most is your own ear. If you can hear an infinitesimal break between the two halves of the word *truant*, and can hear that there is no such break in the word *noise* [nɔɪz], you will not find syllabication difficult.

Exercise 3.11.   Count the number of syllables in these words.

1. coin	_____	2. coincidence	_____
3. owl	_____	4. only	_____
5. inclination	_____	6. facility	_____
7. pragmatic	_____	8. antidisestablishmentarianism	_____

Stress and accent

There is sense stress and there is syllable stress. *Sense stress* indicates what part of a phrase or sentence will be accented, and we will discuss this at length in the chapter on conversational speech. For the present, however, we will worry primarily about syllable stress or, more correctly, *syllable accent*. Syllable accent is very important in any language. Even the meanings of words depend upon it. What is the meaning of the word *present?* You cannot possibly tell until someone pronounces it either as [prɪzɛnt] or [prɛzənt]. The noun refers to a gift; the verb does not.

Exercise 3.12.   Underline the syllable that is accented or stressed in each of these words:

farthest	paper
basketball	complete
university	insurance
alphabet	present (verb)
antique	present (noun)

(If you noticed that polysyllabic words gave you some trouble, it is because they have both primary accent and secondary accent. This problem we will also leave for a later chapter.)

Syllable stress affects the pronunciation of a word, and you must sharpen your listening skills to hear the alteration of pitch, duration, or intensity that occurs on the accented syllable. You must also become highly aware of accentuation, because in the International Phonetic Alphabet there are three pairs of symbols whose only differences occur in whether they are stressed or not. Two of these pairs were discussed in Chapter 2: the two symbols for *uh*, as in the word *above* [əbʌv], and the two symbols for the *er*, as in *further* [fɝðɚ].

A final pair of symbols with stressed and unstressed forms are the [i] and the [ɪ], and this one is the hardest to justify. As we told you at the beginning of this chapter, the *ee* sound in the word *machine* is written [i], [məʃin]. But, if the *ee* sound is in an unaccented syllable, as in the word *pity*, the [ɪ] symbol is used by phoneticians to indicate that lack of stress: [pɪtɪ].

All of these symbol variations will be taken up later in far more detail, but you will be encountering these symbols over and over again in your transcription, and from this discussion you should have a modicum of familiarity with them. We will provide you with one exercise for practice. Remember:

STRESSED VOWEL			"SOUND"		UNSTRESSED VOWEL	
[ʌ]	up	[ʌp]	uh	[ə]	about
[ɝ]	earn	[ɝn]	rrr	[ɚ]	eager
[i]	please	[pliz]	ee	[ɪ]	become

Exercise 3.13.   Underline the stressed syllable in these words.

mɝdɚ	əkɝ	bɪliv	ɛmfəsɪs	kɑndəkt
ʌndɚ	mɛnɪ	əgɛn	kəmjunɪkeʃn̩	kəntɛnt
bɪtwin	ovɚ	θauzənd	ɪresɚ	pɝmɪt
mʌðɚ	hʌndrɪd	vɪdʒələns	dɛzɚt	pɚmɪt

Establishing a strong association between a sound and its phonetic symbol

This final hint is one that you should begin to use right now, and continue using throughout this course.

A few students neglect to build a solid foundation for their phonetic skills. They never become absolutely sure in their reading of certain symbols. Their reading bogs down in guesswork. When they have to transcribe, they search painfully and often inaccurately for the necessary symbol. If you are to become adept in the phonetic skills you must have the symbol–sound associations on the tip of your tongue and pen. They must become almost involuntary, entirely automatic. You must know immediately what sound is represented by the [æ] or [ʊ] or [tʃ]. You should not have to search for, or even think of, a key word to indicate its pronunciation. The symbol should come to you as soon as you hear the sound.

The way to do this most effectively is to use as many of your senses as you can as you learn each new symbol. *Look* at the symbol as you *say* it aloud. *Listen* to the way you say it. Write the symbol in the air as you say it, moving whole arm through its convolutions. This is using your kinesthetic sense. "Write" the symbol with your fingers on paper, sandpaper, on your forehead, on your backside, anywhere, so the tactual sense—the sense of touch—is being utilized, too. If you do all this at the introduction of each symbol, and occasionally afterward, you should never have any difficulty.

Name _____ Date _____ Score _____

Hand this in to your instructor.

1. Circle the word in one of the right-hand columns which has the same vowel sound as that in the left column on the same line. *Example:* Is the vowel sound in the word *queen* the same as the vowel sound in the word *feet* or as in the word *been?*

queen	feet	been
though	sew	cough
farm	warm	harm
said	beat	fed
aisle	height	wait
worm	irk	store
break	pear	crate
psalm	sell	odd

2. The following words are arranged in groups of three. Which of the second and third words in each group ends with the same as the first word? Circle your choice. *Example: Fix* ends with an *s* sound. Does *tick* or *less* end with the *s* sound?

fix	tick, less	breathe	tooth, smooth
blow	now, toe	dismay	quay, croquet
fan	scene, condemn	frog	huge, fatigue
charm	warn, thumb	cough	through, bluff
was	fleas, fuss	tease	fuse, cease
walked	fast, wagged		

3. We have many "silent" letters in English spelling, such as the *p* in *pneumonia.* In the following words cross out all silent consonants—consonants which represent no sound in the word. *Example:* There is no *l* sound in the word *salmon* = sa~~l~~mon. (Not all of the words have silent consonants.)

cat   salmon   walk   bend   island   hymn   sprint

4. Underline the words which have only two sounds. *Example: Though* is made up of only two sounds; *th* and *o*.

though	buy	off	ought
wry	axe	tough	itch
pew	shoe	use	low
know	cough	ash	elm

5. Underline the words which have exactly three sounds.

caught	laugh	shoot	throw
fade	sauce	shin	saw
half	box	church	sting
quick	taught	wrong	shape
cheese			

6. Which of the following words use the same vowel *sound* twice? Underline your choices. *Example: Ballad* will not be underlined because the two vowel sounds are not the same; [bæləd].

ballad	Alabama	bottom	mystic	visit
emblem	Boston	common	unsure	

7. Here are some simple words written in spelled form and in phonetics. Five of them are written *in*correctly in phonetics. Find them and circle them, referring to the phonetic alphabet given earlier for keys to the pronunciation of any unfamiliar symbols.

trick	trɪk	whose	huz
tooth	tutθ	sign	saɪn
each	itʃ	keys	kis
gorge	gɔrg	should	ʃud
of	ʌf	talk	tɔlk
meadow	mɛdo	fell	fɛl

8. After the following words, a series of dashes indicates the number of sounds in each. There are only as many sounds as there are dashes. Your task is to be able to pronounce these sounds, one for each dash. Diphthongs [aɪ aʊ ɔɪ] each count as a single sound.

Mississippi _____	wreck ___	bring ____	crew ___
soaked ____	does ___	boiler ____	dish ___
issue ___	extra _____	guide ___	check ___

9. Count the number of sounds in each of the following words, and fill in the blanks with the proper number.

fill _____	freeze _____	tried _____
fight _____	gnaw _____	feather _____
wait _____	palms _____	mix _____
shift _____	foreign _____	reached _____
clams _____	highly _____	

10. The three words in each of the following groups start with the same *sounds* (not necessarily the same spellings). Using the definitions as a guide, fill in the blank spaces, then write out the word in phonetic transcription.

a. sigh   to make an audible respiration   _____
   sigh_   the power of seeing; vision   _____
   ci_____   mention by way of eulogy   _____

b. cu_   a mongrel dog   _____
   cu__   rudely concise   _____
   cu_____   a window hanging   _____

c. m_   belonging to me   _____
   m___   5280 feet   _____
   m___   gentle in nature or behavior   _____

   fa__   to drop   _____
   fa___   a failing or flaw   _____
   fa____   to move unsteadily   _____

11. In the following list, underline all the words that have the [s] *sound*. Disregard English spelling.

soap	certain	paste	hats	beast
cede	please	mission	his	pronounce
complex	fashion	peace	present	sure

12. Each of the following words is phonetically reversible. By saying the last sound first, and then the first sound last, try to discover the word-opposite for each. Write them in English. *Example: Kin* said backwards is *nick.*

kin	_____	sick	_____	keep	_____
pass	_____	gnat	_____	ice	_____
nap	_____	knit	_____	mash	_____
stop	_____	fix	_____	peace	_____
back	_____	dare	_____	pole	_____
isle	_____	spill	_____	nuts	_____

13. By referring to your key words of the phonetic symbols, work out the following words. Write them in English.

sef	_____	du	_____	kɔrn	_____
mɛn	_____	no	_____	klæs	_____
pliz	_____	sɪŋ	_____	ni	_____
kæp	_____	hu	_____	brum	_____
nɛt	_____	hwɪsḷ	_____	ræbɪt	_____
ðɛn	_____	hænd	_____	wɑndɚ	_____

14. Read the words below and write them in English spelling.

sɑm	_____	ɔlðo	_____	mjutʃuəl	_____
dɛt	_____	lɪkt	_____	ʌv	_____
kuʃən	_____	ruʒ	_____	haɪt	_____
trɛʒɚ	_____	kɔʃən	_____	ni	_____
itʃ	_____	sɪnəmən	_____	hɔk	_____
ækʃən	_____	wɪzdəm	_____	trenz	_____
tʃɚtʃ	_____	skiz	_____		

40

15. Opposite some of the words below there are blanks. Using your answers from question 14 above as hints, write one word in each blank in which the italicized letter does not represent the sound.

    b as in boy, but not as in *debt* (no *b* sound)
    d as in doll, but not as in *stepped* (the *d* is pronounced *t*)
    f as in fall, but not as in _____
    g as in goat, but not as in _____
    h as in house, but not as in _____
    k as in king, but not as in _____
    l as in large, but not as in _____
    p as in paper, but not as in _____
    s as in sand, but not as in _____
    t as in table, but not as in _____
    w as in walk, but not as in _____

4 The Familiar Consonantal Symbols
b m f t d n p v g k w h s z l r

We now reintroduce all of these familiar consonantal symbols, one after another. Each of these phonemes is described according to the place and manner of articulation, since these are among the basic features which give each of these sounds its identity. In addition, you are provided with short reading passages, loaded with the phonemes which each symbol represents. We all learn to read before we learn to write. In these reading passages we will use broad rather than narrow transcription, and transcribe the words as though they were uttered separately rather than in connected speech. We do this to make it easier for you as you begin to master your skills. Later on, you will see how pronunciation of certain words changes when they are strung together in sentences.

[b]

The [b] is a bilabial plosive. It is produced by closing the lips together rather tightly, creating air pressure behind them, then suddenly exploding the air in a little puff. It is a voiced sound.

hau tu gɛt rɪd əv bɛdbʌgz

bɛdbʌgz ɑr bæd tu hæv| vɛrɪ bæd|| ðe baɪt ɪn̩ ðə naɪt|| maɪ brʌðɚ bɪl hæd ə bætʃ əv ðɛm ɪn hɪz bɛdrum ænd ɔlso ɪn hɪz bæθrum|| so bæd wɚ ðe| bɪl bɛrlɪ dɛrd sɪt daʊn|| so hi gɑt hɪz bɪg hɛrɪ frɛnd nemd bozo| hu hæd ə bɪg brʌʃɪ bɪrd| ænd hi pʊt hɪm ɪn hɪz bɛd|| ðɛn hwɛn ɔl ðə bʌgz faʊnd bozo ænd bɛrɪd ðɛmsɛlvz ɪn hɪz bɪrd| brʌðɚ bɪl gɑt ə besbɔl bæt ænd bæŋd ðɛm ovɚ ðə hɛd hwɛn ðe kem aʊt əv ðɪ ʌndɚbrʌʃ||

[m]

The [m] is a bilabial, continuant, nasal, voiced sound. The lips are closed, but the voiced airflow is emitted through the nose.[1]

mɪstrɪs mɛrɪ| mɪk ænd mɛsɪ| mɪændɚd daʊn ðə mɪsɪsɪpɪ| mʌntʃɪŋ ɛm ænd ɛmz ænd mʌʃɪ marʃmɛloz|| ʃi mɛrɪd maɪk ænd med ə vaʊ tu maɪnd hɚ mænɚz fɔrɛvɚmɔr||

---

[1] The [p], [b], and [m] are called *homorganic* sounds because they are produced in much the same way by the lip action, differing mainly in the presence or absence of voice or nasality.

[f]

The [f] is the voiceless labio-dental fricative, the cognate of [v] and is articulated in the same way.

tru ɔr fɔls

sʌm prəfɛsɚz ar fɚoʃəs| ʌðɚz ar frɛndlɪ| sʌm no ðɛr stʌf| ʌðɚz ar frɔdz|| bʌt ɔl əv ðɛm kæn bi kand ɔr fuld ɪf ju no hau|| ɪf ðe ar fɛrlɪ jʌŋ ænd əv ðɪ apəzɪt sɛks ju kæn flɝt wɪð ðɛm|| ɪf ðe ar old ju læf frikwɪntlɪ æt ɔl ðɚ farfɛtʃt dʒoks|| ɪf ðe ar ɪn bɪtwin ju put ə fæsɪnetɪd luk an jur fes ænd flætɚ ðɛm æftɚ klæs baɪ θæŋkɪŋ ðɛm fɔr ðə fæntæstɪk lɛktʃɚ||

[t]

The [t] is the cognate of [d]. It is an unvoiced lingua-alveolar plosive, articulated just like the [d].

ɑn ə tri baɪ ə wɪlo sæt ə lɪtl̩ tɑm tɪt
sɪŋɪŋ wɪlo| tɪtwɪlo| tɪtwɪlo
ænd aɪ sɛd tu hɪm| bɝdɪ hwaɪ du ju sɪt
sɪŋɪŋ wɪlo| tɪtwɪlo| tɪtwɪlo
ɪz ɪt wiknɪs əv ɪntəlɛkt| bɝdɪ aɪ kraɪd
ɔr ə ræðɚ tʌf wɝm ɪn jur lɪtl̩ ɪnsaɪd||
wɪð ə ʃek əv ɪts pur lɪtl̩ hɛd hi rɪplaɪd
tɪtwɪlo| tɪtwɪlo| tɪtwɪlo||

A little vowel help

In order to have words to work with we now provide the phonemic symbols for three of the vowels: [u], [o], and [ɛ]. The first of these is quite familiar (but you must think of it as *oo* instead of *you* since the latter has two sounds in it; the *y* [j] and the [u]. So we have such words as [mun], [krun], and [lun] representing *moon*, *croon*, and *loon*. The second symbol is also familiar. [o] sounds like *Oh*, like "Oh, say can you see?" We use it in words like *oak* [ok], *stone* [ston], and the dog's [bon], but not as in the word *dog* [dɔg]. Our third vowel is the [ɛ] which represents the *short e*, of such words as *slept* [slɛpt], [wɛt], and [tɛnt]. We will discuss and present these and other vowels later in detail, but now we need just these few to enable us to read and transcribe words.

Exercise 4.1.   Transcribe these words.

boom _____	bet _____	to _____
moot _____	boat _____	tomb _____
oaf _____	tome _____	moat _____

Exercise 4.2.   Write these words in English spelling.

[but]   [tut]   [fom]   [bot]   [mɛt]   [bɛt]
____   ____   ____   ____   ____   ____

Exercise 4.3.   Read these words aloud, then write them in English.

1. [but   dum   fud   hum   lus] _____

44

2. [bot dom foks groz kolz] _____

3. [bɛl dɛlt flɛm gɛs klɛnz] _____

4. [sut kroz mɛnt pul sɛd] _____

Exercise 4.4.   Which of these are not real words? Say them aloud, then underline the real words.

1. [up kon sɛl pul tron spɛn sud lɛd kul mon]

2. [mɛlo foks spos drɛst pol skool glukos]

Exercise 4.5.   Transcribe these words.

1. croup _____   2. wounds _____   3. wren _____

4. tomb _____   5. dreamt _____   6. rogue _____

7. spool _____   8. owed _____   9. phlegm _____

Exercise 4.6.   Read the following sentences as swiftly as you can. Go over them twice. Then write them in English in the spaces provided.

1. [tu rɛnz nɛsts hɛld tɛn ɛgz] _____

2. [hu hɛlpt ðə lud rog] _____

3. [tu krom spulz brok lus] _____

4. [ðə ful komd ðə kolts nɛk] _____

5. [huz tɛksts dɪd lulu luz ɪn skul] _____

[d]

The [d] is the voiced lingua-alveolar plosive produced by placing the tongue tip against the upper gum to block the airway, then suddenly lowering it to release the impounded air. The vocal folds are vibrating.

[ðə duk ænd ðə dʌtʃəs sæt daʊn tu ti|
ðiz bʌnz ɑr dɪsgresful| maɪ diə sɛd hi||
maɪ lɔrd hæv sʌm ʃugə| ʃi sɛd wɪθ ə saɪ|
ænd gev hɪm tɛn lʌmps raɪt ɪn ðɪ aɪ||]

Transcribe these words: dupe _____ mood _____ debt _____ food _____
dome _____ boned _____ doom _____ fed _____

[n]

The [n] is a lingua-alveolar nasal continuant phoneme. It is voiced. The tongue position is homorganic, or the same as for the [t], but it is held fixed and the airflow and voice come out of the nose.

nɝvəs nɛlɪ nidəd nəstɝʃəmz fɔr hɝ gɑrdən bʌt ʃi ɪnkaʊntɝd hɝ nebɚ nætəlɪ ɛngedʒd ɪn nɝsɪŋ ænts n̩ wɝmz ɪn æntik pats æz pɛts|| hwʌt nɝtʃɚz ænts n̩ wɝmz| ʃi æskt|| nid ju æsk| nebɚ nætəlɪ ænsɚd|| nəstɝʃəmz ɑr ðer nætʃɚəl fud||

Transcribe these words: nude _____ den _____ phone _____ nest _____
any _____ noon _____ know _____ spoon _____

45

[p]

The [p] phoneme is a bilabial, voiceless plosive, articulated in the same way as its voiced cognate, the [b].

pipḷ tɛl ʌs ðæt pitɚ paipɚ pɪkt ə pɛk əv pɪkḷd pɛpɚz‖ kwait ɪmpɑsɪbḷ‖ pɛpɚz gro ɪn gardṇ plats| nat pɪkḷ pats‖ ɪts plɔzɪbḷ ðæt pitɚ wʌz pɪkḷd ɔr patɪd hɪmsɛlf‖

Transcribe these words: peg _____ spend _____ pool _____ loop _____
open _____ troop _____ pet _____ scope _____

[v]

The [v] is a labio-dental fricative consonant. It is sonant, not surd. The lower lip is lifted to make a loose contact with the upper teeth.

lʌv ɪz ə fivɚ ju trit wɪθ kəntɛnt|
lʌst wants ə vɪktɪm dʒʌst fɔr ə vɛnt|
lʌst ɪz ə vɪktɚ hu nidz tu ɛnslev|
lʌv noz ɪts switɚ tu gɪv ðæn bɪhev‖

Transcribe these words: vote _____ vend _____ groove _____ prove _____
drove _____ vest _____ move _____ heavy _____

[g]

The [g] is the voiced, lingua-velar plosive phoneme. It is produced by humping the back of the tongue until it makes firm contact with the velum or soft palate; then the contact is broken and the puff of air is released.

ðə gros grin gablɪn gritɪd ðɪ ʌglɪ gargɔɪl‖ go sʌk ə ɛgǃ hi sɛd‖ ðə gargɔɪl grʌmpt ænd graʊld‖ ai gɛs jur grin wɪð ɛnvi| ju gros grin gablɪn‖ no| no| gæspt ðə gablɪn‖ aim grin bɪkɔz aim gardɪŋ gret bægz əv grin mʌni frʌm gridɪ gargɔɪlz‖ ðə gargɔɪl gritəd hɪz tiθ ænd gæləpt əwe‖

Think up two words that have a [g] and an [u] in them, two for [g] and [o], and two for [g] and [ɛ].

_____ _____ _____
_____ _____ _____

[k]

The [k] is the unvoiced cognate of [g], and is made in the same way except that the vocal folds do not vibrate. It is a lingua-velar plosive.

ketɪdɪdz ar ɪnsɛkts ðæt lʊk laik græshapɚz| bʌt ðe hæv ðə krezi hæbɪt əv ətræktɪŋ itʃ ʌðɚ bai klɪkɪŋ ænd skrepɪŋ ðɛr wɪŋz tʊgɛðɚ| ə sɛks kɔl ðæt kæn bi hɝd fɔr sɪks mailz an ə kul munlɪt nait‖ ɛnɪwʌn traɪŋ tu kætʃ fɔrti wɪŋks wʊd wɪʃ ðæt ketɪdɪdz dɪdṇt‖

46

Underline all the words that have the [k] sound in them:

keep	Christmas	school
cool	extra	knife
scratch	know	came
accept	king	ankle

[w]

The [w] phoneme is classified as a bilabial voiced glide sound. It begins with the tongue posture for the [u] and continues immediately into the following vowel. Remember that there is no word in English where the [w] is followed by a consonant sound.

wi wɪlɪ wɪŋkɪ rʌnz θru ðə taʊn|
wipɪŋ ænd welɪŋ ænd swɪŋɪŋ əraʊnd||
wɪl wi wɪlɪ wɪŋkɪ hæv ə gʊd de||
hi wɪl ɪf hi wɪʃəz tu wɑndɚ əwe||

Transcribe only the words with the [w] sound in them:

swoop	_____	own	_____	wren	_____
woe	_____	owl	_____	quote	_____
marshmallow	_____	went	_____	flow	_____

[h]

The [h] phoneme is classified as an unvoiced glottal fricative. It is produced in the larynx itself; the friction noise is caused by air rushing through the constricted glottis. However, when it begins a syllable (and it never ends one) it always contains the breathy release of the sound which follows it. It has no fixed mouth position. If we say *hoop*, the mouth is shaped for the [u] during the [h], and if we say *hope*, the mouth is shaped for the [o] even before the [h] is uttered. It is a chameleon sound, taking the color of its surroundings, but always there is the flow of whispered friction.

ho| ho| ho| sɛd ðə hæpɪ hʌntɚ| aɪ si ju haɪdɪŋ ɪn ðə hɛn haʊs|| kʌm hapɪŋ aʊt| ju hæplɪs hɛr|| aɪ wont hɑrm ju|| laɪk hɛl ju wont| hɪst ðə hɛr| aɪl sɪt hɪr tɪl ðə kost ɪz klɪr||

One difficulty you might encounter with this group of consonants is with the words *who* and *whose*. They are transcribed [hu] and [huz]. There are no [w] sounds in those words. Also, you know the sounds of [t] and of [h], but usually when you see them together in the English alphabet, neither of the *sounds* is used; *the, this, that, there, these*, and so on, all begin with a single sound before the vowel—[ð]—and the words *thin, thick*, and *theater*, begin with the single sound [θ]. Once in a while the *th* combination will use the [t] and the [h]; *cathouse* [kæthaʊs] and *fathead* [fæthɛd], but don't count on it, ordinarily.

[s]

The [s] is a lingua-alveolar fricative. This sibilant sound is produced by lifting a narrowly grooved tongue up behind the upper teeth. The hiss of the [s] sound is created by blowing unvoiced air through this narrow channel.

sɪlɪ sælɪ sæt ænd sod ɑn sɪstɚ suz sketɪŋ saks‖ ɑr ju sɚtən ðə stɪtʃəz ɑr strɔŋ ɪnʌf‖ æskt su‖ ðɛr so strɔŋ ðe wɪl stɑp jur sɚkjuleʃən‖ sɪlɪ sælɪ sɛd‖

[z]

The [z] is the voiced partner of the lingua-alveolar fricative [s]. It also is a continuant. Its manner of production is exactly the same as the [s] except that the vocal folds are vibrating.

The letter *z* is much more phonetic than is the *s*, but the *sound* of [z] is often represented by other spellings. Most frequent of these is the *s*, as we have seen in the plurals of nouns, such as *rooms* [rumz] and *beds* [bɛdz], and the endings of verbs: *goes* [goz], *runs* [rʌnz], *believes* [bɪlivz]. You will find other *s* letters having the sound of [z] in such words as *these* and *easy*.

Exercise 4.7.   Write these words in phonetics. Say each one aloud, so you can hear if you are using the silent [s] or the voiced [z].

moves	_____	crest	_____
hiss	_____	graze	_____
zest	_____	zoom	_____
hose	_____	exist	_____

Exercise 4.8.   Transcribe the following.

pɪnokɪoz noz groz ænd groz əntɪl ɪts gros‖ ɪf hi bloz hɪz noz ɪn ə kwaɪət zon ðə nɔɪz kud kɔz ə dɪzæstɚ‖

Exercise 4.9.   Pluralize these words by adding the appropriate phonemic symbol.

[dræg__   brɪk__   fon__   hɛd__   hɪt__   læmp__]

[l]

The [l] sound is a glide consonant. The tongue and alveolar ridge are used in producing the [l] sound; the front part of the tongue is pushed against the back of the upper gum ridge, and the air comes out laterally on either or both sides of the tongue. The [l] can serve as a consonant, or as a sort of vowel. For now, we will treat it solely as a consonant.

lɚnɪŋ ðə lɛtɚz əv ðɪ ɪŋglɪʃ ælfəbɛt wʌz lats hardɚ ðæn jul faɪnd lɚnɪŋ ðɪs ælfəbɛt‖ ðə lɔz əv prənʌnsɪeʃən ɑr lɛs lus ðæn ðə lɔz gʌvɚnɪŋ spɛlɪŋ‖

Exercise 4.10.   Write these words in phonetics.

elbows	_____	fooled	_____
lose	_____	old	_____
loose	_____	legs	_____

[r]

The [r] sound is a lingua-palatal glide. It is voiced. It, like the [l], can either be a semivowel or a consonant; but, again, we will be considering only its consonantal qualities here. You find the consonantal [r] in words such as *run* [rʌn], *rags* [rægz], *dream* [drim], *attract* [ətrækt], and *wring* [rɪŋ].

Exercise 4.11.   Write this in phonetics.

Who will ring the bell when we swipe it from the crude, crafty rogues?

AVOIDING TRANSCRIPTION ERRORS

Now that you have had an opportunity to wrestle with the task of recording the pronunciation of the more familiar consonant symbols, you have become aware of the discrepancies between the letters and the sounds which compose certain words. You have probably made some errors and found some uncertainties. Let us help you a bit. One of your errors was probably that of recording a sound which just was not there. As you found in the last chapter, many words in our language have letters which represent no sound whatever. We have written and spelled these words so long that we almost seem to hear them with our eyes, perceiving sounds which do not exist. Is there an [l] sound in *salmon*, or a [b] in *tomb?* One of the most frequent offenders is the *w.* We already have mentioned *who* [hu] and *whose* [huz], but also, there is no [w] in *wrong* [rɔŋ], *owed* [od], *write* [raɪt], or *fellow* [fɛlo].

Exercise 4.12.   All of these words have silent letters. Cross out the silent letters after you have pronounced each word.

1. debt   2. pneumonia   3. knight   4. doubt
5. sword   6. ghost   7. walk   8. two
9. gnat   10. column   11. half   12. whole

PLURALS

We have already mentioned the confusion produced when verb endings and plurals of certain words end in the letter *s*, but the actual sound is [z]. The rule is as follows: When the sound just before the *s* is voiceless, then the voiceless [s] is used—*hits, mocks, laps, cuffs.* However, if the next to the last sound is voiced, you use a [z] sound—lids [lɪdz], rubs [rʌbz], craves [krevz], brags [brægz]. Remember that a vowel is always voiced, so *ways, frees, toes,* are written phonetically, [wez], [friz], [toz].

Exercise 4.13.   In the spaces after these words write the final sound only. Be sure to say the word aloud and perhaps prolong the last sound a little.

1. crops _____   2. sneezes _____   3. brides _____
4. seats _____   5. seeds _____   6. corps _____
7. moons _____   8. guests _____   9. waits _____
10. wades _____   11. eggs _____   12. six _____
13. boys _____   14. gems _____   15. through _____

Another problem occurs in the past tense of regular verbs. They end in *d* or *ed*, but some are pronounced as [t]. The rule is the same as for the *s* and *z* endings: When the sound just before the *d* endings is voiceless, the [t] sound is used—walked [wɔkt], cuffed [kʌft], mopped [mɑpt]. But if the next to the last sound is voiced, you use the [d] sound—rubbed [rʌbd], craved [krevd], bragged [brægd]. We will give you a few of these to work on.

Exercise 4.14.   Write just the last sound in these words.

1. joked _____
2. guessed _____
3. knitted _____
4. gazed _____
5. cracked _____
6. begged _____
7. banked _____
8. waited _____
9. waded _____
10. loaded _____
11. fished _____
12. skis _____
13. welds _____
14. wheeled _____
15. praises _____

Now let's look more closely at some of the other confusing ways consonant sounds are spelled in English, and thereby help you avoid some [fənɛtɪk bubɪ træps]. The *p* is silent in several words, such as pneumatic [numætɪk] or psychology [saɪkɑlədʒɪ]. How is it spelled in *hiccough?* When the *p* is combined with *h*, it generally represents the [f] sound, as in *physique* [fɪzik], but what sound does this combination produce in the name *Stephen?* In some words it is omitted from the spelling, as in such a word as *warmth*, even though most of us utter a tiny [p] between the *m* and the *th*.

As we have said, the *b* is usually phonetic in English, but there are words where the letter is silent, as in *subtle* and *thumb*. You already have read or written other words that have a silent *b*. Can you remember what they are? ([tum] and [daʊt]). Like the letter *p*, the *b* is often written doubly within a word, although only one sound is spoken: [klʌbd] and [stɑpt]. If only one sound is spoken, only one symbol is written.

The letter *k* is generally phonetic, but often when it is followed by an *n*, it is silent: *knight, kneel, know,* and *knot* [naɪt, nil, no, nɑt]. The letter *c* is not used in phonetic transcription of normal English speech, since the two major sounds it represents are the [s] or the [k]; *cat* [kæt] or cent [sɛnt]. And when we trancribe a word like *cello*, we use the *ch* [tʃ] to give us [tʃɛlo]. Our symbol [k] always represents the *hard c* sound, as in the words *can, cool,* and *catastrophe*, as well as the letter *k* in such words as *keep, kick,* and *ski*. Remember, too, that the letter *x* often represents the [ks] combination. *Styx* and *sticks* are pronounced exactly alike: [stɪks]. In discussing the [k] sound it is impossible to neglect the *q*. At the beginning of a syllable it is usually pronounced *kw: quick* [kwɪk], *quote* [kwot], *inquire* [ɪnkwaɪr], *piquant* [pikwənt]. And, at the end of a syllable it has a single *k* sound: *torque* [tɔrk], *pique* [pik].

Name _____ Date _____ Score _____

Hand this in to your instructor.

1. Transcribe these words.

blue	_____	strolls	_____	bread	_____
ooze	_____	elves	_____	guessed	_____
smells	_____	scent	_____	folks	_____
debts	_____	knew	_____	pseudo	_____
bellows	_____	cents	_____	elbow	_____
close	_____	next	_____	toasts	_____
wooed	_____	ghosts	_____	womb	_____
quotes	_____	tests	_____	wound	_____

2. What is the first *sound* of the following words? Write the symbol in the space provided.

knot	_____	psychology	_____	knows	_____
write	_____	physician	_____	who	_____
hour	_____	xylophone	_____	demand	_____
hair	_____	cracked	_____	were	_____
heir	_____	pneumonia	_____	cyst	_____
wrist	_____	reason	_____	catch	_____

3. Mark an X after each word that contains the [s] sound.

means	_____	system	_____	massive	_____
meets	_____	flags	_____	as	_____
accept	_____	certain	_____	ass	_____
eggs	_____	whose	_____	Missouri	_____
exact	_____	falls	_____	hers	_____

4. Now that you have breezed through the first three questions, we are hitting you with a rough assignment. Write these sentences in English, even though there are many symbols which you have not learned yet. The content of the sentences should help you, since all of the statements contain material you have just learned.

ðə p ænd b saundz ar boθ baɪlebɪəl plosɪvz| ðə fɜˑst ɪz sɜˑd ænd ðɪ ʌðɚ ɪz sonənt||

ðɪ m ɪz ə baɪlebɪəl nezl̩ kəntɪnjuənt|| ðə lɪps ar klozd ænd ðə saund ɪmɜˑdʒəz θru ðə nastrɪlz||

ðə f ænd v ar kɔld lebɪodɛntəlz bɪkɔz ðe ar med baɪ lɪftɪŋ ðə loɚ lɪp ʌp əgɛnst ðɪ ʌpɚ tiθ|| ðe ar frɪkətɪv kəntɪnjuənts| ænd ɪtʃ ɪz ðə kagnet əv ðɪ ʌðɚ||

ðə t ænd d ar kagnet lɪŋgwədɛntl̩ plosɪvz|| ðə tʌŋtɪp ɪz plest əgɛnst ðɪ ʌpɚ tiθ| ðɛn sʌdənlɪ puld daun tu rɪlis ə pʌf əv ɛr||

ðə k ænd g ar med ɪn ðə rɪr əv ðə mauθ baɪ rezɪŋ ðə bæk əv ðə tʌŋ ʌp əgɛnst ðə sɔft pælət ɔr viləm| ðɛn sʌdənlɪ puld daun tu rɪlis ðə stɔrd ʌp ɛr prɛʃɚ|| ðe ar kɔld vilɚ plosɪvz|| ðe ar stap kansənənts| nat kəntɪnjuənts||

ðə s ænd z ar sɪbɪlənt saundz| prədust baɪ lɪftɪŋ ə nɛrolɪ gruvd tʌŋ ʌp bɪhaɪnd ðɪ ʌpɚ tiθ|| ðɪ ɛr flo daun ðɪs gruv kriets ðə hɪsɪŋ saund ðæt meks ðɛm frɪkətɪvz||

ðə r| w| ænd l ar glaɪd kansənənts|| ðɪ r glaɪdz əwe frʌm ðɪ ɜˑ vauəl ɪntu ðə vauəl ðæt faloz ɪt|| ðə w muvz əwe frʌm ðɪ u|| ðə l muvz əwe frʌm æn ʌpθrʌst tʌŋ pəzɪʃn̩ əgɛnst ðə bæk əv ðɪ ʌpɚ gʌm rɪdʒ||

ɪf ju faund ðɪs tu bi ə mɪzɚəbl̩ ɛksɚsaɪz| go əhɛd ænd kɜˑs væn raɪpɚ ænd smɪθ| bʌt rɪmɛmbɚ| ju gat əkwentɪd wɪθ jur nu ælfəbɛt||

5 Some Vowels

Before we begin intensive practice of some of the vowel phonemes, you should remember that a phoneme is a *family* of sounds. The [i] phoneme is pronounced *ee*, but the way you say [i] will be slightly different for different words, and for different times, and it will be slightly different from the way other people say it. The difference is not meaningful, in that the word will mean the same thing, but the difference will be perceptible. As we have said, the various vowel sounds are produced by the mouth opening and the humping of the tongue, and sometimes your tongue might hump infinitesimally higher or lower than usual as you say a certain vowel. Consider the word *intrigue*. The position of the tongue for the first vowel is just one "notch" lower than its position for the second vowel, and when talking, the two tongue humps might be almost identical.

In the next three chapters we will be presenting the *phonemes* (sound families) rather than allophones. We will save the discussion of individual variations of pronunciations—the allophones—for the last several chapters.

[i]
The Vowel [i] as in *eat* [it]

ðə ʃli ɪz wi
ænd mɝ·sɪ mi
ju kænɑt tɛl
ðə hi frʌm ʃi
bʌt ʃi·noz wɛl
ænd so dʌz hi

The [i] is the vowel sound in such words as *eat*, *she*, and *need*. Probably this symbol was chosen by the creators of the International Phonetic Alphabet because in most of the European languages this letter represents this sound. The Spaniard says, "Sí, sí, señor," the Frenchman says, "Oui, oui." Even we who speak English often use words in which the letter *i* is pronounced *ee*, words such as *unique* and *ski*. The [i] is classified as a high, front, tense vowel.

iiiiiiiiiiiiiiiiiiiiiiiiiiiiiiiiiiiiiiiiiiiiiiiiiiiiii

hau ðɪ i ɪz spɛld ɪn ɪŋglɪʃ

Although the [i] sound in English is usually spelled with the letter *e*, either singly as in *he* or doubled as in *meet*, there are many other ways in which this sound is represented. If you were a native of Timbuktu trying to learn how to speak English from a book [ju wʊd hæv wʌn dɛvɪl əv ə taɪm] because in some words *ea* or *ae* or *ay* or *ie* are sounded out as [i]. English spelling is far from consistent. It is only partly phonetic. There are too many symbols or symbol combinations for any one sound. By the use of the phonetic alphabet, where each sound has but one symbol, we eliminate much confusion. To help you appreciate this for the sound of [i] we provide the fɑloɪŋ ɛksɚsaɪz‖

Exercise 5.1.   Here is a list of words, most of which (but not all) contain [i] sounds. Discover all the different ways in which the [i] sound is spelled and list the words under each. You will find twelve different ways of spelling [i].

pea	believe	physique	chic
geese	key	Jean	leader
vaccine	people	conceit	receipt
naive	quay	Phoenix	steeple
amoeba	reach	proceed	marine
physical	scene	concede	prestige
Caesar	ski	thief	

(*Example:* ea = pea, reach, leader.)

———— ———— ———— ———— ———— ————
———— ———— ———— ———— ———— ————
———— ———— ———— ———— ———— ————
———— ———— ———— ———— ———— ————

[i] is not pronounced *eye;* it is always pronounced [i].

You'll find no [i] in such words as *mind, hint, icicle,* or *ignoramus.* Remember that the symbols in brackets are always phonetic symbols, not letters of our English alphabet. The [i] therefore is the vowel sound in *heat* but not in *hit,* in *scheme* but not in *skim,* in *freed* but not in *fried.* Write *heat, scheme,* and *freed* in phonetic symbols here : ————;
————; ————. [ju mʌst lɚn tʊ lɪsn̩ nɑt lʊk‖]

As you observed in the last exercise, there are times in English when the letter *i* represents the sound of [i], such as in the words *machine* and *fatigue.* In our phonetic transcription *i* always means [i]. The phonetic word [hit] can never be used with reference to boxing. It is always *hot.*

Exercise 5.2.   Transcribe these words.

scream ————	kneel ————	feels ————
leaves ————	please ————	seen ————
squeak ————	east ————	priest ————
league ————	scene ————	grease ————
eats ————	unique ————	queen ————
niece ————	teepee ————	sheep ————

Now let's do some reading of phonetic script. Be sure to read it aloud.

Exercise 5.3.

1. o haʊ ʃi skwild hwɛn ðə tu maɪs skwikt‖
2. ju sɪt ɑn jʊr sit bʌt ju nil ɑn jʊr ni‖
3. ædəm ænd iv slɛpt‖ sizɚ ænd kliopætrə dɪd tu‖
4. ʃi faɪ ʃo fʌm twɪdl̩ di ænd twɪdl̩ dʌm‖

54

5. sɪks sɪnjɚz wɝ ɑn ðə tim‖
6. kip itɪŋ lin mit bʌt dont it swits‖
7. bɪliv ɪt ɔr nɑt ilz ar gʊd tu it‖
8. ðə mun nɛvɚ bimz wɪðaʊt brɪŋɪŋ mi drimz‖
9. ʃi gev mi ðə dip friz tritmənt‖
10. hwɛn ju skwiz swɪs tʃiz jul sniz‖

It is difficult to describe just how a vowel is produced, but the following picture represents the conventional way in which the vowel [i] is said to be articulated.

Exercise 5.4. Translate this phonemic passage into English.

[tu mek ðə vauəl i ples ðə tʌŋ tɪp əgɛnst ðə bæk əv ðə loɚ frʌnt tiθ‖ ðə saɪdz əv ðə tʌŋ prɛs ʌpwɚd əgɛnst ði ʌpɚ saɪd tiθ‖ ðə frʌnt əv ðə tʌŋ ɪz lɪftɪd æz haɪ æz ɪt kæn kʌmfɚtəblɪ go‖ ðə loɚ dʒɔ ɪz drɑpt slaɪtlɪ so ðæt ðə tiθ ar bɛrlɪ partɪd‖ ðə lɪps ar nɑt protrudɪd‖ ðə mʌsl̩z əv ðə tʌŋ ænd ðoz dʒʌst bɪlo ðə tʃin ar tɛnst‖]

The [i] is termed a *front vowel* because the tongue is bunched forward in the mouth. It is called a *high vowel* because only a narrow gap separates the upper surface of the tongue from the hard palate. It is called a *tense vowel* because the muscles are more highly tensed than they are for the [ɪ] vowel used in the words *pit* or *sit*. If you will say the word *peel* and prolong the vowel a little while feeling the muscles directly under the chin, you will find them tensed. If you relax these muscles and the tongue, the *peel* will become *pill*. These two vowels, the [i] and the [ɪ], might be said to be next-door neighbors in another way too. In terms of the upward bulging of the tongue's contours, the [i] is the highest vowel while the [ɪ] is the next highest.

Exercise 5.5.   Read these words.

prɛstiʒ	kənsid	sin	əmibə
mərin	prosid	ritʃ	naiv
stipl̩	finɪks	ki	væksin
rɪsit	kənsit	pipl̩	gis
lidɚ	dʒin	bɪliv	pi
ʃik	fɪzik	sizɚ	
θif	ski	fɪzɪkəl	

hæv ju ɛvɚ sin ðiz wɝdz bɪfɔr‖ ju maɪt lʊk bæk ə bɪt‖

Exercise 5.6.   This is one more attempt to help you separate the ear from the eye, to teach you to forget the spelling and listen to the sounds of words. In the following list of words there are eight which are nonsense words, exactly eight. Can you find them?

1. bin	2. dig	3. dip	4. diʃ	5. dim
6. fit	7. git	8. tiθ	9. his	10. lit
11. dʒip	12. tʃiz	13. in	14. iz	15. ist
16. rip	17. kni	18. fri	19. mint	20. strikt

The nonsense words are numbers ＿＿＿ ＿＿＿ ＿＿＿ ＿＿＿

＿＿＿ ＿＿＿ ＿＿＿ .

fɪdl̩ dɪdi fɪdl̩ dɪdi
ðə flaɪ ʃæl mɛrɪ
ðə bʌmbl̩bi

[ɪ]
The Vowel [ɪ] as in *it* **[ɪt],** *business* **[bɪznɪz],** *guilt* **[gɪlt], and** *foreign* **[fɔrɪn]**

[ɪ] is a high, front, lax vowel. The symbol for this common vowel is used in the words *if*, *ship*, or *hit*, and it looks like a small capital I. When you print it, be sure to have not only the vertical line but the bars on top and bottom as well. Not [|] but [ɪ]. Those who do not know phonetics use the diacritical mark [˘] over the letter *i*. [ĭ] or the syllable *ih* to represent the sound. The word *whale* in Russian is written KNT. How would you pronounce it? A friend of ours wrote that he heard it spoken as *kiht*. He was wrong. It is actually pronounced more like [kit] with the [i] sound we studied in the last section. It's hard to tell how a word is pronounced when someone uses the ordinary alphabet.

The sound of [ɪ], like the sound of [i], is spelled in many different ways in English. Look at the last word in the preceding sentence. The first sound of *English* is spelled with an *E* but it is pronounced [ɪ]. Write the word in phonetic script. Do you hear the two [ɪ] sounds in it? Now let's see how many ways the [ɪ] sound can be written in ordinary English spelling. This is good practice, for it helps to free you from the tyranny of the eye; by sorting out the different spellings of a sound you will learn to listen to the sounds themselves.

Exercise 5.7.   There are 11 different spellings for the [ɪ] sound as heard in these 21 words. Sort them out according to their spellings.

flit, guilt, weird, fear, lymph, women, forfeit, jeer, sieve, frontier, myth, pretty, build, palace, mere, example, busy, been, mint, salad, biscuit

1. i, as in mint, flit   2.   3.
4.   5.   6.
7.   8.   9.
10.   11.

Exercise 5.8.   Write all the following words in phonetics.

1. flit _____   2. guilt _____   3. lymph _____
4. women _____   5. sieve _____   6. build _____
7. busy _____   8. been _____   9. mint _____
10. biscuit _____

Exercise 5.9.   Here are some silly sentences loaded with [ɪ] sounds. Read aloud.

1. ɪf bɪl wɪl kɪs lɪl wɪl lɪl hɪt bɪl‖
2. hɪkɚɪ dɪkɚɪ dɪŋk‖ ðɪ il slɪpt daʊn ðə sɪŋk‖
3. tɪz mɛnɪ ə slɪp twɪkst ðə sit ænd ðə sɪt‖
4. bɪg wɪlɪ frʌm pɪkədɪlɪ fɛlt sɪlɪ hwɛn hi mɪkst sɪrəp wɪθ pɪkl̩z fɔr hɪz sɪstɚz bɪskɪts‖

Exercise 5.10.   Transcribe these sentences into phonetic script.

1. His wrist will twist if Bill grips it. (Note: There's no *w* in *wrist*.)

_____

2. Did he fix his deep freeze?

_____

3. If the prince didn't kiss the queen, who did?

_____

4. The pig is so big we will kill and eat him.

_____

5. He dipped deep in the sea, didn't he?

_____

The production of the vowel [ɪ] can best be understood by comparing it with the [i]. In the following exercise, test all the statements and discover which one is false.

1. [ɪn mekɪŋ ðɪ ɪ ples ðə tʌŋ tɪp slaɪtlɪ loɚ əgɛnst ðə loɚ tiθ ðæn ju du for ðɪ i saʊnd‖
2. ɔlðo ðə frʌnt əv ðə tʌŋ ɪz bʌntʃt fɔrwɚd æz ɪn ðɪ i ju wɪl dɪskʌvɚ baɪ plesɪŋ jʊr fɪŋgɚ əbʌv ðə tʌŋ ðæt ɪts ɛlɪveʃən ɪz sʌmhwɑt loɚ‖
3. ðə dʒɔ ɪz loɚd ðʌs pɑrtɪŋ ðə tiθ slaɪtlɪ mɔr ðæn fɔr ðɪ i‖
4. ðɪ ɪ vaʊəl laɪk ðɪ i dɪmændz ðə sem tɛnsnɪs əv ðə tʌŋ ænd mʌslz‖

Use of the symbol [ɪ] in endings of words

Remember that an unaccented _ee_ sound is actually pronounced somewhere between the [i] and the [ɪ]. As you will find in our chapter on narrow transcription, there are ways for you to write this intermediate sound. For now, however, whenever this intermediate sound is used in the unaccented part of a word, write the [ɪ] symbol. Thus, the words _seedy, filly, city, meaty, silly, treaty, pretty, hilly, risky, pity, kitty, misty,_ when written in phonemics, should look like this: [sidɪ‖ fɪlɪ‖ sɪtɪ‖ mitɪ‖ sɪlɪ‖ tritɪ‖ prɪtɪ‖ hɪlɪ‖ rɪskɪ‖ pɪtɪ‖ kɪtɪ‖ mɪstɪ].

Use [ɪ] in unaccented endings of words, even if it sounds like [i] to you. In the word _candy,_ the second syllable is unaccented, and therefore requires the [ɪ] symbol, but in the word _key,_ the whole one-syllable word is accented, and the [i] symbol must be used.

Exercise 5.11.   Here are some words that end in [i] or [ɪ], depending on whether the ending is accented or not. Indicate in the blank following each word whether it ends in [i] or [ɪ].

1. tree _____	2. city _____	3. pity _____
4. employee _____	5. free _____	6. hasty _____
7. tiny _____	8. knee _____	9. guarantee _____
10. deflea _____	11. witty _____	12. thirsty _____

The days of the week fall into the above category. The _day_ at the end of each word is unstressed, and calls for the [ɪ]. This is also true of the _numerical tens:_ twenty, thirty, forty, and so on.

Exercise 5.12.   Fill in the phonemic symbols that are missing, saying the word aloud as you do so.

Monday	mʌnd _____	Miami	maɪæm _____	
Tuesday	tuzd _____	New Jersey	nu dʒɝz _____	
Wednesday	wɛnzd _____	forty	fɔrt _____	
Thursday	θɝzd _____	seventy	sɛvənt _____	
Friday	fraɪd _____	ninety	naɪnt _____	
Saturday	sætɚd _____	twenty	twɛnt _____	
Sunday	sʌnd _____			

The words in the second column are easily recognized as having the unaccented ending [ɪ]. But it is not so easy to hear the [dɪ] endings in the days of the week. If a speaker is stressing the word *Monday*, he will probably say [mʌnde]. However, in everyday conversation the second syllable is partially "lost"—the effort to make a tense [e] sound is too much bother for such an unimportant part of the word. This habit is not considered substandard; our conversational English abounds in examples of the lessening of [ðə tɛnʃən əv] the vowel in the unaccented part of the words. Take the word *interest*. Some people give each syllable its full quality of sound [ɪntɚɛst]. But the second and third syllables are less accented than the first, and thus are subject to being slighted. You will hear the word pronounced [ɪntɚɪst] or even [ɪntrɪst]. All of this may sound confusing, but soon you will be able to hear these differences in pronunciation for yourself.

Another apparent difficulty arises when making a distinction between such words as *posies* and *poses*. If you follow the above rule it would seem that the two words would be identical in phonetic script: [pozɪz]. Actually there is a real difference in the pronunciation of the two words. If you listen closely when a word ending in *y* or *ie* is pluralized, you will hear that the last vowel sound is clearer and longer and has greater stress. In such words the [i] symbol should be used. Therefore, the correct transcription of the plural of *posy* would read [poziz]. Like most rules in phonetics there are some exceptions to this. Sharpen your ears and you will need no rules. Say the following words aloud, taking careful notice of how the last syllable sounds in each word:

daisies	dezɪz	bosses	bɔsɪz
dazes	dezɪz	bossies	bɔsiz
taxes	tæksɪz	purses	pɚsɪz
taxis	tæksiz	Percy's	pɚsiz

In the middle of words when the [i] sound is coupled with another vowel the vowel that is stressed determines whether [i] or [ɪ] is used. (Such words as *piano* and *deity* have another vowel sound coupled with the *ee* sound.) If the *ee* part of the vowel sounds is *un*stressed, we use the symbol [ɪ]; *piANo* is transcribed [pɪæno]. If the *ee* is in the stressed syllable, we use the symbol [i]; *Deity* is transcribed [diɪtɪ]. In the word *react* the *a* is stressed, so the word is written [rɪækt]. *Realize* has the emphasis on the first syllable, and looks like this in phonetics [rɪəlaɪz]. In words such as *reality* and *reecho*, the vowel sound in *re-* is unaccented. Therefore, the words are transcribed in this way: [rɪælɪtɪ| rɪɛko]. In the word *reënter*, both vowels are stressed and the word looks like this: [riɛntɚ]. When in doubt say the word in a sentence to avoid distortion.

Thus, for all doubtful cases the stress within a word itself often determines which symbol [i] or [ɪ] is used. Listen carefully.

Exercise 5.13.   Remembering that [i] tends to become [ɪ] in unaccented or unstressed syllables, fill in the missing sounds of the following words:

1. reMEMber	[r_mɛmbɚ]	2. STORies	[stɔr_z]
3. CANdid	[kænd_d]	4. teases	[tiz_z]
5. Rosie's	[roz_z]	6. roses	[roz_z]
7. HANDicap	[hænd_kæp]	8. eMOTion	[_moʃən]
9. beLIEVE	[b_liv]	10. taxes	[ ]
11. daisies	[ ]	12. piano	[ ]

In syllables where you have a choice of either [i] or [ɪ] before an [r] as in *ear*, *sneer*, *peer*, or *irritate*, the sound you probably use is closer to an [ɪ] than to an [i]. There are a few exceptions but these occur when the speaker splits the [r] diphthong as in saying *HEro* [hiro] instead of *hero* [hɪro]. You probably say [hɪro]. In pronouncing such words, say them swiftly or in a sentence, so that you will speak them naturally and without distortion.

Exercise 5.14.   Read these words as rapidly as you can while thinking of the word meanings.

sip	fist	tɪn	bɪt	spik	gis
sɪp	hɪp	sin	hit	spɪgɪt	grist
nɪr	hip	nɪt	hɪt	bɪn	grɪst
skɪp	tin	nit	mit	bin	
fɪst	sɪn	bit	mɪt	kɪs	

Exercise 5.15.   Transcribe these sentences.

1. We repeat it is easy to keep neat.

_____

2. It seems a pity she seems so weary.

_____

3. Skim milk and beans will slim Lizzie's hips.

_____

4. It's queer the deer will drink beer.

_____

5. Billy is pretty sick since he skipped physics.

_____

Exercise 5.16.   One of our foreign students pronounced this series of words, as recorded phonetically. Which ones have an incorrect [i] or [ɪ]? Underline the correct ones.

1. chin	tʃin	2. believe	bɪliv	3. liberty	libɚtɪ
4. zinc	zɪŋk	5. knitting	nɪtɪŋ	6. village	vɪlɪdʒ
7. sixth	siksθ	8. please	plɪz	9. Friday	fraɪdɪ
10. ditto	dito	11. going	goiŋ	12. gasoline	gæsəlɪn
13. mittens	mitɪnz	14. gym	dʒim	15. guilty	gɪltɪ

[e]
The Vowel [e] as in *pay* [pe]

sleigh	aid	crepe	fate	lay	prey	pray	fail
sle	ed	krep	fet	le	pre	pre	fel

This phonetic symbol is not an *E*. [e] is pronounced *A*. Did the inventors of the International Phonetic Alphabet deliberately plan to confuse you? No! In many of the European languages the letter *e* is sounded as [e]. In Spanish we find it in *peso* [peso], money. In Italian the word *credo* is pronounced [kredo], and *cemb*, the Russian word for *seven*, is pronounced [sem]. Therefore, since the *e* represents what we call the *long A* sound more often than any other sound, [e] it is. In English it is represented often as *a*, or *ay*. However, if you will look at the words above you will see a great many spellings for this [e] sound. The [e] is the vowel sound in these words: *pay* [pe], *bay* [be], *ray* [re], *say* [se], *they* [ðe], *clay* [kle], *weigh* [we], *chase* [tʃes].

Exercise 5.17.   Fill in the blank after each word with the English letters which represent the [e] sound. Some have more than one. For example [stek] is spelled *steak* and also *stake*.

stek	_____ _____	redz	_____	pez	_____
ren	_____ _____	lez	_____ _____	mel	_____ _____
feθ	_____	beð	_____	gret	_____ _____
hwelz	_____	ʃekɪ	_____ _____	kənten	_____
sle	_____ _____	wez	_____ _____		

e e e e e e e e e e e e e

ðɪ e ɪz æn ʌnraundɪd haɪ mɪdl̩ frʌnt tɛns vauəl‖ ðə lɪps ɑr nɑt protrudɪd ɔr raundɪd‖ ðə frʌnt əv ðə tʌŋ ɪz bʌldʒd ʌpwɚd tu ə pəzɪʃən əbaut mɪdwe bɪtwin ðɪ ɪ ænd ðɪ ɛ saundz‖ ðə tʌŋ ɪz ə bɪt tɛnst‖

Exercise 5.18.   Scrambled sentences. Rearrange these words to make sensible sentences.

1. redʒd tuθek wɪð ep ðɪ ə

_____

2. gres fɔr tʃendʒɪŋ ʃem ɑn hɚ edʒ

_____

3. wɛst krezɪ ket wʌz dʒed əbaut

_____

4. bel æt ðə me smɪθ dʒel wevd

_____

5. eprɪl ðel̩ ɑn ðə pe de etθ əv

_____

The [e] symbol is used in phonetics to represent the simple [e] vowel and also all the longer variations of it, such as we find when it glides into another vowel—[eɪ]. Say the word *paid* as we write it in phonetics: [ped]. Then say it again, having the [e] vowel glide into the [ɪ]—[eɪ] [peɪd]. In our country, people use this longer form almost universally in their speech, but for our present transcription purposes we will represent [e] and all its longer variations by the single symbol [e].

We do this because there is no possibility of confusion anyway. There are no two English words identical except for the [e] and [eɪ] sounds. If there were, we would of course have to use the [eɪ] symbol. Many foreigners do use the pure vowel [e] instead of our habitual diphthong. They say [de] instead of our [deɪ], and it truly sounds different. When using phonetics to help foreigners learn English, we always write our words with the [eɪ] diphthong. Thus, if we were teaching a foreigner to speak our language we would transcribe the sentence *He ate at home today* in this fashion: [hi eɪt æt houm tʊdeɪ].

Exercise 5.19. Transcribe these sentences.

1. They placed the ape in the basement.

_____

2. Ray gave Grace a detailed recipe.

_____

3. The whale was placed on a freight train.

_____

4. His waist was wasted away.

_____

5. We paid Abe for the quail.

_____

Exercise 5.20. Reading Passage.

etıet batḷz əv bır an ðə wɔl med etin medz krezı wıθ θɜˑst‖ ðe sizd ðə bır ænd dræŋk ıt ɔl‖ ðen led an ðə tebḷz‖ wetıŋ tu bɜˑst‖

The [ɛ] Phoneme

The [ɛ] phoneme is the vowel sound in the words _wet_, _dress_, _bell_, and _pen_ [wɛt drɛs bɛl pɛn]. It looks like an old fashioned script ɛ, and some people still use it today. If you are one of those people, a graphologist would say that you like the niceties of life, like pink bows, and strive for good grades.

ðə saund ɛ ız fɔrmd baı drapıŋ ðə dʒɔ slaıtlı frʌm ðı ı pəzıʃən‖ ðʌs kozıŋ ðə tiθ tu part ivn̩ fɜˑðɚ‖ ðə lıps ar ın ðer nɔrməl rɛstıŋ pəzıʃən‖ ðə tʌŋ tıp mentenz əpraksımıtlı ðə sem kantækt æz fɔr ðı ı‖ ıf ju wıl ples jur fɔrfıŋɡɚ əloŋ ðə ruf əv jur mauθ ænd prədus fɜˑst ðı ı ænd ðen ðı ɛ ju wıl dıskʌvɚ ðæt ðə tʌŋ ın ðə lætɚ saund ız boθ loɚd ænd slaıtlı rıtræktıd‖

Exercise 5.21. Put the [ɛ] symbol in the blank space in the words below as you say the word aloud, then write the English translation after it.

v__st _____	__b _____	h__vı _____
dr__s _____	int__nd _____	g__st _____
p__nsḷ _____	m__nı _____	__ls _____
b__lt _____	h__d _____	__ko _____
kw__st _____	b__nt _____	s__z _____
p__st _____		

Most often the [ɛ] sound is written in English as an _e_. There are exceptions, however: _ready, chair, feather, says, said_ [rɛdı tʃer fɛðɚ sɛz sɛd].

Exercise 5.22. Write these sentences in phonetics.

1. Many men fell dead.

_____

2. Sell silly Sally seven cents.

_____

3. Lend Ben eleven hens' eggs.

_____

4. His script is easily read.

_____

[æ]
The Symbol [æ] as in *sat*

The symbol looks like a combination of letters or a doodle you might make in your notebook during a boring lecture. But it is actually a unitary symbol and stands for one simple, commonly used vowel sound—the *a* in the words *cat* [kæt], *mantle* [mæntl], *bags* [bægz], *pant* [pænt], and *at* [æt]. The script symbol is made with one continuous stroke, starting at the upper left-hand corner.

This particular sound is an unusual one in that the symbol we use to represent it is almost identical with the letters used to represent the same sound in Old English. In that language the letters *a* and *e* were used for the sound, because its value lay between the Latin *a* and *e*, and they could not decide which sound it resembled most. So they used both symbols to dispel any arguments. From the combination we get our [æ] symbol. Foreigners still confuse it with [ɑ] and [ɛ].

ði æ ɪz ðə lɔɪst əv ðə frʌnt vauəlz‖ ðə tɪp əv ðə tʌŋ kantækts ðə bes əv ðə loɚ tiθ ænd ðə frʌnt əv ðə tʌŋ ɪz slaɪtlɪ hʌmpt‖ ðə loɚ dʒɔ ɪz drɑpt fɚðɚ ðæn fɔr ði ɛ ænd ðə lɪps ɑr rɪtræktɪd ænd sprɛd mɔr ðæn fɔr ɛnɪ əv ði ʌðɚ vauəlz‖

How long does it take you to read these words aloud?

æd	mæd	ætɪk	næstɪ	fænsɪ
bæk	læf	dæns	əgæst	bɪgæn
læm	dæmp	ænt	kræk	æpt
pæk	ræft	æksɛnt	slæpt	næpsæks

Exercise 5.23.   Write these words in phonetics.

fat	_____	lag	_____	sag	_____
cap	_____	back	_____	calf	_____
as	_____	Sam	_____	knack	_____

Now that we have the vowels [ɪ i æ u e ɛ] added to the consonants we know, let's see how fast you can read them.

Exercise 5.24.   Take a speed test, but beware of inaccuracies. Can you read aloud this entire list in 25 seconds?

dɛd	sɛl	sæd	list	bit
did	sɪl	sid	lust	sɪks
dæd	pɛk	sɛd	lɛst	sɛks
dɪd	pɪk	sud	bit	sɪks
rɪd	pæk	lɪst	bɛt	sæks
rud	pik	læst	but	seks

Exercise 5.25.   Now take the above list of words and write them in English. You may find you have been making an error or two. (One word of caution: [lust] is translated *loosed.*)

When the [ɛ] sound is followed by an [r] sound, its quality seems to change. If you say the words *bear* and *bed* quickly, the vowels may not sound alike to you. But take the first word, *bear*, and say [bɛ:], prolonging the [ɛ] sound and then add the final [r]. Do the same with the word *bed*, prolonging the [bɛ:] and then add the final [d]. You will see that the [ɛ] vowel sounds are pretty similar when they are isolated in this way. The final [r] sound only seems to change the vowel which precedes it because it creates a diphthong, or vowel blend.

Try the same experiment with these paired words: *pear–pet*, *air–egg*, *deck–dare*, prolonging the vowel before you add the final sound of the word.

Some of you may feel that you say [dær] rather than [dɛr] and to be perfectly candid, it is possibly true for you as an individual. However, since this book deals with general American phonetics, we will write the word *dare*, and all words that rhyme with it, with an [ɛr] ending.

Exercise 5.26.   Using the consonants of the phonetic alphabet, how many good English words can you make with the [ɛr] ending. *Example:* [bɛr] = *bear*. Here are the consonants:

b d f g dʒ h k l m n ŋ p r s t ʃ tʃ θ ð v w hw j ʒ z

WRITE THESE WORDS IN PHONETICS

1. an _____

2. ant _____

3. rant _____

4. trance _____

5. strand _____

6. stand _____

7. dance _____

8. and _____

9. add _____

10. dʌz ðɪs hæv æn ɛs ɔr ə zi‖ 　　10. lose _____

11. ðɪs ɪz izɪ‖ 　　11. friend _____

12. hwɪtʃ ɪz ði ʌnæksɛntɪd sɪləbl̩‖ 　　12. grouping _____

13. sʌm wɝdz hæv no saɪlənt lɛtɚz‖ 　　13. basket _____

14. dɪto‖ 　　14. neigh _____

15. dont gɛt kɔt baɪ ðə dʌbl̩ ɛf‖ 　　15. staff _____

16. no c ɪn əmɛrɪkən fonɛtɪks‖ 　　16. crypt _____

17. wɝdz ɛndɪŋ ɪŋ y_____‖ 　　17. giddy _____

18. dʌbl̩ tʃɛk ðə fɝst θri saʊndz‖ 　　18. accept _____

19. ju no ðɪs wʌn‖ 　　19. careless _____

20. si nʌmbɚ tɛn‖ 　　20. loose _____

Read these sentences aloud.

ANSWERS

1. ju rʌn ɪntu ðɪs ɔfən ɪnʌf‖
2. hwɑts jʊr ʌŋklz waɪf kɔld‖
3. ðə lændlɔrd rænts hwɛn ju dont pe ðə rɛnt‖
4. ɑr ju ɪn ə stupɚ hwɛn ðə prəfɛsɚ lɛktʃɚz‖
5. ə hæŋk əv hɛr‖
6. naʊ du ju ʌndɚstænd‖
7. kæn ju dæns‖
8. ə kəndʒʌŋkʃən no lɛs‖
9. mebɪ jud ræðɚ səbtrækt‖
10. hɛdz ɔr tɛlz‖ hɛdz aɪ wɪn tɛlz ju luz‖
11. ə dɔg ɪz ə mænz bɛst frɛnd‖
12. mɔr ðæn ə pɛr‖
13. ə tɪskɪt ə tæskɪt‖
14. hɔrsɪz ne‖ dɔŋkiz bre‖ hwɑtdəjudu‖
15. brɛdz ðə stæf əv laɪf‖ waɪnz ðə krʌtʃ‖
16. ðə krip krɛpt ɪntu ðə krɪpt‖
17. hwo‖ æz ɪn gɪdɪjæp hwo‖
18. kəmpɛr wɪð ɪksɛpt ɪn spɛlɪŋ‖
19. bɛtɚ kɛrful ðæn _____‖
20. huz gus ɪz lus‖

1. æn
2. ænt
3. rænt
4. træns
5. strænd
6. stænd
7. dæns
8. ænd
9. æd
10. luz
11. frɛnd
12. grupɪŋ
13. bæskɪt
14. ne
15. stæf
16. krɪpt
17. gɪdɪ
18. æksɛpt
19. kɛrlɪs
20. lus

In general American pronunciation *Mary*, *marry*, and *merry* usually are indistinguishable. Context alone makes sense of an oral "Will you marry merry Mary?" [wɪl ju mɛrɪ mɛrɪ mɛrɪ‖] However, in some parts of the United States and in merry old England each of the three words has a different vowel sound: [wɪl ju mærɪ mɛrɪ merɪ‖].

DISAPPEARANCE OF [ɛ] IN UNACCENTED SYLLABLES

You will sometimes have difficulty deciding what symbol to use in unaccented syllables, in those words in which you would expect an [ɛ] to be used. If you look at the word *hundred* as it is spelled you would probably transcribe it as [hʌndrɛd]. But now say the sentence, "I wrote the [ɛ] symbol a hundred times." In conversation the *e* in the word *hundred* is unaccented and sounds more like [ɪ] (or the unstressed vowel *uh* [ə], which you will learn later). There are many such words in which you might expect the vowel to be transcribed as [ɛ], but if you listen you will hear a different sound.

Regardless of the spelling of the word, the [ɛ] sound often disappears when it occurs in an unaccented syllable. This is no rule, merely a caution to listen. But if you do not listen, you will make many errors.

Exercise 5.27. Read the italicized word in each sentence, first as you would expect it to be transcribed from the spelling. Then listen to the difference in the sound when it occurs in the unstressed part of the word, and is used in conversation.

1. [hardɪst ɔr hardɛst] The *hardest* thing to do is hear the sounds.
2. [ɛndlɪs ɔr ɛndlɛs] Do these lessons seem *endless?*
3. [sɪstəm ɔr sɪstɛm] There must be a *system* to this.
4. [ɛlɪgənt ɔr ɛlɛgɛnt] The word *elegant* looks familiar in phonetics.

Exercise 5.28. The [ɛ] sound requires a keen ear. In only one of the following words is there actually an [ɛ] vowel. Which one?

different   channel   nearness   coldest   explanation

For a while it may be difficult to hear the differences between [ɪ], [ɛ], and [i] because we are so accustomed to following the English spelling of the word. Remember, practice is the only way to make your ear as reliable as your eye.

Exercise 5.29. Here are a list of foolish phrases. Can you read them rapidly—without a mistake?

ɪt hæz ritʃt aʊr kɛn ðæt sʌm əv aʊr kɪn ɑr kin‖
wi pikt æz wi pɪkt ðə pɛk əv pətetoz‖
ðə tinz tʊk tɛn tɪnz tʊ tɪmbəktu‖
rɪd ðə rum əv rɛd ridz‖
ɪts no bɛd əv roziz tʊ bɪd ən bidz‖
fɪl fɛld ðə ful ɑn ðə fild‖

Many foreign-speaking individuals tend to use the [ɛ] or the unfamiliar [ɛɪ] instead of our [æ] vowel as in the words *bat*, *cat*, and *rat*. They mispronounce the vowels in these words so that they sound like [bɛt] [kɛɪt] [rɛt].

Read these words as spoken by a Latvian learning English. Pronounce them accurately.

[mɛθɪmɛtɪks kɛndɪ ɛskɪn hɛmsɛnwɪtʃ slɛɪpt ɛŋgrɪ ɛksɛnt]

This same error is sometimes heard in people who have lost their hearing in the early preschool years.

In the Uncle Remus stories the word *if* is commonly spelled *ef* in order to indicate its pronunciation as [ɛf]. This substitution of [ɛ] for [ɪ] is often found in regional dialects of the United States. You will hear it often in such relatively unaccented words as *in*, *been*, *since*, *as*, or *and*. According to television [wɛstɚn kaʊbɔɪz nɛvɚ sɪt ɑn ðɛr sædḷz| ðe sɛt ɑn ðɛm‖]. Most of these pronunciations are substandard, though some are attaining respectability. In Southern speech the opposite substitution occurs in words where the [ɛ] is followed by *n*. You will hear sentences such as these south of the Mason-Dixon line: [wi liv tɪn ˈwiks fəm ˈwɪnzdɪ‖]

Exercise 5.30.   Write these sentences in phonetic script.

1. Will he be late?

_____

2. We made a date.

_____

3. If he misses the train,

_____

4. We'll wait in vain.

_____

Exercise 5.31.   Read the following paragraph aloud and underline all the [æ] sounds. Then write the entire paragraph in phonetic script.

A man can say many words [wɝdz] easily if he can read the [ðə] key. If he sits and scans the plan and has enough [ɪnʌf] practice, he can translate phonetic script as easily as his family can. [ju dont nid tʊ mek sɛns aʊt əv ðɪs‖ dʒʌst raɪt ðə saʊndz æz ju hɪr ðɛm‖]

Exercise 5.32.   In the words below, fit each of these six vowels into the blank space in the phonetic word. How many actual English words can you obtain from each one this way? The first one gives five words. Write these words in English.

	[ɪ]	[ɛ]	[e]	[æ]	[i]	[u]
[h__d]	hid	head	hayed	had	heed	
[g__s]						
[s__n]						
[r__m]						
[m__t]						
[p__n]						

67

[a]

This vowel sound is not commonly used in general American speech except in the diphthongs [aɪ] and [aʊ]. Indeed, most speakers of this major dialect in America find it a difficult sound to produce in isolation or in words where it constitutes the accented vowel. The best way we can describe it in print is to say that it lies somewhere between an [æ] and an [ɑ]. By forming the mouth posture for the [æ] and holding it as you attempt to say [ɑ], you will approximate the [a] sound. Another method for producing it is to prolong the diphthongs [aɪ] or [aʊ] and to stop suddenly before you make the terminal sound. It may be heard in the speech of eastern New England. Kenyon and Knott say that it is also often heard in New York City in such words as *ask* or *bath*. Even in the part of New England where it is common, the [a] is not used consistently as a substitute for the general American [æ] in all words. This inconsistency often spells exposure to those who affect the so-called "Harvard accent." Only the native born "down-easter" seems to know the 200 or 300 words in which [a] would be used rather than [ɑ] or [æ]. He might use it in *path* [paθ] but would not use it in crash [kræʃ].

[ɒ]

Like the [a] this new symbol represents a sound which is not commonly used in general American speech. The vowel lies midway between the [ɑ] and the [ɔ]. You may approximate its quality by placing your mouth in position for the [ɔ] and holding it fixed therein as you attempt to say [ɑ]. It is frequently heard in stage speech and in British pronunciation. In this country the [ɒ] is heard mainly on the Eastern seaboard as a substitute for [ɑ] in such words as *knotty* [nɒtɪ], *watch* [wɒtʃ], or *cot* [kɒt]. However, it may occasionally be found in a word or two in speakers of general American English. One of the authors of this book, born and bred in Michigan, consistently uses this vowel in only one word, the preposition [fɒr]. We describe the [ɒ] here partly so that you may sharpen your ears to the variations in speech of your fellow students, partly to limber up your tongues, and primarily so that you will be able to read the phonetic transcription of dialect later in this text.

Exercise 5.33.   Read the following very carefully.

[æ ɑ a; a æ ɑ; ɑ a æ; kɑd kad kæd; haf haf hæf; ɑnd and ænd; pæst pɑst past; lɑf laf læf; a a a ɑ a ɑ a ɑ a æ a ask‖]

[ðə kaf draŋk haf əv ə naɪn kwɔrt pel əv mɪlk‖
ðə man laft hwɛn hɪz hat blɪu ɒf‖
dan ran past hɪz ants haʊs‖]

[ɑ]
The Sound [ɑ] as in *father* [fɑðɚ]

ɑ ɑ bɑks ɑ ɑ rɑb ɑ ɑ ɑrmɪ ɑ ɑ

This symbol is made just like a small written *a*, but is not used as frequently as we use that letter in English spelling. It is used only to represent the *ah* sound, and you will find a great many words spelled in English with an *o* which are pronounced [ɑ]. If you have ever studied any of the Romance languages this phoneme will be easier for you to master, for in those languages the [ɑ] is usually pronounced *ah*. The English language, however, creates difficulties. When you see the word [tap] you may be inclined to translate it as *tap* [tæp], and if you are asked to write the word *top* in phonetics you might write [top] which is *taupe*.

The [ɑ] sound is spelled as *a* in such words as *palm* [pɑm], *party* [pɑrtɪ], and *mama* [mɑmə]. It is spelled as *ea* in such words as *heart* [hɑrt], and as *o* in *knock* [nɑk], *hot* [hɑt], *not* [nɑt], *bomb* [bɑm], and *John* [dʒɑn].

ðɪ ɑ saʊnd ɪz nɔn æz ə lo bæk vaʊəl‖ ðə bæk əv ðə tʌŋ ɪz slaɪtlɪ rezd‖ ðə tɪp ænd frʌnt part əv ðə tʌŋ laɪ flæt ɪn ðə maʊθ‖ ðə medʒɚ kɛrɪktɚɪstɪk əv ðə saʊnd laɪz ɪn ɪts opənɪŋ‖ ðə dʒɔ ɪz drɑpt tu fɔrm ðə waɪdɪst opənɪŋ əv ðə spɪtʃ saʊndz‖

Exercise 5.34.   haʊ wɛl kæn ju rid ðɪz nɑnsɛns wɚdz‖

pɑdiwad	atɪla	manɪmid	dɪpaka	tabɪliəs
vɑzet	kadala	sawefɪl	dɛmanid	pizafile

Exercise 5.35.   Read these words aloud, then write them in English script.

bɑm	_____	ark	_____	klak	_____	valɪ	_____
kam	_____	armɪ	_____	stap	_____	pad	_____
dak	_____	alɪv	_____	lak	_____	krak	_____
nat	_____	baks	_____	batl̩	_____	barn	_____
sad	_____	fand	_____	ad	_____	farm	_____

In the exercise above it is very evident that you will have to forget ordinary spelling. Some of the words resemble words you have known in English spelling which have no relation to the phonetic words they actually represent. [sad] looks like something that should make you weep, but there's no need for tears unless your bit of turf has weeds in it. In phonetics this symbol ceases to be the letter *a* and becomes the *ah* sound only.

Exercise 5.36.   In the following paragraph fill in the blank spaces with either the [æ] or the [ɑ] symbol. The content will determine which you use.

ðə m__n sɛd hi kʊd n__t st__p seɪŋ ə l__t əv wɚdz hi h__d pr__ktɪst‖ ɪt simd __d tu hɪm t se ðɪ __saʊnd ɪn wɚdz sʌtʃ __z map hwɪtʃ hi h__d pr__bəblɪ ɔlwɪz spɛld wɪð __n o‖ haʊɛvɚ hi dɪd __n __dmɪrəbl dʒ__b‖

In spite of the fact that general American speech is pretty well standardized, there are some officially recognized variations, and the *ah* sound comes in for its share of them. Have you ever noticed the way some people say *doll?* They make it rhyme with *hall* or *ball* [dɔl]. They are neither more right nor more wrong than those who say [dɑl]. However, most of us say [dɑl].

The word *wash* goes one step further; you will hear three pronunciations of it. Both the *ah* [wɑʃ], and the *aw* [wɔʃ] are permissible, but *warsh* must be considered substandard, no matter how often you hear the error.

Exercise 5.37.   Transcribe these sentences.

1. Molly says olives are delicacies.

_____

2. We parked the car far from the barn on the farm.

_____

3. Tom had the quality of strictest honesty.

_____

4. Are we to place the palms in the park?

_____

[ɔ]
The Vowel [ɔ] as in _crawl_ [krɔl], _song_ [sɔŋ], _bought_ [bɔt]

ɔ| go fɔl ɔf ə lɔg||

This vowel symbol is a small reversed letter _c_. We find it used in an initial position in the word _always_ [ɔlwɪz], in the medial position in _applauded_ [əplɔdɪd], and in the final sound in _straw_ [strɔ]. It is spelled _au_ in _pause_ [pɔz], _aw_ in _paws_ [pɔz], _a_ in _ball_ [bɔl], _o_ in _often_ [ɔfn̩], _augh_ for _caught_ [kɔt], and _ough_ for _fought_ [fɔt]. Since those English letters have many other sound values, you will have to depend on your ears entirely in recognizing this sound.

tu mek ði ɔ saund ju rez ðə bæk əv ðə tʌŋ tu æn ɛlɪveʃən dʒʌst slaɪtlɪ bɪlo ðæt əv ði o bʌt haɪɚ ðæn ðæt əv ði ɑ saund|| ðə dʒɔz əsum ə pɪzɔʃən mɪdwe bɪtwin ðæt əv ðə sem tu vauəlz ænd ðə lɪps ɑr raundɪd ænd dʒʌst slaɪtlɪ prətrudɪd||

Exercise 5.38.   Read these words as quickly as you can. Try for 15 seconds.

hɔl	ɔlso	ɔ	hɔtɪ	pɔz
pɔ	ɔlmost	ɔdɪt	lɔ	brɔt
klɔ	kɔt	sɔs	lɔd	dɔn
slɔ	hɔk	ɔful	nɔ	fɔrk
tɔt	ɔlwɪz	gɔkɪ	ɔlrɛdɪ	kɔf
mɔl				
ɔt				

Exercise 5.39.   Now take the list in the previous exercise and write the words in English.

_____ _____ _____ _____

_____ _____ _____ _____

_____ _____ _____ _____

_____ _____ _____ _____

_____ _____ _____ _____

_____

A certain gentleman I know says [ə frɑg sæt ɑn ə lɑg ɪn ðə bɑg ɑn ə fɑgɪ de||]. Most people in the midwest would say [ə frɔg sæt ɑn ə lɔg ɪn ðə bɔg ɑn ə fɔgɪ de||] What is your choice?

To compound this problem, sometimes you find people who substitute the [ɒ] sound for the [ɑ] and the [ɔ]. This vowel is heard frequently in British speech but rarely in general American. This vowel can be thought of as possessing some of the characteristics of both [ɑ] and [ɔ]. It sounds exactly as it looks; halfway between the [ɑ] and the [ɔ]. Your job is to transcribe what you hear, but be sure you are hearing accurately.

[ðɪs saʊnd ɪz ðə vɛrɪ loːɪst əv ðə bæk vaʊəlz‖ ðə tʌŋ ɪz ɔlmost flæt ɪn ðə maʊθ bʌt ðə bæk əv ɪt ɪz saɪtlɪ rezd‖ ðə lɪps ar raʊndɪd lɛs ðæn fɔr ɔ ænd ðə tiθ ar klosɚ tʊgɛðɚ‖ ðə mʌsl̩z ar nat tɛns‖ ðə tɪp əv ðə tʌŋ ɪz bɪhaɪnd ðə loːɚ tiθ‖ ə gʊd mɛnɪ pipl̩ juzɪŋ dʒɛnrəl əmɛrɪkən spitʃ juz ðɪs saʊnd ɪn ðə wɛˑdz [John] ænd [cloth]‖ sʌm studn̩ts gɛt ɪt baɪ ətɛmptɪŋ ə saʊnd mɪdwe bɪtwin [ɑ] ænd [ɔ]‖‖]

Exercise 5.40.   Read the following very carefully.

[ɔɒ; ɒɔ; ɒ ɒ ɒ; ɑ ɔ ɒ; ɔ ɑ ɒ; ɔd ɒd ɑd; nɔt nat nɒt;
gɒd gad gɔd; dɔl dɒl dɑl; lɒrɪet lɔrɪet; gɒn gɔn gɑn‖
ðə klɒθ gɒt kɒt ɪn ðə dɒr‖
ɪt ɪz nɒt ɒd fɔr ə tʃaɪld tʊ ple wɪð dɒlz‖‖]

Exercise 5.41.   In the following pairs of words, place an [ɑ] in the blank in the first word and an [ɔ] in the blank in the second word. Say the pair aloud, and write in English spelling the words which you get.

```
_____ __d  __d _____        _____ m__l m__l _____
_____ p__rt p__rt _____      _____  t__t  t__t _____
_____ b__rz b__rz _____      _____ k__t k__t _____
_____ l__rd l__rd _____      _____ n__d n__d _____
_____ k__r k__r _____        _____ kl__d kl__d _____
```

Name _____ Date _____ Score _____

Hand this in to your instructor.

1. Transcribe the following words.

1.	chance	_____	2.	cruel	_____
3.	element	_____	4.	fails	_____
5.	renegade	_____	6.	incest	_____
7.	fiends	_____	8.	sandwich	_____
9.	echos	_____	10.	wintry	_____
11.	exists	_____	12.	masking	_____
13.	pasted	_____	14.	wedges	_____
15.	civic	_____	16.	prerequisite	_____
17.	elect	_____	18.	inspect	_____
19.	embrace	_____	20.	English	_____

2. Transcribe these sentences.

1. The pains seem to be getting up into my head.

   _____

2. It is easy to create fancy tableware.

   _____

3. If you fail to say these sentences you will have difficulty.

   _____

4. That crazy man will chase you if you don't take care.

   _____

5. We pitched the hay into the back of the tent.

   _____

TRANSCRIPTION–TRANSLATION

A purist would have good cause for complaint in our use of these two words but, since language is a tool and all good mechanics can adapt tools to their specific use, the word *transcribe* invariably implies a shift *into* phonetics, and *translate* means the shift *into* English from phonetics.

Transcribe the following phonetically.

1. Salve his self-esteem and call him brave.

   _____

2. Safety is not an accident.

   _____

3. Can an apex be an axis?

   _____

4. Mobs maul many meatheads.

   _____

5. Queens quibble if princes reign.

   _____

6. Translate his transcript, please.

   _____

7. We are at the Air Force Base on Navy Pier.

   _____

8. He squawked and squeaked as the squall squealed.

   _____

Translate the following into English.

[rizən dɪktets ðæt wi spɛnd ə gret dil əv ɛfɚt mæstɚɪŋ ðə fonɛtɪk sɪmblz‖ sɪns ɔl ɪksɛpt ə vɛrɪ fju (few) ɑr pɑrt əv aur ælfəbɛt ɪt ɪz boθ iziɚ ænd mɔr dɪfɪkəlt fɔr ʌs‖ ðɪ i sɪmbl̩ fɔr ɪnstɪns ɪz sɛldəm sɪnɑnɪməs wɪð ðɪ (i) ɪn ɪŋglɪʃ‖ fətig ɪz æn ɪksɛpʃən| æz ɪz məʃin‖ ɔlso mɛnɪ pipl̩ fɔrgɛt ðæt pat ɪz nat ə sɪmbl̩ əv əfɛkʃən fɔr ə dɔg ɪksɛpt ɪf hi its frʌm ɪt‖ ɪn ɛnɪ kes æn æplɪkeʃən əv brɛnz wɪl hæv ɪts rɪwɔrd‖|]

TRANSCRIBE THESE WORDS.

1. ðə vauəl ɪz prɪtɪ ʃɔrt‖

2. wɔtʃ ðæt vauəl‖

3. hɪrz jur frɛnd *x*‖

4. ðɪs ɪz izɪ‖

5. no dʌbļ ɛl ɪn fonɛtɪks‖

6. ɪz ðə fɚst lɛtɚ nɛsɪsɛrɪ‖

7. rɪmɛmbɚ plurəl ɛndɪŋz‖

8. gud old *x*‖

9. hwɑts ðə w duɪŋ ðɛr‖

10. jur læst sɪmbəl hæd bɛtɚ bi raɪt‖

11. jur fɚst sɪmbəl hæd bɛtɚ bi raɪt‖

12. boθ vauəlz ɑr trɪkɪ‖

13. θri fonimz onlɪ‖

14. hau mɛnɪ vauəlz‖

15. lɑts əv ɛksɛs bægɪdʒ hɪr‖

16. si nʌmbɚ wʌn‖

17. bi kɛrful əv ðɪ ɛndɪŋ‖

18. gɛt ɔl θri fonimz raɪt‖

19. dɪfɚɛnʃɪet ðɪs frʌm ɪksɛpt‖

20. onlɪ kauɚdz gɪv ʌp‖

1.	queer	_____
2.	moss	_____
3.	box	_____
4.	mask	_____
5.	vacillate	_____
6.	heir	_____
7.	robs	_____
8.	examine	_____
9.	flaw	_____
10.	classy	_____
11.	case	_____
12.	prepares	_____
13.	pawn	_____
14.	meant	_____
15.	brought	_____
16.	eerie	_____
17.	laughed	_____
18.	knees	_____
19.	accept	_____
20.	physiognomy	_____

If you missed an item do the extra work.

ANSWERS

1. deer	___	quick	___	clear	___	1. kwɪr
2. gloss	___	boss	___	class	___	2. mɔs
3. knocks	___	cask	___	oxen	___	3. bɑks
4. task	___	cask	___	ask	___	4. mæsk
5. oscillate	___	facile	___	exacerbate	___	5. væsɪlet
6. honest	___	who	___	hair	___	6. ɛr
7. knobs	___	cops	___	mobs	___	7. rɑbz
8. exist	___	resist	___	contaminate	___	8. ɪgzæmɪn
9. raw	___	saw	___	draw	___	9. flɔ
10. sassy	___	messy	___	saucy	___	10. klæsɪ
11. lace	___	lass	___	laws	___	11. kes
12. repairs	___	pears	___	prevent	___	12. prɪpɛrz
13. dawn	___	don	___	din	___	13. pɔn
14. lent	___	leaned	___	spent	___	14. mɛnt
15. thought	___	fought	___	hog	___	15. brɔt
16. weary	___	bleary	___	merely	___	16. ɪrɪ
17. half	___	left	___	caught	___	17. læft
18. niece	___	knows	___	gnaws	___	18. niz
19. accident	___	ask	___	accede	___	19. æksɛpt
20. idiosyncrasy	___	physical therapy	___			20. fɪzɪɑgnəmɪ

[o]
The Vowel [o] as in *soak* [sok], *though* [ðo], *rope* [rop]

The [o] symbol is in many ways the easiest vowel to learn. In the first place it is shaped like your mouth when you say it, and in the second place it is seldom confused with any other phoneme. As you can see from the words at the top of the page, there are many ways to spell this sound: s*oak*, t*oe*, th*ough*, r*ope*, t*ow*, *oh*, t*au*pe, kn*o*ll, plat*eau*. Here are those same words in phonetics. Read them aloud: [sok to ðo rop to o top nol plæto].

Exercise 5.42.   Have you learned this sound already? Here is a sentence. Say it aloud and underline each word that contains an [o] sound.

Most people look hopeful when ponderous boons are offered to them.

In order to check yourself right away, the answer can be found in saying the next to the last word of the sentence aloud. We are *most hopeful* that you chose the right words.

[æz wi mek æn o ðə lıps ɔlso mek ðə ʃep əv æn o‖ ðe ɑr nat pʌkɚd æz mʌtʃ æz fɔr ði u hauɛvɚ‖ ðə bæk əv ðə tʌŋ ız hʌmpt tɔrd ðə sɔft pælət dʒʌst slaıtlı lɛs ðæn fɔr ði u saund bʌt ðə tʌŋ ız hɛld mɔr tɛnslı‖]

Exercise 5.43.   Say the following words aloud, visualizing the English spelling as you do so.

rob	fɛlo	rod	sop	wındo
bon	ok	gol	sol	blo
noz	rost	rımot	gron	bol
pılo	kod	slo	kroz	toz
nol	ot	hol	hom	rozı
od	bıhold	fon	dont	kold
ozon	pol	non		

Like the [e] vowel symbol, the [o] may represent either a simple vowel or a diphthong, but no distinction is made between the two in broad transcription if the other sounds in the word are identical. The diphthong would be represented accurately by the combination of symbols [ou]. If you say the word *bony* first as [bonı] and then as [bounı], being careful to add the [u] sound as you glide from the [o], you will be able to hear the difference. However, for our transcription there is little necessity for the double symbol since we know the sound we use. Thus, we employ only the single sound [o] to designate the sound and its variations, including the diphthong [ou].

Again with the [o] sound, as with the [e], we find many foreign-speaking people who use a pure short [o] vowel which is readily distinguishable from the one we use. We can help them learn our value for the spoken [o] by using the diphthong version in transcription. Rather than giving the sentence [lɛts go hom sun], in which they would use their pure form of [o], we would write the sentence [lɛts gou houm sun] when working with foreign students. Theirs is the more precise speech. What happens when we say [ou] is that we produce the pure [o], then relax the speech muscles slightly so that an [u] is produced.

1. A couple of silent letters here.   1. knows   _____

2. This rhymes with the word above.   2. nose   _____

3. More silent letters.   3. knees   _____

4. Disregard the spelling; just listen.   4. phrase   _____

5. A breeze.   5. basket   _____

6. So is this one.   6. oboe   _____

7. It'll look funny when you write it.   7. vogue   _____

8. Just the vowel changes.   8. vague   _____

9. Here's that *x* again.   9. hoax   _____

10. Where have we heard that vowel sound before?   10. boss   _____

11. Watch it!   11. ox   _____

12. Only the vowel's different from no. 11.   12. oaks   _____

13. The *s* is the sticker.   13. positive   _____

14. You know the vowel   14. storm   _____

15. No sweat with this.   15. sweat   _____

16. But this is more sugary.   16. sweet   _____

17. Do you like easy ones?   17. indicate   _____

18. Careful of the vowel.   18. wary   _____

19. This doesn't mean we can charge you.   19. feasible   _____

20. Quit school if you don't know this by now.   20. phoneme   _____

ANSWERS

1. Did you remember to put a z at the end? — 1. noz

2. luks fəmɪljɚ dʌznt ɪt‖ — 2. noz

3. ənʌðɚ tʌf wʌn‖ — 3. niz

4. ðɪ r ɪz ðɪ onlɪ sɪmbl̩ ðæt mætʃɪz ðɪ ɪŋglɪʃ‖ — 4. frez

5. dɪd ju ɛnd ʌp wɪð ɪt‖ — 5. bæskɪt

6. izɪ‖ — 6. obo

7. ðə læst tu ɪŋglɪʃ lɛtɚz ar ʌn:ɛsəsɛrɪ‖ — 7. vog

8. dɪto‖ — 8. veg

9. kæn ju spɛl soks ænd foks‖ — 9. hoks

10. nɛvɚ krɔs jur bɔs — 10. bɔs

11. wʌz jur vauəl raɪt‖ — 11. ɑks

12. raɪmz wɪð nʌmbɚ naɪn‖ — 12. oks

13. izɪ wʌznt ɪt‖ — 13. pɑzɪtɪv

14. luks ɔlmost nætʃurəl‖ — 14. stɔrm

15. fɔr ẃʌns wi juz ðə w‖ — 15. swɛt

16. ɪz jur vauəl raɪt‖ — 16. swit

17. dɪd ju mɪs ðɪ e‖ — 17. ɪndɪket

18. raɪmz wɪð vɛrɪ‖ — 18. wɛrɪ

19. ðɪs wʌz prɪtɪ dɪfɪkəlt‖ — 19. fizəbl̩

20. ɪts ə gud ki wɝd fɔr ðɪ o ænd i‖ — 20. fonim

[u]
The Vowel [u] as in [mun]

ʃut tuθ buθ suð flut truθ dʒus glu

When you see this phonetic symbol in the future you must remember that it is not pronounced *you* [ju] but [u]. *Cute* has four sounds in it: the [k], the [j], the [u], and the [t] to make [kjut]. *Coot* is the name of a species of duck, and is pronounced [kut]. Remember: [u] is not [ju].

u u u u u u u u u u u u u

This vowel symbol should not be too difficult for you to acquire since there are many words in English in which the letter *u* alone or in combination with other vowels is pronounced the same as the phonetic symbol. For example, we have such words as *chute* [ʃut], *gnu* [nu], *flu* and *flue* [flu], as well as *through* [θru] and *suit* [sut]. However, the letter *u* can also represent other sounds such as [ʌ] as in [ʌp], so use your ear rather than your eye. Listen to the sounds and ignore the spelling.

Exercise 5.44. Transcribe into phonetics only those words which require the [u].

1. cup _____   2. two _____   3. coo _____
4. own _____   5. run _____   6. booze _____
7. stool _____   8. zoo _____   9. pull _____
10. look _____   11. slewed _____   12. bruise _____

wi səgdʒɛst ðæt ju fɪnɪʃ raitiŋ ði ɛksərsaɪz bɪfɔr ridiŋ fɚðɚ bɪkɔz wɪr nau givɪŋ ju sʌm kluz tu ði ænsɚz‖ nʌmbɚz wʌn| fɔr| faɪv| naɪn| ænd tɛn ʃud nat hæv bɪn rɪtn̩‖ ɔl ði ʌðɚz du hæv ði u saund‖ hau wɛl dɪd ju du‖

That last passage was difficult to read. Let's give you an easier one.

Exercise 5.45. Read these sentences, then write them in English.

1. ju hæv ə nu blu sut‖

_____

2. du nat bruz jʊr niz an ðə raks ɪn ðə ruɪnz‖

_____

3. hu kæn əsum hi dɪdn̩t ful hɪz rum mets‖

_____

4. numætɪk tulz ar hændl̩d izɪlɪ baɪ ðə kru‖

_____

5. stud prunz me bi kɔld ɪnibrɪetɪd frut‖

_____

The sound [u] is termed a *high back vowel* because the *back* part of the tongue is bulged upward toward the soft palate. The elevation of this rear part of the tongue is higher than for any other of the back vowels [ʊ] [o] [ɔ]. It is also termed a *lax vowel* because the tension of the muscles in the mouth and throat is relatively less than it is for such vowels as the [ʊ], as in *cook* [kʊk]. Finally, it is called a *rounded vowel* because the lips form a round opening. This opening for the [u] is the smallest used in producing any English vowel [ðɪ u ðɛn ɪz ə læks raʊndɪd haɪ bæk vaʊəl‖]

Exercise 5.46.   Here are some of the spellings of the [u]. Find one word representing each and write it in the blank space.

1. oo ____cool____   2. u _____   3. oe _____
4. ue _____   5. ui _____   6. ew _____
7. eu _____   8. ault _____   9. ough _____
10. wo _____

uuu u u u u u u u u uuuu u u u u u uuu u u u

Exercise 5.47.   Transcribe into phonetics.

1. Whose tune did he play.

_____

2. Stay cool even if the moonbeams dance on the waves.

_____

3. He'll expand the news to include the true rules.

_____

4. The zoo contained a gnu and two elephants.

_____

[ʊ]
The Vowel [ʊ] as in *put* [pʊt]

ðə kʊk tʊk ðə krʊk|
pʊt hɪz fʊt ɪn sʌm sʊt‖
hi ðɛn sɛd| bʊlɪ|
aɪv tɔt hɪm fʊlɪ
tu lʊk fɔr ðə kʊk| ɔr hiz hʊkt‖

This [ʊ] sound may be a bit difficult for you to isolate at first. You hear it as the vowel sound when you say the words *put* and *push*. It is represented in English spelling by the letter *u* as in *full* [fʊl], by *oo* as in *wood* [wʊd], and *ou* as in *could* [kʊd]. It is seldom used at the end of a word in our language and is used at the beginning of words only for such things as foreign words and anglicized foreign words, such as *umlaut* [ʊmlaʊt].

[tu mek ðɪ ʊ saʊnd hʌmp jʊr tʌŋ ʌp ɪn bæk| wɪð ðə tʌŋ bled ænd tɪp pɔɪntɪŋ daʊnwɚdz‖ ðə hʌmp ɪn bæk ʃud nat bi rezd æz haɪ æz ɪt ɪz hwɛn mekɪŋ ðɪ ʊ saʊnd bʌt ɔlmost æz haɪ‖ ðə lɪps ɑr prətrudɪd mɔr ðæn fɔr ðɪ o bʌt nat æz mʌtʃ æz fɔr ðɪ u‖]

Exercise 5.48.   Write the following words in phonetics, prolonging the [ʊ] sound long enough to enable you to write the symbol four times. This sound is sometimes difficult to prolong without modifying it. Use each word five times.

put   look   book   would   full   poor

Exercise 5.49.   Read the following words aloud.

brʊk   pʊl   pʊsɪ   bʊlɪ
tʊk   gʊd   stʊd   kʊks
nʊks   kʊd   bʊk   lʊk
fʊl

The [ʊ] sound is sometimes confused with the [u] vowel, and in some speech the two sounds may be interchanged. Have you ever heard anyone say [aɪ tʊk ə gʊd lʊk ætɪm‖]: What foreign dialect might this be? There are also some words where the [ʊ] and the [u] may be interchanged in good standard English. *Roof* is one; [rʊf] is acceptable, as is [ruf]. Take care, however, for there are only a few such words. Most often just one or the other vowel is standard.

Exercise 5.50.   In the following pairs of words place an [ʊ] symbol in the blank in the first word and an [u] symbol in the blank in the second word. Then read the pair of words aloud, listening carefully to the difference between the vowels before you proceed to the next pair.

b__k   b__t   h__d   h__t   n__k   n__d   p__l   p__l
f__t   f__d   l__k   l__p   t__k   t__n   k__k   k__p

Exercise 5.51.   Fill in the following blanks with either the [u], the [o], or the [ʊ] symbol.

[ɪf hi hæd p_t mɔr n_z ɪnt_ ðə pepɚ hi k_d hæv med ə g_d prɑfɪt‖ ɪt w_d tek _nlɪ ə l_k t_ si ðæt ɪt w_d bi wɝθ rɪdɪŋ‖]
[ju ʃʊd hæv fɪld ɪn sɪks blæŋks wɪð ðɪ ʊ‖ pɚhæps sɛvɪn ɔr et ɪf ju sɛd ɪntu ænd tʊ æz ju kʊd hæv dʌn hwɛn spikɪŋ fæst‖]

Some English words can be correctly pronounced with either the [u] or the [ʊ] vowels. Here are some of them: *roof*, *root*, *hoof*. How would you transcribe your own pronunciation of these words? A word of caution; there are very few words which enjoy this ambivalence.

Exercise 5.52.   Transcribe these pairs of words.

pull	_____	pool	_____	who'd	_____	hood	_____
look	_____	loot	_____	lock	_____	Luke	_____
would	_____	wooed	_____	stood	_____	stewed	_____
shoed	_____	should	_____	spawn	_____	spoon	_____
crook	_____	crock	_____	poor	_____	pour	_____

Exercise 5.53.   Transcribe these sentences.

1. Two books fell off the wooden table.

2. Who'd have stood for being pushed into the pool?

_____

3. The crook couldn't have been hit with the horse's hoof.

_____

4. You choose your cook usually for good food rather than for looks.

_____

Exercise 5.54.   Read these words swiftly.

sʊt	huts	grup	kʊk	rus
hup	pʊl	rumɪnet	pul	hu
sut	wʊl	rʊf	mjul	uz
gʊd	kul	klu	lʊk	brʊks

1. Listen carefully to both vowels.	1. endure	_____
2. Don't be hasty.	2. prune	_____
3. This is easy.	3. bookmobile	_____
4. So is this.	4. nook	_____
5. Two easy vowels.	5. handfull	_____
6. Remember this word?	6. prayer	_____
7. dont sɛl ði old homstɛd pæpɪ‖	7. poorfarm	_____
8. Use the [ɚ] if you make it two syllables.	8. drawer	_____
9. ðɛrz nʌθɪŋ laɪk ə dem ɔr æpḷ paɪ‖	9. drool	_____
10. How do you transcribe y endings?	10. bully beef	_____
11. Same as above.	11. ordinary	_____
12. Oh, those silent letters.	12. morgue	_____
13. Here's a hint; there are two vowels.	13. suet	_____
14. ðə daɪnɪŋ rum tebḷ‖	14. footrest	_____
15. Don't let no. 14 throw you off	15. bootblack	_____
16. kʊks tʊrz ɪn jurəp ɑr gʊd wʌnz‖	16. tour	_____
17. Need we mention—no c.	17. electric	_____
18. Don't get this vowel wrong.	18. proof	_____
19. Don't let a *cough* throw you *off*.	19. cough	_____
20. Pay attention to the last sound.	20. looked	_____

							ANSWERS
1. boor	——	bore	——	sew	——	1. ɪndʊr
2. prove	——	plumes	——	broom	——	2. prun
3. automobile	——	mobile	——	eel	——	3. bʊkmobil
4. took	——	soot	——	suit	——	4. nʊk
5. grandpa	——	bull	——	fall	——	5. hændfʊl
6. spray	——	mare	——	dare	——	6. prɛr
7. harm	——	lure	——	moor	——	7. pʊrfɑrm
8. roar	——	rural	——	draw	——	8. drɔr
9. spool	——	full	——	prude	——	9. drul
10. roof	——	wooly	——	fully	——	10. bʊlɪbif
11. extraordinary	————		ordinance	————		11. ɔrdɪnɛrɪ
12. [ə spʊkɪ spɑt nɑt fɔr fulɪʃnɪs‖]						12. mɔrg
13. [sʊɪt suts ðə gʌlz‖]						13. sʊɪt
14. boot	——	book	——	bought	——	14. fʊtrɛst
15. brook	——	booze	——	boot	——	15. bʊtblæk
16. lore	——	tune	——	tore	——	16. tʊr
17. electricity	————		egocentric	————		17. ɪlɛktrɪk
18. cruel	——	roof	——	true	——	18. pruf
19. calk	——	caught	——	cod	——	19. kɔf
20. cook	——	crook	——	crooked	——	20. lʊkt

Name _____ *Date* _____ *Score* _____

Hand this in to your instructor.

1. In the following passage, underline the words in which an [ɪ], [i], or [ɛ] vowel symbol is used incorrectly. There are five.

[ɪt sɪmz ðæt ɪt iz hɑrd tu tɛl hwɪtʃ sɪmbl̩ tu juz ɪn ðiz wɝdz‖ wi mʌst sɪ ɪf wi kæn tɛl ðə rɛl dɪfrəns ɪn ðə saʊndz‖]

2. Here is a list of words for you to transcribe. Say them aloud and write them exactly as you say them.

trade	_____	fence	_____	giddy	_____
prune	_____	feed	_____	lose	_____
leap	_____	feet	_____	group	_____
creep	_____	feat	_____	accept	_____
crept	_____	head	_____	neigh	_____
basket	_____	guess	_____	new	_____
please	_____	staff	_____	to	_____
ready	_____	mane	_____	two	_____
cent	_____	brood	_____	too	_____
dream	_____	brute	_____	who	_____
track	_____	bliss	_____	pity	_____
straight	_____	niece	_____	many	_____
tomb	_____	fancy	_____	came	_____
eat	_____	friend	_____	crab	_____
loose	_____				

3. Transcribe the following paragraph.

We must train ourselves to watch for some new things. Since we found out about accent, we will be more conscious of what is stressed and what is unstressed. If this lesson has seemed boring at times and you felt unable to finish it, we hope it's at least given you something to make phonetics seem easier [izɪɚ].

4. In the following paragraph you will find five words in which the [ɔ] symbol *should* have been used. Read the transcription aloud, underline the error words, and write the correction above the words.

[aɪ ðə pipl̩ sɔ ðæt ðə lɔ wʊd hæv tʊ bi kald ɪn‖ ɪt ɔt tʊ bi told ðæt ðə bɔl hæd gɔn θru ə hatɪ mænz wɪndo‖ hi kʊd ivn bi brɔt tʊ dra ə gʌn‖ hæv ju bɪn kat an ɔz jɛt‖]

5. Underline the ten errors in the following passage. Then write the words the way they should be written.

[ðə kʊk put ðə soup in bolz‖ it simd tu hat tu it so wi watɪd θri mɪnɪts‖ ɛftɚ ɪt kʊld wi swalod ɪt kwiklɪ‖ ɪt tastɛd gʊd‖]

6. In the words below, fit each of the ten vowels into the blank space in the phonetic word. How many actual English words can you obtain from each one this way?

[ɪ]   [i]   [æ]   [ɛ]   [e]   [ɔ]   [a]   [o]   [u]   [ʊ]

[h__d]
[p__r]
[k__l]
[n__k]
[sp__nz]
[f__t]
[n__t]

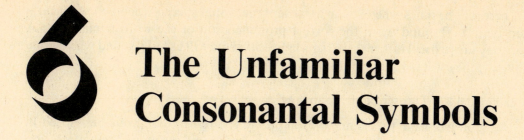

The Unfamiliar Consonantal Symbols

[j]
The Sound [j] as in *you* [ju] and *canyon* [kænjən]

In phonetics, the [j] is the symbol for the first sound in *yet* and *yellow*. You have already been introduced to it in your study of the [u] symbol, as it is sometimes necessary to use it before that vowel: *use* [juz] or [jus], *few* [fju], and *cue* [kju]. This symbol has no relation to the *jay*, or *j* of the English alphabet. Instead, it signifies the sound usually associated with the *y*.

The [j] sound is never used at the end of words. It is a glide sound and is always followed by a vowel. Since many words have this sound without there being a corresponding *y* letter in the English spelling, students consider it one of the more difficult phonemes: *acute* [əkjut], *future* [fjutʃur], *argue* [argju]. Study carefully the following phonetic passage.

[hwɛn ju mek ði j saund ju ɑr mekɪŋ ə glaɪd saund‖ ju bɪgɪn baɪ plesɪŋ jur mauθ ænd tʌŋ ɪn ə pəziʃn̩ sɪmɪlɚ tu ðæt fɔr ði ɪ ɔr i saund‖ ðə vɔɪs kʌmz ɪn æz ju muv frʌm ðɪs pəziʃn̩ tu ðæt əv ðə fɑloɪŋ vauəl‖ ðʌs ə vɔɪst trænzɪʃən frʌm ði ɪ ɔr i tu æn u vauəl prədusɪz ðə wɝd jul‖ ðə vɔɪs ɔlwɪz əkʌmpəniz ðə tʌŋ ænd mauθ muvmənt‖]

Exercise 6.1.   Read the following list of words aloud, all the way through. Then go back to the beginning, say each word aloud as you write it in English, and before going on to the next word, write it in phonetics, again saying the word.

jɛt _____	ju _____	jɑrd _____
junjən _____	əbjuz _____	əbjus _____
jɑt _____	jist _____	jɛs _____
mɪljən _____	əmjuz _____	jild _____
jæmz _____	jɔn _____	jɑrn _____
jur _____	jɪp _____	jɛl _____

Exercise 6.2.   Say each of the following words aloud. Write in phonetics only those words which have a [j] sound.

excuse _____	yacht _____	school _____
tulip _____	yield _____	wayside _____
cute _____	request _____	music _____
just _____	onion _____	canyon _____

There will be times when you are transcribing actual speech when you will hear a person omit a [j] sound when the correct pronunciation of the word demands it. A person may say [rɛgələ] rather than [rɛgjulə]. Still others will use a [j] sound where none is required; they will say [kɑljəm] for [kɑləm].

Exercise 6.3.   Transcribe the following.

You will have to use many examples if you're to attain your best speed in phonetics. It may take a year for you to get used to rapid script, and sometimes you will find yourself confused. But you can make a supreme effort to increase your rate.

The ideal which you are supposed to reach in reading phonetics is to be sure how to pronounce every phoneme, so that even if you are reading an unknown foreign language, or a dialect, you can rattle off the words with no hesitation. If you depend on context to assist you, you might come a "cropper."

Because this symbol is probably the most difficult of all IPA symbols to learn, due to our utter familiarity with the English letter *j*, take a few minutes to say these words aloud as you write them in phonetics.

ju	jæm	fju
juz	jɛstɚde	fɪgjɚ
jʊr	jɛlo	ɑrgju
jo ho ho		

Exercise 6.4.   Reading Passage

ɑɪ jɝn tu lɝn tu jodl‖ jɛt ju əkjuz mi əv biiŋ jɛlo hwɛn ɪt kʌmz tu jɛlɪŋ wɪθ ɪnʌf vɑljʊm tu bi juzd ɪn æktʃuəl kɑmpətɪʃn̩‖

[hɛlpfʊl hɪnts]

1. ðɛrz ə j hɪr| bʌt nɑt hwɛr ɪt simz||
2. baɪ naʊ ju no ðɪs||
3. ɪt ɪznt̩ ɪmbu||
4. wɔtʃ ðə læst vaʊəl||
5. no dʌbl̩ l||
6. dʌbl̩ tʃɛk ðə vaʊəl||
7. waɪ æz ɪn jɑn||
8. nɑt argu||
9. si hɪnt nʌmbɚ wʌn||
10. ju me juz ðə sɪlæbɪk l̩||
11. ju dɪd ðɪs ə fju lɛsənz əgo||
12. ɪt ɪz nɑt sɪmɪlɚ tu ðə wʌn əbʌv||
13. se ðɪs ə kʌpl̩ əv taɪmz hwaɪl ju lɪsn̩||
14. ə tʃɚtʃ pju ɪz rɪtn̩ ðʌs pju||
15. ðə fɚst fonim ɪz ði onlɪ izɪ wʌn||
16. lɔŋ bət izɪ||
17. nʌmbɚ naɪn wɪl start ju ɔf||
18. ent ðɪs ə bjut||
19. θɪŋk bæk tu ðə lɛsn̩ an ðɪs ɛndɪŋ||
20. kɛrful||

1. fury _____
2. your _____
3. imbue _____
4. regulate _____
5. yellow _____
6. yore _____
7. yarn _____
8. argue _____
9. beauty _____
10. yodel _____
11. poor _____
12. pure _____
13. endure _____
14. ampule _____
15. fuse _____
16. speculate _____
17. beautiful _____
18. cue _____
19. yesterday _____
20. pewter _____

ANSWERS

1. præktɪs raɪtɪŋ ju ænd jur‖   1. fjurɪ

2. ʃur ɪts jur‖ kjurɪəs bʌt aɪm ʃur‖   2. jur

3. ju ʃud bi ebl̩ tu hɪr ðɪ ju‖   3. ɪmbju

4. ə snɪkɪ wʌn‖   4. rɛgjulet

5. du ju it jɛlo dʒɛlo‖   5. jɛlo

6. ɪn dez əv . . .‖   6. jɔr

7. ʃi jɔnz æt hɪz jarnz‖   7. jarn

8. hæv ju æn argjumənt fɔr ðɪs‖   8. argju

9. bebiz hæv butiz‖ bebz hæv bjutɪ‖   9. bjutɪ

10. jo di jo di ja di je‖   10. jodl̩

11. ovɚ ðə hɪl tu ðə purhaus mʌðɚ‖   11. pur

12. ʃi wʌz pur bʌt pjur‖   12. pjur

13. ju me se ɪndjur ɔr ɪndur‖   13. ɪndjur

14. æn ovɚsaɪzd pɪl‖   14. æmpjul

15. ðə fjuz rɪfjuzd tu bɝn   15. fjuz

16. ju me spɛkjulet an jur fet‖   16. spɛkjulet

17. djutɪ ɪz bjutɪ‖   17. bjutəful

18. ʃi hɪt hɪm ovɚ ðə hɛd wɪð ə kju   18. kju

19. . . . wʌz wʌns təmaro‖   19. jɛstɚdɪ

20. kəmpjutɚz ar nat med əv pjutɚ‖   20. pjutɚ

90

[ʃ]
The Sound *sh*

The single sound we know as *sh* in English, is represented as [ʃ] in phonetics. It is the sound which we find at the beginning of the words *shoe* [ʃu] and *ship* [ʃɪp]. We also hear it in the middle of the word *bushel*, and at the end of the words *lash* and *fresh*.

[hwɛn wi mek ðə ʃ saund ðə tiθ ar brɔt ɔlmost təgɛðə‖ ðə bæk əv ðə tʌŋ ɪz tɛns ænd ðə saidz əv ðə tʌŋ tʌtʃ ðɪ ʌpɚ tiθ‖ ə strim əv ɛr ɪz sɛnt θru ə brɔd gruv daun ðə sɛntɚ əv ðə tʌŋ‖ ɪt hɪts ðə kʌtɪŋ ɛdʒ əv ðə frʌnt tiθ ɪn ə brɔd strim‖ ɪt‖ laɪk ðɪ ɛs‖ ɪz ə sɪbɪlənt saund‖]

Exercise 6.5.　Read these sentences and copy them in ordinary script.

1. ʃɛrɪ ʃod ðə ʃɛf hau tu ʃrɛd ʃarks flɛʃ‖

2. ɪn ðə ʃæk nɪr ðə marʃ ʃmɪtɪ kæʃt ðə prɛʃəs ʃɛlz‖

3. ʃnɪtsəlbaum ʃevz onlɪ wɪð ə ʃɪk rezɚ‖

4. o ʃɔ ʃrʌgd ðə ʃik hwɛn hi sɔ hɚ ʃep‖

5. ʃi ʃrikt ʃrɪlɪ hwɛn hi tʌtʃt hɚ ʃæŋk‖

6. ʃud ʃi ʃrɪŋk ðə ʃɚt ʃɔrtɚ ɪn ðə ʃauɚ‖

7. tu ʃɪps wɛnt aut æftɚ oʃən ʃrɪmp‖

8. ʃe hauʒ əbaut ənʌdə lɪl ʃnɔrt əv ðæt ʃnʌps‖

9. ʃev bɪfɔr ju tek ʃɛrɪ tu ðə let let let ʃo‖

10. ðə ʃmu ʃi ʃrikt‖ hiz ʃur tu ʃʌk hɪz ʃraud‖

In one way the [ʃ] sound is quite consistent. [hwɛn wi hæv æn ɛs etʃ rɪtn̩ ɪn ðə wɚd], we expect it to be pronounced [ʃ]. However, there are other letters which are sounded as [ʃ]. Among them are *t*, *s*, *ss*, and *c*. We find them in the words *lotion* [loʃən], *sugar* [ʃugɚ], *issue* [ɪʃu], and *ocean* [oʃən]. The [ʃ] sound is also spelled as *ch* in the word [məʃin], and as *x* in the word [æŋkʃəs]. [əgɛn ðə lɛtɚz juzd ɪn spɛlɪŋ du nat tɛl ʌs ɛnɪθɪŋ dɛfɪnɪt‖]

Exercise 6.6.   Write these words in phonetics.

1. fresh _____   2. chef _____   3. ratio _____
4. shelter _____   5. thresh _____   6. mesh _____
7. machine _____   8. selfish _____   9. pressure _____
10. censure _____   11. flesh _____   12. ashes _____
13. precious _____   14. shoot _____   15. shows _____
16. shells _____   17. chutes _____   18. shoals _____
19. cashew _____   20. social _____

When you are transcribing the actual speech of an individual you may find cases in which the [ʃ] sound is used incorrectly. A person with a lateral lisp may use the [ʃ] where the [s] is ordinarily used. He may say [ʃe wɪl ʃʌmwən tɛl mi ðə lɛʃən‖]. Still others with no actual speech defect will interchange the *s* and [ʃ]. If you hear someone ask for a pair of [ʃɪzɚz‖ ɪt me min onlɪ ðæt hi hæz ə paɪp bɪtwin hɪz tiθ‖] Or someone else will say [aɪ sʊd go hom pɪtɪ ʃun‖]—and he probably should. Children are often conspicuous "baby talkers" because they have not yet mastered the [ʃ] sound and will say [si ge mi ə nu sʌvəl‖]

Exercise 6.7.   Read these sentences over until you can read them swiftly.

1. ʃi ʃod su tu blu ʃuz wɛt ænd mɛsɪ frʌm splæʃɪŋ ɪn ðɪ oʃən‖
2. no ɪgzæmɪneʃən kæn ʃo ɪf hiz ə vɪʃəs bist‖
3. wi ʃæl ʃut ðə ʃark ðæt ʃuk ænd smæʃt ðə mɛʃɪz əv aur nɛts‖
4. ʃi sɛlz si ʃɛlz tu ðə məlɪʃə‖
5. ðə mɪʃən tu rʌʃə med ʌs ɔl æŋkʃəs‖

92

1. bɛtɚ gɛt ðə vauəl raɪt‖

2. ðə læst vauəl ɪz ðɪ ə‖

3. dɪto‖

4. pronauns ɪt ɪn gud old əmɛrɪkəniz‖

5. ə krɪstəlɪn rɑk‖

6. skiɪŋ ɪn ə stret laɪn‖

7. tʃaɪldz ple‖

8. ɛnd ɪt ɪn ən ɚ‖

9. wɑtʃ ðæt faɪnəl saund‖

10. ðə temɪŋ əv ðə

11. dont ju dɛr mɪs ðə fɚst saund‖

12. izɪ‖

13. ɪz ðə fɚst saund æksɛntɪd‖

14. ðɛrz no o hɪr‖

15. ju hæv tu tʃɔɪsɪz fɔr ðə mɪdl̩ vauəl‖

16. pe ətɛnʃən tu ðə dɪfθɔŋ‖

17. ə sɪntʃ‖

18. ju hævn̩t hæd ðə tʃ jɛt‖

19. si nʌmbɚ sɪkstin‖

20. ðɪs hæz θri dɪfɚɪnt minɪŋz‖

1. shame	_____	
2. motion	_____	
3. passion	_____	
4. sheik	_____	
5. schist	_____	
6. schuss	_____	
7. shoots	_____	
8. shoulder	_____	
9. shows	_____	
10. shrew	_____	
11. sure	_____	
12. pension	_____	
13. emotion	_____	
14. evolution	_____	
15. Chicago	_____	
16. seashore	_____	
17. action	_____	
18. cellos	_____	
19. cashier	_____	
20. squash	_____	

	ANSWERS
1. ʃem an ju ɪf ju mɪst ðɪs‖	1. ʃem
2. ə wumənz tʌŋ ɪz ɔlwɪz ɪn pəˈpetʃuəl	2. moʃən
3. ɔfn̩ saundz laɪk æzmə‖	3. pæʃən
4. ʃi ʃrikt hwɛn ðə ʃik græbd hɝ‖	4. ʃik
5. saundz laɪk dʒɪalədʒɪ‖	5. ʃɪst
6. wi wɪʃ wi kʊd ʃus‖	6. ʃus
7. hi ʃuts ðə ʃuts‖	7. ʃuts
8. ðə soldʒɝ laɪks ə sɔft ʃoldɝ‖	8. ʃoldɝ
9. ɪt goz tu ʃo hu ʃoz ʃuz‖	9. ʃoz
10. ə wumən wɪð ə maus fɔr ə hʌzbənd‖	10. ʃru
11. ɪf ju mɪst ðɪs raɪt ɪt tɛn taɪmz‖	11. ʃur
12. old foks nid əm‖	12. pɛnʃən
13. dont gɛt ɪmoʃənəl‖	13. ɪmoʃən
14. darwɪn wʌz ə stʌtɝɝ‖	14. ɛvəluʃən
15. netɪvz se ʃɪkɔgo‖	15. ʃɪkago ʃɪkɔgo
16. ʃiz sɔr æt ðə siʃɔr‖	16. siʃɔr
17. ·aɪm æŋkʃəs fɔr ækʃən æt ði ɔkʃən‖	17. ækʃən‖
18. tʃɛlɪsts kɔl ðɛm ðɛr dɔg hauzɪz‖	18. tʃɛloz
19. wi snik ə tuθpɪk hwɛn ʃiz nat lukɪŋ‖	19. kæʃɪr
20. ə hɛləvn̩ ɪkskjus fɔr ə vɛdʒtəbl̩‖	20. skwɔʃ

[ʒ]
The Sound [zh]

The [ʒ] sound (the long-tailed z—[ʒʒʒ]) is never found at the beginning of a word in English. It is the sound found in the middle of the words *usual* [juʒʊəl] and *vision* [vɪʒən], and at the end of the word *rouge* [ruʒ].

[ðə ʒ saund ɪz prənaunst ɪgzæktlɪ laɪk ðə ʃ saund ɪksɛpt ðæt ðə brɛθ ɪz vokəlaɪzd‖ traɪ tu se ə ʃ saund—ɪt ɪz ə hwɪspɚd saund‖ nau mek ðə sem saund ænd vɔɪs ɪt‖ put jur fɪŋgɚz laɪtlɪ ɑn jur θrot tu fil ðə vaɪbreʃən hwɛn ju vɔɪs ɪt‖ ðæt ɪz ðə ʒ saund‖‖]

Exercise 6.8. Do these things.

1. tres ə ʒ sɪmbəl ɪn ðɪ ɛr wɪθ jur fɔrfɪŋgɚ seɪŋ ʒ əlaud æz ju du so‖
2. se ʒ ɪn grups əv θri ɔltɚnetɪŋ ɪt wɪð ðə ʃ saund‖
3. faɪnd wʌn ɪŋglɪʃ wɝd bɪgɪnɪŋ wɪð ə ʒ saund ænd jur ɪnstrʌktɚ wɪl pe ju faɪv dɑlɚz‖

Exercise 6.9. Copy the following syllables and nonsense words in the spaces provided, saying them distinctly as you write them.

1. oʒu _____	2. ɛʒo _____	3. oʒɛ _____
4. uʒo _____	5. tuʒ _____	6. stroʒ _____
7. ʃuʒ _____	8. moʒup _____	9. puʒɛk _____
10. skruʒ _____		

Exercise 6.10. Find words showing three different English spellings for the sound of [ʒ].

1.
2.
3.

The [ʒ] sound is not a native English sound. We do not find it in Old English. It comes to us from the French in such words as *garage* [gərɑʒ], *beige* [bɛʒ], *loge* [loʒ], and *camouflage* [kæməflɑʒ]. These words have the same meanings in both languages. Many of these seem to be becoming anglicized so that we hear [gərɑdʒ] almost as frequently as we hear [gərɑʒ]. Also in substandard speech we hear [plɛʒɚ] instead of [plɛʒur], though this is not acceptable. When intoxicated, people often use [ʒ] instead of [z]. [ðe se aɪ ʃɔ ə zibrə ɪn ðə ʒu] when in this condition. Some individuals with lateral lisps also use this [ʒ] instead of the [z].

Exercise 6.11. Transcribe these words.

1. Asia _____	2. rouge _____	3. aphasia _____
4. beige _____	5. garage _____	6. prestige _____
7. menage _____	8. casual _____	9. usual _____

Exercise 6.12. Read these sentences, then translate them.

1. pɝʒə ɪz ɪn eʒə sɛd ðə rɑdʒɑ‖

2. ðə mɪraʒ an ðɪs əkeʒən wʌz ə vɪʒuəl ɪluʒən‖

_____

3. ɪt wʌz ə plɛʒɚ tu faɪnd ðə trɛʒɚ æt maɪ lɛʒɚ‖

_____

4. hɪz kəmpoʒɚ wʌz ənjuʒuəl‖

_____

5. hɪz dɪsɪʒən wʌz tu baɪ ðɪ æʒɚ pəriʒən hoʒɚɪ‖

_____

Don't peek at the next page until you have written all twenty of the words.

1. ðɛrz no dʒ saʊnd æt ðɪ ɛnd əv ðɪs‖

2. raɪmz wɪθ trɛʒɚ‖

   ðiz ɑr ɔl mʌtʃ tu izɪ tʊ gɪv ju ɛnɪ mɔr hɛlp‖

1. prestige	_____
2. azure	_____
3. fusion	_____
4. usual	_____
5. closure	_____
6. vision	_____
7. loge	_____
8. Frazier	_____
9. cohesion	_____
10. rouge	_____

Students frequently make errors in failing to distinguish between the [ʃ] and the [ʒ] sounds and in interchanging these symbols or substituting them for the [s] or the [z]. The following words may help you to keep out of these booby traps.

θruaʊt ðiz wɝdz ju wɪl faɪnd æn əkeʒənəl jus fɔr ðɪ ə sɪmbl̩ hwɪtʃ wi hævn̩t stʌdid jɛt‖ baɪ nau ju ʃʊd bi ebl̩ tʊ mek æn ɛdʒʊketɪd gɛs‖ haʊɛvɚ ju wɪl nɑt bi pinəlaɪzd ɪf ðə mɪsjus əv ði ə ɪz jʊr onlɪ ɛrɚ‖

11. social	_____
12. seizure	_____
13. precious	_____
14. teased	_____
15. lettuce	_____
16. census	_____
17. bruised	_____
18. provision	_____
19. mission	_____
20. garages	_____

ANSWERS

1. hwɑt prəfɛsɚz dont hæv ɪn ðɪs kʌntrɪ‖　　　1. prɛstiʒ

2. ɔr blu skaɪz‖　　　2. æʒɚ

3. fjuʒən brɪdz kənfjuʒən‖　　　3. fjuʒən

4. ɪn kæʒuəl spitʃ ðə læst vauəl ɪz ɔfṇ omɪtɪd‖　　　4. juʒuəl

5. æd ðə wɚd mauθ tu ðɪs ænd si hwɑt ju gɛt‖　　　5. klozɚ

6. sɛnts ænd sɪnɚz hæv əm‖　　　6. vɪʒṇ

7. fænsɪ tɚm fɔr ə bɑks sit‖　　　7. loʒ

8. ə skɑtɪʃ nem‖　　　8. freʒɚ

9. stɪkɪŋ təgɛðɚ‖　　　9. kohiʒṇ

10. frɛntʃ fɔr rɛd‖ hwɑts ə vɪzɑz ruʒ　　　10. ruʒ

hwaɪ dont ju kwɪt fɔr ə hwaɪl ænd go du sʌmθɪŋ sɪlɪ‖ it ə goldfɪʃ‖ puʃ ə bɛd‖ sɛrɪned ðə dɪn‖ laɪfs ʃɔrt bʌt nid ju wɛr sʌtʃ ə lɔŋ fes maɪ fæthɛdɪd frɛnd‖

11. ʃæl sæl so æt ðə soɪŋ soʃəl　　　11. soʃəl

12. sizɚ wʌz ɛpɪlɛptɪk‖ hi hæd sizɚz‖　　　12. sizɚ

13. maɪ most prɛʃəs pəzɛʃən ɪz maɪ old paɪp‖　　　13. prɛʃəs

14. gɚlz laɪk tu bi tizd bʌt nɑt baɪ gɚlz‖　　　14. tizd

15. lɛt ʌs hæv no mɔr lɛtəs‖　　　15. lɛtəs

16. ə sɛnsəs sʌmtaɪmz əgriz wɪð ə kənsɛnsəs‖　　　16. sɛnsəs

17. hi bruzd hɚ lɪps‖ hi ʃud hæv rɪmuvd hɪz kætʃɚz mæsk‖　　　17. bruzd

18. prəvaɪd ðə prəvɪʒən‖ ʃut ðə ʃɚbɚt tu mi hɚbɚt‖　　　18. prəvɪʒən

19. hɪz stetɪd mɪʃən wʌz tu kɪs ə fimel tubə pleɚ‖　　　19. mɪʃən

20. aɪ prɪfɚ ðə dɛzɚts mɪrɑʒɪz tu ðə sɪtɪz gɚrɑʒɪz‖　　　20. gɚrɑʒəz

[θ]
The Sound [θ] as in *thick* **[θɪk] and** *teeth* **[tiθ]**

This unvoiced *th* [θ] sound has occasionally been presented to you before, but not nearly so often as its partner, the voiced *th* which we will study next. The [θ] is a single sound and is made by drawing an oval with a line through its center. The [θ] is the commonly used sound we find at the beginning of the words *theme* [θim], *thing* [θɪŋ], and *thick* [θɪk]. It is also heard in the middle of the word *breathless* [brɛθlɪs], and at the end of the words *oath* [oθ] and *path* [pæθ].

[ðə saund θ ɪz æn ʌnvɔɪst kəntɪnjuənt‖ hwɛn wi mek ɪt ðə tɪp əv ðə tʌŋ ɪz plest dʒʌst fɑr ɪnʌf fɔrwəd tu mek ə slaɪt opənɪŋ bɪtwin ðə tiθ‖ ðə brɛθ ɪz ðɛn fɔrst daun ðə sɛntər əv ðə tʌŋ θru ðə slɪt‖ ju kæn hɪr ðə saund ɪn ðə wɜːd θɪsl̩ ɔr hwɛn ju hwɪspər ə ti etʃ saund‖ ɪt ɪz ə frɪkətɪv saund‖‖]

Exercise 6.13.   Read the following list of words aloud. Then say them a second time and write them in English.

θɪn	θro	nʌθɪŋ	fɪfθ	θɛft
θaɪ	θɪm	θʌndər	θru	mauθ
feθ	θɔt	tɛnθ	nɔrθ	θæŋk
hɛlθ	dɛθ			

Exercise 6.14.   Now write the following in phonetic symbols.

1. Through thick and thin we'll both take a bath.

_____

2. He held his breath until he gained the depths.

_____

3. The throne had three thorns on its thick seat.

_____

Some children and some adults who have first spoken some language other than English find the voiceless *th* sound difficult to master and will substitute a *t* sound for it. They will say [aɪ tɪŋk aɪl tek ə bæt]. This results when the person fails to put the tongue tip in the opening between the teeth.

Exercise 6.15.   Read each of the following groups aloud, and then say it again, substituting the [θ] for the [t]. Write this second word in the space provided. (In order to understand exactly what a child or foreigner does when he mistakes the [θ] for a [t], prolong a *th* [θ] sound, then switch to a *t* sound.)

tɔrn	_____	pæt	_____	fet	_____
tɪn	_____	tru	_____	tɪk	_____
fɔrt	_____	tæŋk	_____	bæt	_____
dɛt	_____				

Another common misuse of the [θ] sound results from a lingual lisp. A person with such a lisp will use a [θ] when he is supposed to use the [s] sound. Such a lisper would say [aɪ θi ju θe θʌm əv ðə θem wɜːdð ɪn ə fʌni wel‖].

Most foreign language words have no *th* sound. German equivalents of our words which start with the *th* sound usually start with the letter *d*. We find the same in the Scandinavian languages and in Dutch. The absence of the *th* is one of the most obvious characteristics of a foreign dialect and is one of the first sounds you can teach to a foreigner who wants to Anglicize his speech. The Greeks gave us the phonetic symbol [θ]. In their language it is called *theta*.

Exercise 6.16.   In the following paragraph, fill in the blank spaces with either [θ], [t], or [s].

[ə fɔrɪnɚ sʌm‿aɪmz‿ɪŋks hi kænat gɛt‿ru ðə ti etʃ wɝd hwɛn hi ɪz lɝnɪŋ tu‿pɪk ɪŋglɪʃ‖ hi maɪt ‿ɪŋk əv ə ‿auzənd ɪn hɪz on læŋgwɪdʒ ænd nɑt faɪnd ə‿ɪŋgl saund hwɪtʃ kem fɔr‿ æz ə θ‖ if ju gɪv hɪm ‿ʌtʃ gud hɛlp ðæt hi kæn mæstɚ ðə saund nʌ‿ɪŋ wɪl hɛlp hɪz spitʃ mɔr‖ hi wɪl ‿æŋk ju fɔr ɛvrɪ‿ɪŋ ju hæv dʌn tu ‿itʃ hɪm ə saund hwɪtʃ ɪz nu tu hɪm‖‖]

One other substitution you will hear occasionally is [f] for the [θ] sound in childish speech or in black English. You probably have heard a child say [fæŋk ju] or [aɪm fɝstɪ].

[ð]
The Phoneme [ð] as in *this* [ðɪs], *brother* [brʌðɚ], and *loathe* [loð]

This is a phoneme which must be very familiar to you by now. It is almost impossible to write more than a sentence or two without using *the* [ðə], *this* [ðɪs], *those* [ðoz], or *another* [ənʌðɚ]. The [ð] is the voiced *th*, the vocal partner of the [θ] phoneme. The lips, tongue, mouth, and teeth all assume the same position as they do in making the [θ], and the only major difference between the two phonemes is that when you say [ð] you vibrate your vocal folds, whereas when you say [θ] you give the air a clear passageway all the way up to the teeth.

There are several pairs of phonemes besides the [ð] and [θ] whose only difference is in the voiced or unvoiced quality. Can you think of the others? Here's a bit of help; since vowels by their very name are vocal, you can ignore them in this exercise.

Exercise 6.17.   On the first line list all the consonantal symbols we have studied so far, then on the second line pair those phonemes which are identical except for their vocal quality. Put the unvoiced phoneme first, then the voiced. *Example:* [θ–ð].

[ɪf ju fɔrgat ðə s–z pɛr jul bi ʃat æt sʌnraɪz‖‖]

The [θ] and [ð] are paired in more ways than their similarity of production. The meanings of some words are vocally distinguishable only by the use of the [θ] or [ð]. *Loath*, meaning *reluctant*, is [loθ], whereas *loathe* (*abominate*) is [loð]. [tuθ] and [tuð] is another pair. Can you spell these words correctly?

One very common word may properly be pronounced either with a [θ] or a [ð]. Read the preceding sentence aloud. Did you say [wɪð] or [wɪθ]?

Exercise 6.18.   Here are some nonsense words to say aloud. There is no better way to become proficient with the phonemes of the IPA.

æðon roðiruθ gæðɪpɚð aɪðbuð ðinwɪð sɔðzæð

Exercise 6.19.   Say the following words aloud, then translate them into English.

ðæn	kloð	bɑðɚ	iðɚ	ðɛm
ðɛn	gæðɚ	mʌðɚ	brɪð	ðʌs
fɑðɚ	sʌðɚn	ðɑu	ənʌðɚ	tugɛðɚ
ðiz	bɛð	fɛðɚ	ræðɚ	wɛðɚ
ʌðɚ	ðɛr	ðo	niðɚ	saɪð

Probably the most common misuse of the voiced *th* sound is the substitution of the *d* sound for it. [ɪt ɪzn̩t ɔlwɪz gæŋstɚz ænd tʌf kɛrɪktɚz ɪn muviz hu se "dɛn aɪ tol doz gaɪz də wɛdɚ wʌz tu bæd"‖] Even in the hallowed halls of higher learning you might hear this substitution. It is seldom caused by a real inability to make the [ð]. It usually results from carelessness.

Exercise 6.20.   Read these pairs of words aloud.

ðaɪn	daɪn	niðɚ	nidɚ
ðe	de	fɑðɚ	fɑdɚ
ðo	do	brɪð	brɪd
ðɛn	dɛn	saɪð	saɪd

Did you notice that they are all real words? A *kneader* [ɪz wʌn hu nidz do‖]. If you will make the [d] and then the [ð] sounds you will see why this is considered a lazy substitution.

Usually a person who substitutes a [d] for the [ð] will also use its voiceless counterpart, the [t] sound, for the voiceless *th* [θ]. Occasionally you will hear a person substitute a [z] for the voiced [ð]. This occurs more often when a person has learned English as a foreign language.

Exercise 6.21.   It's time for a transcription passage.

Those who heard the third theme got thirsty when the author was brought forth and led to the dais. His "Ode To A Waterfall" was so realistic that there was no other course but to mouth their approval. The other authors oozed oaths as they soothed their own feathers with assumed enthusiasm.

1. rɪvju	1. birth	_____
2. onlɪ θri sɪmbl̩z	2. through	_____
3. watʃ ðə vauəl	3. hearth	_____
4. dʌz ɪt raɪm wɪθ faðɚ	4. bother	_____
5. luk æt ðə nɛkst wɚd bɪfɔr ju raɪt	5. lathe	_____
6. si əbʌv	6. lath	_____
7. wi lʌv ðoz ɛksɪz	7. sixth	_____
8. dont ju dɛr mɪs ðɪs	8. their	_____
9. gɛt ðə raɪt ti etʃ	9. rather	_____
10. no haɪfən nidɪd	10. brother-in-law	_____
11. dont juz fɔr sɪmbl̩z	11. thumb	_____
12. ðɪs ɪzn̩t æz hard æz ɪt luks	12. thwart	_____
13. nid wi se no si	13. thence	_____
14. raɪmz wɪθ hɛd	14. crossthread	_____
15. luks fʌnɪ ɪn fonɛtɪks	15. oath	_____
16. ɪz jurz pevd wɪθ gud ɪntɛnʃənz	16. path	_____
17. ðɪs ɪz trɪkɪ se ɪt əlaud	17. paths	_____
18. ste ɑn jur toz	18. throes	_____
19. hæv ju sin ðɪs bɪfɔr	19. phoneme	_____
20. bi kɛrful əv ðə θɚd sɪmbl̩	20. theater	_____

ANSWERS

1. ɛvɚ hɪr əbaut ðə mæn hu daɪd ɪn hɪz bɝθ

    1. bɝθ

2. hi θru ðə bɔl θru ðə wɪndo

    2. θru

3. sʌm de jul hæv lɪtl̩ spræts æt jur harθsaɪd

    3. harθ

4. dont baðɚ faðɚ

    4. baðɚ

5. ðə plurəl əv leð ɪz leðz

    5. leð

6. hi hu læfθ læθt lɪθpθ

    6. læθ

7. kæn ju se sɪksθs

    7. sɪksθ

8. ðer ɪz no hɛr ɑn ə tɝtl̩‖ ɪts bɛr

    8. ðer

9. aɪðɚ ɔr iðɚ‖ aɪd raðɚ juz ræðɚ

    9. ræðɚ

10. jur mʌðɚɪnlɔz sʌn ɔr jur sɪstɚz hʌzbənd

    10. brʌðɚɪnlɔ

11. kʌm kʌm no bi ɪn θʌm

    11. θʌm

12. ju ʃud hæv bɪn θwækt fɔr ðæt ɛrɚ

    12. θwɔrt

13. ðɛns ɔr hɛns‖ nɑnsɛns

    13. ðɛns

14. hau dɪd ðɪs sɪlɪ wɝd gɛt ɪn hɪr

    14. krɔsθrɛd

15. ju me tek ðɪs bʌt nɑt gɪv ɪt

    15. oθ

16. dɪd ju pæθ θaɪkɑlədʒɪ

    16. pæθ

17. ɪt tʃendʒɪz ɪn ðə plurəl

    17. pæðz

18. ʌp

    18. θroz

19. fon hu

    19. fonim

20. nʌkl̩hɛdz juz ən e ɪn ðɪs wɝd

    20. θiətɚ

[hw]
The Phoneme [hw] as in *whether* **[hwɛðɚ]**, *when* **[hwɛn]**, and *why* **[hwaɪ]**

As you can see, the [hw] is a double phoneme and perhaps needs no special section of its own. The [h] and the [w] you already know, and the [hw] is simply a combination of the two. However, since there are so many [hw] words, and since the combination is spelled backwards in English, a bit of practice won't hurt. There is no such thing as a *wh* phonetically; when both sounds are used back to back the [h] always precedes the [w]. The only thing you need to get this combination correctly every time is an accurate ear. Say these words aloud: *what, why, which.*

The sounds [hw] are begun with forced breath as in pronouncing an *h*, even though the lips are rounded to make the *w* sound. The [hw], like the [w], is a glide since it is always made as a movement, and it is pronounced only when the mouth is in motion.

Sometimes the sound [hw] is written as [ʍ] in phonetics to indicate that it is a single sound, the equivalent of an unvoiced [w], but in this country the [hw] symbol seems to have attained the greatest usage. [ænd ɪts dʒʌst əz wɛl‖ fɔr ði ʍ lʊks tu mʌtʃ laɪk ðə m‖]

Exercise 6.22. Say each of the following words aloud, and underline those which are nonsense words.

hwito	hwɛn	hwɪt	hwʊd	hwɪtʃ
minhwaɪl	hwel	ihwaɪn	ɛnɪhwɛr	hwaɪt
hwaɪl	hwetɪ	əhwaɪl	hwɑtɛvɚ	hwæz
ɑhwɪt	hwɛns	hwinz	hwit	hwɪl

The *h* part of the [hw] sound is sometimes omitted entirely in conversation and you will hear such snatches as [wɛr wɪl aɪ mit ju æn wɛn‖ wɪtʃ pis əv waɪt pepɚ ʃæl aɪ raɪt ɑn‖]

This substitution of the *w* is the most common mispronunciation of the [hw]. This tendency seems to be growing swiftly in common usage, and perhaps one hundred years from now the [hw] may never be heard in colloquial speech. Even the most careful speaker will drop the *h* in this sound when speaking hurriedly. [ɔl raɪt‖ ɔl raɪt‖ so ju nɛvɚ du‖ so lɛts dʒʌst se jur ði ɪksɛpʃən‖]

Exercise 6.23. Transcribe the following.

Why, which, what, and *when* are found at the beginning of many questions. Anywhere you see them written in phonetics they look somewhat similar. Why is it that the word *who* looks so unusual in phonetic script? Everywhere you hear people use it to initiate questions, too.

Exercise 6.24. Now answer the question that was asked in the preceding exercise. Answer it phonetically.

[tʃ]
The Sound *ch* as in *church* [tʃɝtʃ]

[tʃ] and [dʒ] are called *affricate* sounds. They are homogenized consonant blends. The two symbols for each indicate their components. This is the sound we know as *ch* [tʃ]—the sound which begins the word *chair* [tʃɛr], ends the word *itch* [ɪtʃ], and is in the middle of the word *nature* [netʃɚ]. It is often written in English as *ch*, but there are exceptions. The words *venture* [vɛntʃur] and *tincture* [tɪŋktʃur] are examples.

[dʒʌst æz vauəlz kəmbain tu fɔrm difθɔŋz so ɔlso du sɝtən kansənənts‖ ðə si etʃ kambineʃən kəmbainz ænd blɛndz ðə stap kansənənt t wið ðə kəntinjuənt ʃ‖ fɝst wi əsum ðə tʌŋ pəziʃən fɔr t ænd ðɛn rilis ðə dæmd ʌp ɛr θru ðə brɔd tʌŋ gruv əv ðə ʃ‖ it iz ʌnvɔist‖ it iz kɔld æn əfrikətiv saund‖]

Exercise 6.25. Fill in the blank spaces in the phonetic script below with the [tʃ] sound as you read through it. Say the [tʃ] sound alone as you write the symbol [ænd ðɛn se ði intair wɝd əlaud bifɔr ju rid fɝðɚ‖].

[i__ əv mai__ʌmz wa__iz kips gud taim‖ bai vɝ__u əv ðis mai fonɛtiks ti__ɚ kæn vau__ fɔr mai biiŋ pʌŋk__uəl‖ mʌ__ əv ðə taim ai əpro__ ðə klæs wið ə kæ__ kwɛs__ən sʌ__ æz ðis‖ hwai did ju __uz ðə tʃ saund tu lɔn__ʌs an ðiz nu kansənənts‖]

Exercise 6.26. Read the following words aloud.

rɪtʃ	tʃap	hætʃit	mætʃiz	ritʃt	tʃɛri
sɝtʃ	lætʃ	tʃaim	tʃiz	tʃɛn	titʃ
tʃes	trɛntʃ	tʃir	bitʃ	pitʃɚ	tʃildrin
tʃin	kætʃ	tʃæt	kitʃən	tʃæns	lʌntʃ
tʃok	witʃ	tʃu	itʃ	tʃɔk	

Exercise 6.27. Here are some nonsense words to read aloud. Is there a real word among them?

tʃubotʃu	tʃuməʃʌmo	tʃamitʃu	ɝtʃin	mabolɛtʃ
ɔtʃotʃo	retʃibaʃ	ætʃitoz	tʃimbəti	ʃibolatʃ
ædotʃai				

Exercise 6.28.   Write the words below in phonetics [bʌt sʌbstɪtut ðə tʃ fɔr ðə ʃ ɪn ðə wɝd‖] Underline any in the [tʃ] list which are *not* real words.

ʃip	_____	ʃɛl	_____
kæʃ	_____	mæʃ	_____
dɪʃ	_____	ʃek	_____
ʃɪn	_____	ʃuz	_____
klæʃ	_____	krʌʃ	_____
ʃap	_____	liʃ	_____

[ju ʃud hæv faund onlɪ θri wɝdz tu ʌndɚlaɪn‖]

In the above exercise you can see that there is some resemblance between the [ʃ] and the [tʃ]. Actually, the [tʃ] is a combination of [t] and [ʃ], as the symbol denotes. Say these two sounds slowly in this order [ɪt . . . ʃi ɪt . . . ʃi]; keep saying them in that order, decreasing the pause between. When you are saying them rapidly with no pause between, you get a good [tʃ] sound. Some people actually substitute [ʃ] for [tʃ]—[kæʃ ðə bɔl‖ ɪf ju ar lɪsṇɪŋ tu ə pɝsən wɪð ə skatɪʃ daɪəlɛkt] you will find his [tʃ] sound is very harsh and throaty. It has a quality unlike that of [tʃ] in any other English or American dialect.

Children sometimes find the [tʃ] difficult to learn at first, and will often substitute a *t* or *ts* for it. They may say [aɪ gat sʌm tsɛri pʊdɪŋ ɔn maɪ tɪn‖] or [lɪsṇ tu ðə tɝt bɛlz taɪm‖] They also confuse the [ʃ] and [tʃ] sounds, sometimes reversing them completely: [ðə pʌpɪ ʃud maɪ tʃu‖ aɪm goɪŋ tu tʃɪkago‖].

Exercise 6.29.   Transcribe the following words.

1. Chinese	_____	2. bleachers	_____	3. Christian	_____
4. Dutch-cheese	_____	5. chipmunk	_____	6. splotch	_____
7. chains	_____	8. chicken	_____	9. chimney	_____
10. trench	_____	11. nature	_____	12. creation	_____
13. chisel	_____	14. hatchets	_____	15. anxious	_____
16. sketched	_____	17. thatched	_____	18. chinks	_____

Transcribe these sentences.

1. Each child reached for a peach.

_____

2. He pitched a cherry into the ketchup.

_____

3. The bachelor chased the wretched wench up the beach.

_____

Circle the words which are not transcribed correctly:

1. chance [tʃæns]	2. spuds [spʌdʒ]	3. visual [vɪdʒuəl]
4. individual [ɪndɪvɪdʒuəl]	5. which [wɪtʃ]	6. douche [duʃ]
7. serge [sɝtʃ]	8. chalk [tʃɔlk]	9. ache [etʃ]
10. negligee [nɛglɪdʒe]	11. Betsy [bɛtsɪ]	12. exchange [ɪkstʃendʒ]

[dʒ]
The Sound *j* as in *jelly* [dʒɛlɪ]

[ðə dʒ saʊnd ɪz med ɪgzæktlɪ laɪk ðə tʃ ɪksɛpt ðæt ɪt ɪz vɔɪst‖] It is the first sound in the words *jump* [dʒʌmp] and *jam* [dʒæm], the middle sound in the words *angel* [endʒəl] and *magic* [mædʒɪk], and the final sound in the words *edge* [ɛdʒ] and *page* [pedʒ].

The [dʒ], like the [tʃ], is really two sounds produced almost simultaneously, and therefore is represented by two symbols. Try it for yourself; say [dʒ] just once, but continue saying it for a count of ten. Notice that after the first instant you are saying only [ʒ].

Exercise 6.30.　Write these in English, and again in phonemics.

dʒo	_____ _____	dʒʌst	_____ _____
dʒɛlɪ	_____ _____	dʒæm	_____ _____
ɪndʒɔɪ	_____ _____	edʒ	_____ _____
kedʒ	_____ _____	lɑrdʒ	_____ _____

You may have some difficulty for a while, confusing the symbol [j] with the [dʒ] sound, because in English spelling you have learned to connect the letter *j* with the sound that you are learning now. [ju wɪl hæv tu bɪld ə nu kənɛkʃən‖]

Exercise 6.31.　Say the following pairs of words aloud, underlining the ones which have the [dʒ] sound [æz ju se ðem‖].

jæm	dʒæm	dʒok	jok
jɛlo	dʒɛlo	jul	dʒuḷ
dʒɛt	jɛt	dʒɑt	jɑt
dʒɛld	jɛld	jus	dʒus

Undoubtedly, the most common variation in the use of the [dʒ] sound in English is the substitution of the unvoiced [tʃ]. [lɛmi tɛl ju ə fʌnɪ tʃok‖] In foreign languages and dialects the [dʒ] is one of the sounds most often confused. This is probably due to the fact that there was no *j* letter in the Latin alphabet, which was the basis of Western European scripts. So when the letter *j* was introduced it was given different values in different languages. In Scandinavia and Germany the letter *j* is sounded as our [j] symbol. In English it is [dʒ], and in French it is [ʒ]. Germans also often use the unvoiced [tʃ] where we would use the [dʒ].

This inconsistency accounts for the carry-over of sound usages by people from those countries who have learned English as a second language. [ju dont hæf tu bi ə dɪtɛktɪv bʌt ju wɪl prɑbəblɪ səspɛkt] that a person who says [aɪ jʊst vɑntu tɛl ɪm ə jok‖] isn't too far removed from Norway or Sweden!

We can tell the difference in the [tʃ] and [dʒ] sounds by putting our fingers lightly on our throats and feeling the vibration as we voice the [dʒ]. Or you can get a similar sensation by plugging your ears with your fingers as you say both sounds.

Exercise 6.32.　In the following words, substitute the [dʒ] sound for the [tʃ]. Write the words which you get in phonetic script.

batch	_____	chip	_____
choke	_____	etching	_____
rich	_____	char	_____
lunch	_____	cheap	_____
chin	_____	chunk	_____

Exercise 6.33.   Transcribe the following words.

1. orange _____
2. January _____
3. gauged _____
4. sponge _____
5. sergeant _____
6. justice _____
7. image _____
8. genial _____
9. jonquil _____
10. jungle _____
11. geography _____
12. garbage _____
13. manages _____
14. Egyptian _____
15. cottage _____

Exercise 6.34.   Transcribe the following word pairs.

cheering _____   jeering _____   chin _____   gin _____
Jerry _____   cherry _____   jokes _____   chokes _____
buds _____   budge _____   chest _____   jest _____
pats _____   patch _____   rich _____   ridge _____
choose _____   Jews _____   sins _____   singe _____
leisure _____   ledger _____   junk _____   chunk _____

1. ðɛr ɑr mɛnɪ kaɪndz əv ðɪzɪz‖   1. cheeses   _____

2. ɪz onlɪ gʊd ɪn sauɚkraut‖   2. cabbage   _____

3. gɪv ə pitʃ əv ə spitʃ‖   3. speech   _____

4. bɪgæn ɪn həwai‖   4. hoochy-koochy   _____

5. bæŋglz ɔlwɪz dæŋgl‖   5. beads   _____

6. ɪz nidɪd tu mek æn ɪnveʒən ə səksɛs‖   6. evasion   _____

7. watʃ ðə θɝd saund‖   7. raging   _____

8. onlɪ fɔr saundz ɪn ðɪs‖   8. butcher   _____

9. kæn ju tek ɪt æz wɛl æz . . . . ɪt aut‖   9. dish   _____

10. bɪwɛr ðə spaɪ ɔr ðɪ ɪnʃurəns kaɪnd‖   10. agents   _____

11. bɪfɔr ju vot‖   11. register   _____

12. ɪmædʒɪn ə kɪŋ ɪn hɪz bæθtʌb‖   12. majestic   _____

13. ðɛm æz kæn dʌz‖ ðɛm æz kænt titʃɪz‖   13. teacher   _____

14. ɪts ənʌðɚ wɝd fɔr kɪdɪŋ‖   14. joshing   _____

15. nɑt laɪk sɪv ɔr liʒ ɔr beʒ‖   15. siege   _____

16. kʌm ʌp ænd si maɪ____   16. etching   _____

17. ənʌðɚ wɝd fɔr vænɪtɪ‖   17. prestige   _____

18. aɪv ə laɪkɪŋ fɔr ðɪz‖   18. lichen   _____

19. pliz raɪt ðɪs raɪt‖   19. pleasure   _____

20. dont gɛt ɪmoʃənəl‖   20. motion   _____

REMINDERS

æ æz ɪn æz, ʒ æz ɪn ruʒ, ɔ æz ɪn bɔdɪ, e æz ɪn eprɪl, ɪ æz ɪn ɪn, ɛ æz ɪn ɛg, ʊ æz ɪn kʊks, ɑ æz ɪn fɑðɚ, aɪ æz ɪn aɪs, i æz ɪn inimini, ə æz ɪn əbaut, ɚ æz ɪn kritʃɚ, ɝ æz ɪn gɝl, ʌ æz ɪn ʌp, o æz ɪn moʃən

Transcribe these for items you missed.

ANSWERS

1. please	_____	seizes	_____	1.	tʃiziz
2. rabbit	_____	bridge	_____	2.	kæbɪdʒ
3. spits	_____	preach	_____	3.	spitʃ
4. brooch	_____	cute	_____	4.	hutʃɪkutʃɪ
5. bids	_____	seeds	_____	5.	bidz
6. occasion	_____	elation	_____	6.	ɪveʒən
7. page	_____	fashion	_____	7.	redʒɪŋ
8. much	_____	butch	_____	8.	butʃɚ
9. fish	_____	squishy	_____	9.	dɪʃ
10. pages	_____	engines	_____	10.	edʒənts
11. just	_____	red	_____	11.	rɛdʒɪstɚ
12. majesty	_____	major	_____	12.	mədʒɛstɪk
13. preaching	_____	feature	_____	13.	titʃɚ
14. jaw	_____	slosh	_____	14.	dʒɔʃɪŋ dʒɑʃɪŋ
15. seeds	_____	sledge	_____	15.	sidʒ
16. edging	_____	itches	_____	16.	ɛtʃɪŋ
17. college	_____	vestige	_____	17.	prɛstiʒ
18. reckon	_____	bacon	_____	18.	laɪkən
19. treasure	_____	seizure	_____	19.	plɛʒɚ
20. lotion	_____	emotion	_____	20.	moʃən

Exercise 6.35.   Transcribe these sentences.

1. Jack jumped up and made a jewel of a catch.

_____

2. The gypsies were put in jail after they outraged the village.

_____

3. The bridge was damaged as the car plunged into the gorge.

_____

4. In college we tend to fudge a bit on genuine study.

_____

[ŋ]
The Sound [ŋ] as in *sing* [sɪŋ], *banging* [bæŋɪŋ], and *wrong* [rɔŋ]

We have saved the easiest of the more difficult consonantal symbols for the last. Even though there is no English letter like the [ŋ] it would take a real dunderhead not to guess what sound it stands for. The [ŋ] is not found at the beginning of words, and except for substandard speech, always follows a vowel. It is found at the ends of words (*strong* [strɔŋ]) and in the middle of words (*ankle* [æŋkl̩]).

[ɪn mekɪŋ ðə ŋ saʊnd ðə bæk əv ðə tʌŋ ɪz prɛst əgɛnst ðə loɚd sɔft pælɪt‖ ðə saʊnd ɪtsɛlf kʌmz aʊt θru ðə noz ænd ɪz ə kəntɪnjuənt saʊnd‖ ɪt ɪz vɔɪst‖ rɪmɛmbɚ ðæt ðɪs ɪz ə sɪŋgl̩ saʊnd hwɪtʃ kæn nɑt bi dɪvaɪdɪd‖]

Exercise 6.36.   Write one line each of the following short words in phonetic script. Prolong the final [ŋ] sound.

rɪŋ   bæŋ   hʌŋ   swɪŋ   lɔŋ

Exercise 6.37.   Here are some nonsense words for you to try. Do not follow [ŋ] with [g] unless it is so written.

pæŋobɔŋ   ɪŋgotɪŋ   tɪŋtən   nɔŋwɔŋ   nebɪŋ   bɪŋlɪŋ   zɪŋgæn

Exercise 6.38.   Spell the following words aloud.

mæŋgl̩	brɪŋ	kɪŋ	sɪŋgl̩	fɪʃɪŋ
kæmpɪŋ	rʌnɪŋ	pæsɪŋ	dʒʌmpɪŋ	hʌŋ
sɔŋ	lɔŋ	sʌŋ	ræŋ	sprɪŋ
drɪŋk	lɪŋk	sɪŋɚ	kʌmɪŋ	goɪŋ
wɪŋ	duɪŋ	raɪtɪŋ	klemɪŋ	
rʌŋ	tæŋ	hʌŋgɚ	tʌŋ	

A very common error made by beginners is to combine [n] and [k] in words like *thank*, *ink*, and *sunk*. Each of these words has the [ŋ] before the [k]. Try saying these pairs of words: [sɪn:k sɪŋk‖ bæn:k bæŋk].

Undoubtedly, the most common error in the use of the [ŋ] sound is the substitution of the [n] for it. [ɪn most kesɪz ɪt ɪz onlɪ bɪkɔz əv lezɪnəs ðæt ə pɚsən wɪl ɔlwɪz seɪ aɪm duɪn æz mʌtʃ sɪŋɪn æn jɛlɪn æz aɪ kæn‖]

Another error you must watch for if you are to transcribe speech accurately is the exploded *g* ending of a [ŋ] sound in the middle of a word when such is not called for: [aɪm brɪŋgɪŋ maɪ lɛsənz ɪn bʌt aɪm lɔŋgɪŋ tu kʌt klæs‖].

In a few English words, the use of *ng* in the middle of the word calls for an added exploded *g* sound. You will have to listen closely to hear which words these are. Among them are [æŋgɚ fɪŋgɚ strɔŋgɪst‖ kæn ju θɪŋk əv ʌðɚz‖].

Exercise 6.39. Transcribe the following.

Uncle Angus banged his ankle on an unguarded angle of the range. He blinked with anguish, incurring the sympathy of the unkempt beggar whose stinking clothes were hanging loosely in the sink.

Exercise 6.40.　Transcribe these word pairs.

bagging	_____	banging	_____	bacon	_____	baking	_____
anchor	_____	anger	_____	sinning	_____	singing	_____
guarding	_____	garden	_____	pan	_____	pang	_____
thing	_____	think	_____	wink	_____	wing	_____
stung	_____	stunk	_____	rung	_____	wrong	_____

Read these aloud.

1. ɪŋkɪ dɪŋkɪ duduldidu
2. wɝdz laɪk ðɪs mek ju æŋgrɪ
3. gɛt ə gud æŋgl̩ hwɛn ju si ðɪs wɝd
4. hau ændʒɛlɪk du ju fil nau
5. æŋzaɪətɪ ɪz ən æsɪd
6. ðe hʌŋ dʒan braunz badɪ frʌm ə tri
7. hwat ju fil hwɛn hi nʌzlz ju
8. bi an gard əgɛnst ðoz sʌnz əv si kuks
9. ðɪs minz jus
10. wi bɛt jur nat filɪŋ ðɪs tɔrd nalɪdʒ
11. wɪl kʌm tu ðæt bjutəfəl fɔrhɛd
12. ɪz ðɛr ə faɪnəl g
13. hau əbaut ɪt dʒæk
14. ænd ju bɪsaɪd mi fɔrtɪ jɪrz əgo
15. ɪndɪgo ɪz blu‖ hau ar ju
16. ɝdʒɪz bɪkʌm ɝdʒənt ɪn sprɪŋ
17. sɪn no mɔr bʌt dʒʌst æz mʌtʃ
18. hu wʌz bɔrn ɪn ə mendʒɚ
19. taɪm fɔr ə
20. ʃi kɔt hɚ fɪŋgɚ ɪn ðə rɪŋɚ

1. ink _____
2. anchor _____
3. angel _____
4. angle _____
5. anxious _____
6. honk _____
7. tingle _____
8. sunguard _____
9. function _____
10. hunger _____
11. wrinkling _____
12. throng _____
13. jangle _____
14. moonglow _____
15. indignant _____
16. urging _____
17. wrongdoing _____
18. ranger _____
19. change _____
20. linger _____

Transcribe these words if you missed the item.

ANSWERS

1. think	_____	stinker	_____	1. ɪŋk
2. canker	_____	tanker	_____	2. æŋkɚ
3. hwɛr du ðə bʌfəlo rendʒ				3. endʒəl
4. wɝ ju ɑbtus ɔr əkjut				4. æŋgl̩
5. handkerchief	_____			5. æŋkʃəs
6. donkey	_____	drunk	_____	6. hɔŋk
7. things	_____	twinkle	_____	7. tɪŋgl̩
8. yard	_____	hum	_____	8. sʌngɑrd
9. ʌŋkʃən minz hwɑt				9. fʌŋkʃən
10. lung	_____	finger	_____	10. hʌŋgɚ
11. twinkling	_____	sprinkling	_____	11. rɪŋklɪŋ
12. long	_____	wrong	_____	12. θrɔŋ
13. angel	_____	ankle	_____	13. dʒæŋgl̩
14. idiosyncracy	_____			14. munglo
15. runt	_____	dig	_____	15. ɪndɪgnənt
16. virgin	_____	merging	_____	16. ɝdʒɪŋ
17. song	_____	bluing	_____	17. rɔŋduɪŋ
18. danger	_____	stranger	_____	18. rendʒɚ
19. mange	_____	shift	_____	19. tʃendʒ
20. longer	_____	stringer	_____	20. lɪŋgɚ

Name _____ *Date* _____ *Score* _____

Hand this in to your instructor.

1. Transcribe the following words.

mule	_____	yellow	_____	shoes	_____
coach	_____	chef	_____	leisure	_____
you__	_____	length	_____	shoals	_____
ji____ing	_____	cute	_____	yolk	_____
__sh	_____	chewing	_____	shrewd	_____
choose	_____				

2. Underline the words which are incorrectly transcribed.

uncle [ʌŋkl̩]	cushion [cʊʃən]	these [ðiz]
hungry [hʌŋrɪ]	onions [ʌnjənz]	precious [prɛʃəs]
sugar [ʃʊgɚ]	illusion [ɪluʃən]	feather [fɛθɚ]
whistle [hwɪsl̩]		

3. Only one word in each of these sentences is incorrectly transcribed. Circle it.

   1. ðiz madən wɪmɪn gɛt æŋgrɪ hwɛn ju trit θɛm tu kæzuəlɪ
   2. wɪθɪn ðə lɛŋθ əv tu mʌnθs ðə wɛðɚ tʃɛndʒd grɛtlɪ
   3. jɛlo fjuʃəz ar nat onlɪ junik ðe ar butɪful

4. Write these sentences in phonetic script.

   1. She went to the booth to change her [hɝ] bathing suit.

   _____

   2. Joe's wrench, when it fell, hit the seventh rung.

   _____

   3. The usual show will change next week.

   _____

   4. Then thinking we'd use a check we joked with the clerk. [klɝk]

   _____

5. Transcribe these word pairs.

   gin   _____   chin   _____
   sheep   _____   cheap   _____
   edge   _____   etch   _____
   buds   _____   budge   _____
   age   _____   H   _____
   Joyce   _____   choice   _____
   marsh   _____   march   _____
   bridges _____   breeches _____
   joke   _____   choke   _____

7 More Vowels and Diphthongs

In Chapter 3 you were told how syllable stress affects the way we write certain symbols in the International Phonetic Alphabet; the *ee* sound is written [i] in a stressed symbol and [ɪ] in the unstressed syllable, as in *meaty* [mitɪ]. Also, the *uh* sound is written as [ʌ] when it is in a stressed syllable, as in *under* [ʌndɚ], and it is written [ə] in an unstressed syllable, as in *upon* [əpɑn]. This rule is difficult to understand, but you might find it easier to convince yourself if you try this: say only the vowels in the word *above*. Can you hear that there is greater stress and length and, probably, higher pitch on the second *uh* sound? There are minimal differences in their production, for the mouth, lips, and tongue are essentially in the same position.

The four vowels that we introduce here, are actually two pairs of very similar sounds: [ʌ], [ə], [ɜ], and [ɚ]. They are the *uh* sounds in *above* [əbʌv], and the *er* sounds in *further* [fɜðɚ]. Since the *uh*'s seem so much alike, and so do the *er*'s, why have separate symbols for each? The usual reason offered is that the two vowels in each pair differ enough in stress and length to be considered different phonemes. There are linguistic scholars who deny there are such differences and state that [ʌ] is merely the accented [ə] and [ɜ] is merely the accented [ɚ]. However, whether we can justify them or not, we have two symbols for each of these closely related sounds and no student of phonetics can ignore them.

We have found that more students make transcription errors because of their failure to scrutinize for stress than for any other single reason. They write [ʌraʊnd] instead of [əraʊnd] for *around*. They transcribe *earlier* as [ɚlɪɜ] instead of its correct form [ɜlɪɚ]. Or they fail to recognize the final [ə] in the word *consistent* [kənsɪstənt], writing it instead as [kənsɪstɛnt]. The most common vowel used in English speech is the unaccented [ə]. If you fail to master the scanning of words for stress you will never be sure whether you should use [ʌ] or [ə], [ɜ] or [ɚ]. You will make mistakes continuously. So let's study this business of stress and accent.

Exercise 7.1.   Write the following passage in English, making sure to grasp the facts presented.

[əl'ðo wi juz ðə wɝdz strɛs ənd 'æksɛnt intɚ'tʃendʒəblɪ ðɛr ɪz ə slaɪt 'dɪfrɪns in 'minɪŋ‖ ðə wɝd 'æksɛnt ɪz juzd 'onlɪ ɪn 'rɛfɚəns tu ˌplʊrəsɪ'læbɪk wɝdz| ænd rɪ'fɝz tu ðə 'sɪləbl̩ hwɪtʃ rɪ'sivz ðə 'gretɚ 'ɛmfəsɪs‖ in ə tu 'sɪləbl̩ wɝd sʌtʃ æz ə'nɔɪ| ðə 'sɛkənd 'sɪləbl̩ ɪz sɛd tu bi 'æksɛntɪd‖ ðɛr ɪz mɔr 'ɛmfəsɪs plest ɑn ðə 'sɛkənd part əv ðə wɝd‖]

ðɛr ɑr ˈvɛriəs wez tu ˈɪndɪˌket ˈɛmfəsɪs ɑn ə ˈsɝtən ˈsɪləbl̩ wɪˈðɪn ə wɝd hwɛn
ˈspikɪŋ‖ ju me ˈɔltɚ ðə pɪtʃ əv jur vɔɪs| ju me ˈlɛŋkθən ðə durˈeʃən| ɔr ju me ɪnˈkris
ɪts ɪnˈtɛnsɪtɪ‖ ˈjuʒuəlɪ wi juz ə ˌkɑmbɪˈneʃən əv ðiz θri‖ ðə ˌkɑmbɪˈneʃən ˈvɛrɪz frəm
wɝd tu wɝd ɪn ən ˌɪndɪˈvɪdʒuəlz spitʃ| ænd ˈɔlso ˈvɛrɪz frəm ˈpɝsən tu ˈpɝsən‖ ði
ˈæksɛntɪd ˈsɪləbl̩ wɪˈðɪn ə wɝd rɪˈmenz ˈkɑnstənt| bət ðə we ju prəˈdus æk ˌsɛntʃuˈeʃən
dʌz nɑt‖

ðɛr ɑr tu ˈdɪfrənt kaɪndz əv ˈæksɛnt| ɔr ˈræðɚ| tu dɪˈgriz əv ˈæksɛnt‖ praɪmɛrɪ
ˈæksɛnt mɪnz ðə ˈstrɔŋgɪst ˈsɪləbl̩ ɪn ə wɝd| bʌt ɪn wɝdz ðæt hæv mɔr ðæn tu ˈsɪləbl̩z
ðɛr me bi ənˈʌðɚ ˈsɪləbl̩ gɛtɪŋ sʌm æk ˌsɛntʃuˈeʃən‖ ðə strɛs ɑn ðɪs ˈsɪləbl̩ wɪl ˈnɛvɚ
bi əz strɔŋ æz ðə wʌn ˈhævɪŋ ˈpraɪmɛrɪ strɛs‖ ðɪs ɪz kɔld ˈsɛkənderɪ ˈæksɛnt‖ ɪn ðə
wɝd ˌɪndɪˈkeʃən| ðə ˈsɪləbl̩ ke hæz ˈpraɪmɛrɪ ˈæksɛnt| ænd ðə ˈsɪləbl̩ ɪn ɪz ˈgɪvən
ˈsɛkənˌderɪ ˈæksɛnt‖ ðə ˈsɛkənˌderɪ ˈæksɛnt mɑrk ɪz plest bɪˈfɔr ænd ˈslaɪtlɪ bɪˈlo
ðə ˈsɪləbl̩‖‖

In many languages there is a specific pattern governing the location of accent in
plurisyllabic words. In Spanish the tendency is for the next-to-the-last syllable to be
accented, providing that the word ends in a vowel. If it ends in a consonant, however,
the accent would be on the last syllable.

Most other languages have their own peculiar pattern, and to a very minor extent
this is true of the English language. We tend to stress the next to the last syllable, just
as in Spanish, but there are so many exceptions to this tendency that to accept it as a
rule would be more confusing than helpful. The only trustworthy guide will be your
listening ability or a good phonetic dictionary.

Accent marks are important. There are some perfectly familiar words whose
pronunciation you cannot be sure of without accent indication. How would you pronounce *conflict?* It can be pronounced *con*flict or con*flict.* There are many of these
noun-versus-verb words. The noun has the emphasis on the first syllable, and the verb
has the emphasis on the second syllable: "He up*set* the plans." "The *up*set caused
dismay."

If we consider isolated words only, we find that there are different degrees of stress
or forcefulness. We can detect at least three such conditions in such a word as *indicate.*
The strongest syllable is the first; the weakest of all three is the second; the second
strongest is the third. Accordingly, we speak of *primary* and *secondary* stress and use
the word *unstressed* for those syllables which have neither primary nor secondary stress.
The ordinary dictionary puts the accent mark *after* the syllable with primary stress, but
in phonetic transcription we place the stress mark in front of the syllable concerned.
Thus *Webster's New Collegiate Dictionary* gives the pronunciation of *deceive* as dĕ.sēv´,
whereas our phonetic transcription of this word would be [dɪˈsiv]. Remember this:
[ples ði ˈæksɛnt mɑrk ɪn frʌnt əv ðə ˈsɪləbl̩‖‖].

Webster's dictionary recognizes two degrees of stress and shows them by marks
of different width. The syllables having primary stress are inked more heavily than those
with secondary stress. Unstressed syllables receive no markings. Thus the dictionary
shows the pronunciation of *idiotic* in this way: ĭd´ĭ.ŏt´ĭk. The primary stress is on the
third syllable, *ot,* and the accent mark is darker and heavier than it is on *id,* the syllable
with secondary stress. We do it a bit less clumsily in phonetic transcription. The syllable having primary stress is preceded by the vertical mark *above* and *before* the syllable.
To show secondary stress we place the vertical mark *below*—but also in front of the
syllable. Thus *idiotic* is transcribed [ˌɪdɪˈɑtɪk]. With this brief introduction, let us provide
some training in scanning for stress. Remember that the vowel sounds usually change
when the accented syllable changes: [ˈkɑn flɪkt] [kən ˈflɪkt].

Exercise 7.2.   In the parentheses following the italicized words, place the number 1 or 2 to indicate whether the first or second syllable has the primary stress.

1. His *conduct* (   ) was so terrible we had to *conduct* (   ) him out of there.
2. He was *content* (   ) with the *contents* (   ) of the box.
3. Don't *desert* (   ) me in this terrible *desert* (   ).
4. We could not *permit* (   ) him to drive without a *permit* (   ).

Exercise 7.3.   Put both primary and secondary stress marks in the words of this group.

saɪəntɪfɪk   ʌndɚstændɪŋ   prapəzɪʃn̩   rɛprɪzɛntɛʃn̩   lɔsændʒəliz
palɪsɪlæbɪk   əpalədʒɛtɪk   madəfɪkeʃn̩   kanstæntɪnopl̩   fənamɪnəl

Here are some hints for improving your ability to detect stress.

1. aɪsəletəd wɚdz əv wʌn sɪləbl̩ ɔlwɪz hæv praɪmɛrɪ strɛs‖
2. most tu sɪləbl̩ wɚdz hæv ðɛr æksɛnt an ðə fɚst sɪləbl̩‖
3. kampaʊnd naʊnz sʌtʃ æz melmæn juʒuəlɪ hæv ðə praɪmɛrɪ strɛs an ðə fɚst sɪləbl̩‖
4. kampaʊnd vɚbz sʌtʃ æz ovɚtek juʒuəlɪ hæv ðɛr praɪmɛrɪ strɛs an ðə sɛkənd vɚb‖
5. ðɛr ar ɪksɛpʃənz tu ɔl ðiz rulz‖

Exercise 7.4.   Here are some groups of words. In each group all the words but one have the same pattern of primary and secondary syllabic stress. Find the exception and write it in the blank.

1. election, deliver, celery, connection, relieving   _____
2. carrot, issue, wouldn't, healing, correct   _____
3. icicle, condiment, syllable, abandon, similar   _____
4. electrical, accuracy, philosophy, methodical   _____
5. delicate, evident, mineral, consonant, material   _____
6. continental, population, catastrophe, hesitation   _____
7. Chicago, emphasize, believing, extinguish, November _____
8. Emily, difficult, populate, cosmetics, yesterday   _____
9. onion, among, connect, conceive, relief   _____
10. biological, abbreviation, incapacitate, recognizable   _____

Exercise 7.5.   One of the words in each of these groups has the accent mark incorrectly placed. Find it and write it correctly in the space at the end of each series.

1. ˌægrə'veʃn̩, 'kansɚˌveʃn, 'ɛləfənt, 'æspɚɪn   _____
2. 'fɔrtʃənətlɪ, ɪn'dɪkəˌtɪv, 'fɔrgɛt, ˌdʒɚ'usələm   _____
3. 'ægət, sɪ'lɛkt, 'ɚθɪ, 'pɪˌæno, 'mɛθədɪst   _____
4. 'pɛtrəˌfaɪ, mɛkə'nɪzm̩, ˌstu'pɪdɪtɪ, ˌɪk'sɛpʃənəl _____

There are some special problems in recognizing the stress characteristics of compound words. You will have to listen a bit more carefully to know where to put the accent marks. Some of these compounds even have two primary stresses, or *level stress*. The words *fifty-fifty, can-can,* and *hand-made* are examples. There are not many of these. Most compound words show primary and secondary stress, as in ['postmən].

[ʌ]
The Sound [ʌ] as in *up* [ʌp]

The [ʌ] sound is heard in the words *utmost* [ʌtmost], *must* [mʌst], and *dull* [dʌl]. It is represented in different ways in English spelling: *buck, blood, some, touch*. It is the *accented uh* sound. It is therefore to be found both in one-syllable and polysyllabic words.

[hwɛn wi mek ðɪ ʌ saund wi du nɑt muv iðɚ ðə frʌnt ɔr bæk əv ðə tʌŋ‖ ɪt laɪz fɛrlɪ kwaɪətlɪ ɪn ðə mauθ bʌt ðə mɪdl̩ əv ðə tʌŋ ɪz juʒuəlɪ ɛlɪvetɪd ə traɪfl̩ ænd tɛnst‖ ɪn sʌm spikɚz ðə tɪp me bi rɪtræktɪd slaɪtlɪ‖ ɪts pəzɪʃən ɪz klos tu ðə pəzɪʃən əv ðə tʌŋ ɪn saɪlənt briðɪŋ‖

Exercise 7.6.   Read the following words aloud. Which one is not a meaningful word?

tʌf	nʌt	stʌmp	sʌdz	tʌb
dʌl	bʌk	sʌp	trʌk	bʌmp
rʌst	mʌs	fʌn	pʌmp	wʌn
gʌn	mʌnɪ	flʌb	tʌn	kʌn
pʌp				

Exercise 7.7.   Read the following words and mark the syllable with the primary stress. Then write in phonetic script the words in which the [ʌ] is required.

some	upstart	study	balloon	afraid
aside	raven	become	salute	bumped
subway	rough	must	summit	custom
banana	agree	rustic	dusty	

_____ _____ _____ _____ _____

_____ _____ _____ _____ _____

_____ _____ _____ _____ _____

_____ _____ _____ _____

[ju ʃud hæv faund twɛlv wɝdz tu raɪt‖ dɪd ju mɪs ðə wʌn sɪləbl̩ wɝdz‖]

There is one group of words in which we shall find more than one syllable with almost equal stress. This is the large group of words with an *un* or an *up* prefix. In these words, we use the stressed symbol [ʌ]. Three exceptions are the common words *unless*, *upon*, and *until*.

Exercise 7.8.   Read the following words aloud, and you will see that the first syllable, as well as another one, receives noticeable stress.

ʌnped	ʌndu	ʌnbolt	ʌntold
ʌphɪl	ʌprɔr	ʌpsɛt	ʌplɪft
ʌnkwot	ʌnhuk	ʌnsɛd	ʌptek

Reading passage for [ʌ]

wʌns| wʌn sʌmɚ sʌnsɛt‖ wʌn dʌm dʌk‖
tu| tu hʌŋgrɪ hʌntɚz‖ θri fri ʃʌts frəm gʌnz‖
fɔr gem wɔrdn̩z kʌm‖ mʌtʃ lʌk?‖ nʌn‖ nʌn?‖
hʌm‖ wʌn dʌk‖ bæd lʌk‖ kʌm‖

120

wʌn hʌntɚ rʌnz‖ stʌmblz‖
ʌðɚ hʌntɚ rʌnz‖ tʌmblz‖
lʌgd tʊ dʒʌg‖ faɪv mʌnθs ɪn dʒel‖
juv ə grʌdʒ ju dʌm old dʒʌdʒ‖
wʌn hʌndrəd bʌks kəntɛmt‖
sʌtʃ lʌk‖ wʌn dʌk‖ wʌn hʌndrəd bʌks‖ ʃʌks‖
wʌn dæm dʌk‖
tu dʌm hʌntɚz tu dæm hʌŋgri‖
θri ənlʌki ʃʌts‖ fɔr rʌf gem wɔrdn̩z‖
faɪv mʌnθs ɪn dʒel‖ no bel‖
nʌts‖

Exercise 7.9.   Transcribe the following words.

1. blood _____   2. mud _____   3. hung _____
4. chugs _____   5. chunk _____   6. rough _____
7. Dutch _____   8. shove _____   9. young _____
10. brother _____   11. does _____   12. thumb _____
13. thus _____   14. judge _____   15. uncle _____

Exercise 7.10.   Reading passage.

ə hɪroɪk tel

ðʌs æz ðə dʌtʃ bɔɪ sɔ ðə flʌd ʃʌv rʌflɪ æt ðə daɪk hi θrʌst hɪz θʌm ɪntu ðə mʌdɪ hol ænd hʌŋ ðer əntɪl ðə kostgard tʃʌgd ʌp ɪn ə lɔntʃ ænd rɛskjud ðə jʌŋstɚ dʒʌst ɪn taɪm‖

Exercise 7.11.   Transcribe these sentences.

1. The other bum was the one who won the sum of money.

_____

2. The hunter grabbed his gun when one of the pups flushed the covey.

_____

3. No one under the sun could be so ugly as my beloved Uncle Slug.

_____

4. Honey, who hung sonny up in the mulberry tree?

_____

5. The guppy's husband gulped when he saw the dozens of puppy guppies.

_____

Exercise 7.12.   Read this [sɛksɪst poəm] with feeling.

rʌbədʌb dʌb
wʌn mæn tʊ ɚn grʌb
wʌn wɛntʃ hu kn̩ skrʌb
ðel sun hæv ə kʌb
fɔr ðe θɪŋk ðæt ɪts lʌb
rʌbədʌb dʌb

The unstressed [ə] is made in exactly the same way as the [ʌ], but the middle of the tongue is not tensed, and the use of the symbol is different. It is one of the most commonly used sounds in phonetic transcription and is represented in English spelling by all the vowel letters—*a, e, i, o, u*: remn*a*nt, fragm*e*nt, an*i*mal, p*o*tato, gam*u*t. In ordinary transcription it is the sound used to represent the article word *a* [ə mæn] and the last sound of the word *the* [ðə dɔg], as both these words are unstressed in common usage. Later we will find it combined with *r* in unaccented syllables to make *er* [ɚ]: bett*er* [bɛtɚ]. [ə] also occurs at the end of words which are spelled with the final *er*, but in which the *r* is "dropped" as in eastern and southern localities: [bɛtə].

The [ə] sound is called a *schwa* or weak vowel because the tongue, lips, and jaws may stay in the resting position and still be able to produce this sound. It is the most neutral vowel so far as distinctiveness is concerned. It is also probably the most frequently used vowel in American English. Another weak, or schwa, vowel is the unstressed [ɪ] as in *cousin* or *important*, but the [ə] is the weakest of all. Remember that this sound is used only in syllables having no primary stress. We provide the following exercise to help you contrast the unstressed with the primary stressed.

Exercise 7.13.   Transcribe each of the following words as you say them aloud, but put the articles *a* [ə] or *the* [ðə] alternately before each successive word. *Example:* [ə mʌg] [ðə kʌt]

1. mug _____ 2. cut _____ 3. rug _____
4. skunk _____ 5. truck _____ 6. bunny _____
7. run _____ 8. hug _____ 9. pump _____
10. spud _____

Exercise 7.14.   These words have either the stressed [ʌ] or the unstressed [ə] in them. Transcribe them carefully. One word has both sounds.

1. alone _____ 2. utmost _____ 3. running _____
4. above _____ 5. neutral _____ 6. fussy _____
7. convey _____ 8. obvious _____ 9. patrol _____
10. across _____

Exercise 7.15.   Reading passage. Definitions.

1. kətæstrəfɪ‖ ə dʌtʃəs wɪθ ðə hɪkəps‖
2. ɛnəmɪ‖ ɛnɪ ʌðɚ pələtɪʃn̩‖
3. dʒʌŋk‖ ʌðɚ pipl̩z væluəbl̩ prapɚtɪ‖
4. dʒɛntl̩mən‖ ə sosɪələdʒɪkəl rɛmnənt əv ðə dez əv ʃɪvəlrɪ‖
5. ʃɪvəlrɪ‖ ɪt ɪzn̩t ðə dez əv ʃɪvəlrɪ ðæt ɚ dɛd‖ ɪts ðə naɪts‖
6. əflɪkʃən‖ ðə juʒuəl dɔrmətərɪ sæləd‖
7. əhɔɪ‖ əhɔɪ– əhɔɪ‖ ɪf ju dont hæv ə hɔɪ θro mi ə rop‖
8. blʌfɪŋ‖ mɪrlɪ kəˈrabɚətɪv ditel ɪntɛndɪd tu gɪv ɑrtɪstɪk ˈvɛrəsɪmɪlətud tu ə bɔld n̩ ʌnkənvɪnsɪŋ nɛrətɪv‖
9. sofə‖ hwɛr græmpə gat hɪz kæləsɪz‖
10. pəlaɪtnəs‖ ə plɛzn̩t we fɚ ə mæn tu gɛt nohwɛr wɪð ə gɚl‖‖

In this section describing the phenomenon of stress we attempted to emphasize that in unstressed syllables most vowels tend to change into [ə] or [ɪ]. Of these two, the [ə] is most frequently used. Compare *cup* [kʌp] and *hiccough* [hɪkəp], *chase* [tʃes] and *purchase* [pɝtʃəs], or *rate* [ret] and *desperate* [dɛspɚət]. Many students never learn to listen to the sounds of the unstressed syllables; they fail to recognize the presence of the [ə] or [ɪ] vowels therein; they are affected by the look of the word and so they continue to make errors. This exercise may help you to avoid their mistakes.

Exercise 7.16.   Transcribe these pairs of words, watching for the schwas.

1. meant	_____	tenement	_____
2. lice	_____	Alice	_____
3. man	_____	woman	_____
4. mass	_____	Christmas	_____
5. fast	_____	breakfast	_____
6. bell	_____	rebel	_____
7. able	_____	abominable	_____
8. nest	_____	meanest	_____
9. lace	_____	palace	_____
10. Ted	_____	rented	_____
11. Kate	_____	delicate	_____
12. men	_____	specimen	_____
13. site	_____	opposite	_____
14. lance	_____	vigilance	_____
15. ate	_____	immediate	_____
16. ally	_____	royally	_____

It is also possible to have several [ə] sounds in a single word of several syllables. We would never write *grub* as [grəb]; it must be written [grʌb]. But in words such as *unutterable* [ənʌtɚəbəl] we may find three [ə] sounds and one [ʌ]. How many [ə] sounds are there in *unconditional*? In *unrepresentative*? In *suspiciousness*? In these unstressed syllables it is sometimes difficult to determine whether you are saying [ə] or [ɪ]. So weak are these sounds when buried in words which are hidden in sentences that they are difficult to remember once they have been spoken. Moreover, different speakers use different schwa vowels. One person will say [pɑsəbɪlətɪ] while another from the same community will say [pɑsɪbɪlɪtɪ]. How do you say it?

Exercise 7.17.   Ask three different people to say these words. Record their pronunciation of the schwa vowels. Ask them also to use the words in sentences.

1. lett*u*ce _____ _____ _____
2. pal*a*ce _____ _____ _____
3. com*i*cal _____ _____ _____
4. hatch*e*t _____ _____ _____
5. test*i*fy _____ _____ _____

In most instances the difference will be found to be so slight that we will not be far wrong if we use the [ə] sound for those syllables with little stress.

Now let's go back and review the contrast between the [ʌ] and the [ə] sound, remembering that the first is used in syllables having primary stress only, while the [ə] is reserved for those of secondary stress or those which are unstressed.

Exercise 7.18.   Transcribe these words after first putting down the primary stress marks.

1. above _____ 2. couplet _____
3. around _____ 4. among _____

5. salad _____	6. remnant _____
7. slovenly _____	8. gallop _____
9. suppose _____	10. kingdom _____
11. shovel _____	12. asleep _____
13. immediate _____	14. Episcopalian _____
15. fundamental _____	

Exercise 7.19. Spell these words aloud as swiftly as you can.

dɛsələt	əfɔrd	bənænə	əwek	lʌvɚ
sɝkəs	notəbḷ	sɛkʃən	aɪdiə	raɪtʃəs
əpɪnjən	wɪljəm	maɪkəl	əgɛn	θauzənd
maɪnəs	wumən	səpoz	ɛlə	kʌplət
ʃʌvəl	kənsit	gæləp	əbten	ɪsɛnʃəl
pɪdʒən				

Exercise 7.20. Read aloud the following words saying the symbols exactly as they are written. You will find that the accent will also change. These words as written are all mispronounced.

kəntri   əgli   tɛstʌmɛnt   həŋgri   tʌhɪtɪ   məstɚd

There are some words in which the [ə] is merely suggested in pronunciation, but we do not need to write the symbol. This occurs in some words when we find an unstressed syllable ending in *m*, *n*, or *l*. In such syllables the tongue either remains in contact from the preceding consonant, or makes such a slight shift that no vowel really comes in. We can hear it easily in the words *apple* [æpḷ] and *button* [bʌtṇ]. The sounds are designated as syllable-forming ones by placing a small dot [.] beneath the *l*, *m*, or *n*: [æpḷ]. [du ju se bʌbəl ɔr bʌbḷ‖] These three consonants are the ones that most often become *syllabic consonants*, although there are others. In ordinary speech we might say [ə pis y̩ paɪ‖]

Exercise 7.21. Read these words aloud. Remember there is no noticeable shift from the preceding consonant to the syllabic one.

bʌtṇ	baɪsɪkḷ	kændḷ	kæmḷ	bɑtḷ
kɪtṇ	blɑsm̩	tebḷ	pipḷ	rɪðm̩
bʌbḷ				

Now read the list again slowly. Notice how the tongue remains in contact for the syllabic marked sound and the consonant just preceding it.

All of these words in which a syllabic consonant is used can also be said with the vowel [ə] plus the ordinary consonants *l*, *m*, or *n*. But in many of the words this would give us a formal kind of pronunciation which is not acceptable. Read the following pairs of words and listen to the difference.

lɛsṇ	æpḷ	rɪzṇ	prɪzm̩	opṇ
lɛsən	æpəl	rɪzən	prɪzəm	opən

Whether to use the syllabic consonant in transcription or the [ə] plus the consonant will depend on the speaker's presentation. Listen to his usage.

Occasionally the nasal consonant [ŋ] (the final sound in the word *ring*) is syllabic: [aɪm mekŋ̩ ə paɪ‖]. Here the back of the tongue remains in contact with the velum

124

through the [k] and [ŋ] sounds. We usually find this in informal conversation. You also hear a syllabic [ŋ] in the following phrase: [aɪm tekŋət bæk‖].

[ɝ]
The Sound *r* as in *church* [tʃɝtʃ]

The [ɝ] is the *r* vowel when it occurs [əkɝz] in the accented syllable: *word* [wɝd]. In English spelling it is often written in combination with *i, o, e, u,* or *ea: mirth, worth, term, purr, learn.* But these vowel letters are phonetically meaningless. The [ɝ] is the only vowel in these words.

Much like the [ʌ] and the [ə], our two new sounds, the [ɝ] and the [ɚ], represent the stressed and unstressed forms of the sound we call the *retroflexed central vowel.* The word *retroflexed* refers to the curling shape of the upper tongue surface. You might think of [ɝ] or [ɚ] as camel-like sounds because the tongue has two humps, the front one being higher than the back. Some speakers curl the tip of the tongue backward to make the high hump, others merely shove up the blade of the tongue. The sound can be made correctly either way, but as any speech therapist knows, the coordinations are complex; this is a difficult sound for children to learn, and it is difficult to teach. In general American speech we always use [ɝ] for the vowel in syllables having primary stress just as we use the [ʌ] in such syllables. Similarly, in the unstressed syllables or those having secondary stress we utter another vowel much like the [ɝ] but which we symbolize by [ɚ]. The formation of this vowel also requires a double-humped contour of the tongue.

At this time, however, let us concentrate our study on the [ɝ]. The symbol is similar to the number 3 with a hook at the upper end. Some phoneticians put the hook at the bottom end, thus [ɚ], but the sound is the same. It is the vowel sound in *earth*.

[ðɪ ɝ vauəl ɪz med ɪn tu medʒɚ wez‖ ðə rɪr part əv ðə tʌŋ ɪz rezd tu ðɪ əprʌksɪmət pəzɪʃən əv ðɪ u saund‖ ðə frʌnt part əv ðə tʌŋ ɪz rɪtræktɪd ænd ɛlɪvetɪd haɪɚ ðæn ðə rɪr pɔrʃən‖ sʌm pɪpḷ kip ðə tʌŋ tɪp lo ænd rez ðə bled əv ðə tʌŋ tu produs ðə frʌnt ɛlɪveʃən‖ ʌðɚz prədus ðə frʌnt ɛlɪveʃən baɪ rezɪŋ ðə tɪp ænd sʌmtaɪmz kɝlɪŋ ɪt slaɪtlɪ‖ ðɪs læst mɛθəd prədusɪz hwat ɪz tɝmd ə rɛtroflɛkst ɝ‖]

Exercise 7.22.   Read these words aloud, exaggerating the accented syllable.

bɝn	wɝk	nɝv	bɝdz	ɝn
kɝdḷ	tɝkɪ	vɝs	əkɝd	sɝvɪs
lɝnd	pɝl	dɝtɪ	vɝv	fɝ
sɝtən	tɝtḷ	hɝmɪt	kɝənt	sɝ
mɝkɪ	sɝkɪt	gɝl	kɝtɪəs	

Exercise 7.23.   Transcribe these single-syllable words, using the stressed vowel.

1. heard _____
2. surd _____
3. verse _____
4. perch _____
5. quirk _____
6. third _____
7. yearn _____
8. hearse _____
9. surge _____
10. whirls _____
11. germ _____
12. work _____

Exercise 7.24.   Remembering that [ɝ] is used in stressed syllables, how do these nonsense words sound?

mɝdo	gɝntutɪ	bɝdæt	vɔdɝno
bɪdɚ	ɝlib	tatɪnbɝdo	mutɝn

Exercise 7.25.   Transcribe these words, remembering to put in the primary stress marks.

1. curfew _____
2. unearth _____
3. occur _____
4. emergency _____
5. alert _____
6. incurring _____
7. furnace _____
8. spurts _____
9. convert _____
10. merging _____
11. perching _____
12. serve _____

Reading passage

wʌns ðɛr wəz ə vɝdʒɪn stɝdʒɪn nemd mɝtl̩‖ mɝtl̩ wəz kɝst baɪ ðə tu fɝvənt lʌv əv ə tɝtl̩ nemd ɝnɪst‖ mɝtl̩ dɪdn̩t kɛr mʌtʃ fɚ tɝtl̩z ənd sɝtənlɪ ɝnɪst med hɝ skwɝm‖ aɪ wɑnt no fɝvɚ frəm sʌtʃ ə wɝm sed mɝtl̩‖ ʃi jɝnd ɪnstɛd for ən oʃən pɝtʃ nemd hɝbɚt‖ bʌt mɝtl̩ wʌzn̩t hɝbɚts ʃɝbɚt so hi spɝnd hɝ‖ hɝt n̩ ɝkt baɪ ði ɪmpɝtɪnənt pɝtʃ|mɝtl̩ hwɝld ən swæm ɔf tə sɝtʃ fɚ ɝnɪst ðə tɝtl̩ hu lʌvd hɝ fɝst‖ hau ɝnɪst ɑr ju ɝnɪst sed mɝtl̩ tu ðə tɝtl̩‖ ɝnɪst smɝkt‖ maɪ gɝl hi pɝd| ju ɑr ðə pɝl əv ɔl maɪ wɝld‖ mɝtl̩ bɝnd wɪθ ɝnɪstnəs‖lɛts mɝdʒ ʃi blɝtəd‖ ðə mɔrəl tu ðɪs grusəm tel ɪz| ə vɝdʒɪn stɝdʒɪn nidz sʌm ɝdʒɪn‖

[ɜ]

The symbol [ɜ] (the Eastern *r* sound) corresponds to the [ɝ] in the word [bɝd]. In it the tongue has the same general position as for the [ɝ], but the tip is held low in the mouth and the front elevation is no higher than that of the rear of the tongue. This sound characterizes speech in some eastern and southern parts of our country where a person may say [aɪ si ðə bɜd]. Say the words [bɜd] and [bɝd] aloud and notice how the tongue tip or blade raises as you add the *r* value to the vowel. Practice the two words until the difference is distinct. [ɜ], like [ɝ], is used only in accented syllables or isolated stressed words. Anchor your tongue tip against your lower teeth if you must.

Exercise 7.26.   Read the following pairs of words aloud, slowly enough so you can hear the difference.

hɝd	hɜd	vɝb	vɜb
fɝ	fɜ	tɝn	tɜn
wɝm	wɜm	pɝpl̩	pɜpl̩
vɝs	vɜs	kɝs	kɜs

126

Transcribe the following words putting in the primary stress marks.

REMEMBER

ðæt ðə praɪmɛrɪ strɛs mɑrk ɪz plest əbʌv n̩ bɪfɔr ðə sɪləbl̩‖

tə se ðə wɝd əlaʊd ənd ɪn ə sɛntɪns‖

ðæt ðɪ æksɛntɪd sɪləbl̩ ɪz juʒʊəlɪ haɪɚ ɪn pɪtʃ‖ strɔŋgɚ ɪn ɪntɛnsətɪ‖ n̩ ɪz hɛld lɔŋgɚ‖

tu traɪ tə se ðə wɝd boθ wez æksɛntɪŋ fɝst wʌn sɪləbl̩ ðɛn ðɪ ʌðɚ‖

ðæt ʌ ɪz juzd onlɪ ɪn sɪləbl̩z hævɪŋ praɪmɛrɪ strɛs‖

1. magazine _____
2. affection _____
3. paralysis _____
4. religion _____
5. recollect _____
6. uneasy _____
7. ability _____
8. submit _____
9. economic _____
10. judgment _____
11. emphasis _____
12. delicate _____
13. contentment _____
14. production _____
15. triumphant _____

Which word in each of the following groups is transcribed incorrectly.

16. əlon   ridʒən   ˈkʌpl̩   nutrʌl   fʌdʒ   16. _____
17. kʌf   krɪmʌnəl   plʌmz   əbʌv   əmʌŋ   17. _____
18. ʌkrɔs   dɪstəns   neʃən   əten   mɛθəd   18. _____
19. sɛvrəl   əfɔrd   səbmɪt   sofʌ   əbten   19. _____
20. sæləd   ənælʌsɪs   gæləp   əkaʊnt   dʒʌdʒ   20. _____
21. θʌm   sʌbmɪt   əgɛn   plʌmz   tʃʌnks   21. _____
22. mʌŋkɪ   ərɛndʒ   kʌnɛkt   ʌŋkl̩   dʒʌmpt   22. _____

127

If you missed the item transcribe these parallel words.

ANSWERS

1. gasoline	_____	machine	_____	1.	'mægəzin mægə'zin
2. collection	_____	rejection	_____	2.	ə'fɛkʃən
3. analysis	_____	synthesis	_____	3.	pə'ræləsıs
4. collision	_____	pigeon	_____	4.	rə'lıdʒən
5. connect	_____	reject	_____	5.	rɛkə'lɛkt
6. easy	_____	unequal	_____	6.	ən'izı
7. agility	_____	stability	_____	7.	ə'bılətı
8. admit	_____	remit	_____	8.	səb'mıt
9. economical	_____	comical	_____	9.	ɛkə'namık
10. judging	_____	arrangement	_____	10.	'dʒʌdʒmənt
11. emphatic	_____	thesis	_____	11.	'ɛmfəsıs
12. syndicate	_____	pelican	_____	12.	'dɛləkət
13. contents	_____	contented	_____	13.	kən'tɛntmənt
14. product	_____	producing	_____	14.	prə'dʌkʃən
15. triumph	_____	elephant	_____	15.	traı'ʌmfənt

Here is a collection of transcribed words among which you may find those above. Be sure to correct your answers.

kantɛnts	stəbılətı	pradəkt	izı	ənikwəl	16. 'nutrəl
kəlıʒən	məʃin	pɛləkən	θisıs	ɛmfætık	17. 'krımənəl
prədusıŋ	rıdʒɛkt	pıdʒən	kənɛkt	rımıt	18. ə'krɔs
sındıkət	ərendʒmənt	kaməkḷ	kəntɛntıd		19. 'sofə
prədusıŋ	ædmıt	ɛləfənt	gæsəlin		20. ə'næləsıs
sınθəsıs	ədʒılətı	ɛkənaməkḷ	kəlɛkʃən		21. səb'mıt
gæsəlin	rıdʒɛkʃən	pradəkt	dʒʌdʒıŋ		22. kə'nɛkt

[ɚ]
The Sound *er* as in *banner* [bænɚ]

The symbol represents the combination *er* sound when it is used in an unaccented syllable. It is often found in English spelling as *er*, and is used often at the ends of words such as *mother* [mʌðɚ], *under* [ʌndɚ], *faster* [fæstɚ], and *ever* [ɛvɚ]. It is also spelled *or*, *sailor* [selɚ]; *ur*, *femur* [fimɚ]; and *ar*, *liar* [laɪɚ].

The symbol is written just like the unstressed [ə], but with a hook added: [ɚ].

[ɪt ɪz med ɪgzæktlɪ laɪk ðɪ ɝ ɪksɛpt fɔr ðə tɛnʃən əv ðə mʌs!z ɪnvalvd‖ dʒʌst æz ðɪ ə ɪz æn ʌnstrɛst ʌ so ðɪ ɚ ɪz æn ʌnstrɛst ɝ‖]

Exercise 7.27. Remembering that [ɚ] is used in *unaccented* syllables, say these nonsense words aloud.

pɪntɚon   ɚlændɚ   luzitɚ   tɛpətɚ
dɚmɑt   bɚludi   kɚfoni   sobətɚ

[ɪt hɛlps ɪf ju mɑrk ðɪ æksɛntɪd sɪləb!z fɝst‖]

Exercise 7.28. Read the following words as quickly and accurately as possible.

sʌfɚ   sɚve   nɛvɚ   igɚ   pepɚz
sutɚ   vɪktɚ   soɚ   dæmpɚ   selɚ
ræftɚ   sɪstɚ   suɚ   rɛvɚənt rɛkɚd
bɪldɚ   pɛdlɚ   kʌvɚ   lɛpɚ   ɪntɚækt

Exercise 7.29. In this list there are seven words which use *both* the accented [ɝ] and the unaccented [ɚ]. Find those words and write them in phonetic script.

bother   currant   permit   perturb   burner
murder   purser   perverse   muster   bolder
razor   occur   celery   disperse   overwork
pervade   curler

_____   _____   _____
_____   _____   _____
_____

Because it is unstressed, the [ɚ] is never found in syllables having primary accent, but it can be found in various positions of the word. Here we find it in the first syllable: [pɚhæps], [flɚteʃən], and [sɚmaunt]. Here we find it in the last syllable: [kʌbɚd], [lʌvɚ], [dɑktɚ], and [ʃoldɚ]. It also can be found in words of more than two syllables such as [ˌsɚkəmˈstænʃəl]. Just as we found with [ə] and [ʌ], the [ɚ] and [ɝ] may both be found in the same word. So we have in the word *earner* [ɝnɚ], and in several words in Exercise 7.29, both the stressed and the unstressed retroflexed vowel. There are many of these words and we will test you on them later, but there are three more in the following list. Remember that the syllable with the [ɝ] in it has the primary stress.

Exercise 7.30. Transcribe these words.

1. sugar _____   2. mother _____   3. yesterday _____
4. standard _____   5. memorable _____   6. author _____
7. energetic _____   8. liquor _____   9. river _____
10. curler _____   11. worker _____   12. merger _____

There are also words in which no stressed [ɝ] is found but two or more of the unstressed sounds can be heard. They can even be adjacent. *Stutterer* [stʌtɚɚ] is one of them. You will also remember that [ɚ] could be used in centering diphthongs, although we usually use [r]. In such words as *car*, *bear*, *sure*, *pour*, *fire*, *hour*, and *beer* there are some phoneticians who use the vowel symbol followed by [ɚ], but the prevailing fashion of the moment, which we shall follow, is the use of [r] in centering diphthongs. It is also possible to find a centering diphthong followed by [ɚ], as in explorer [ɪksplɔrɚ].

Exercise-7.31.   Transcribe these words. Watch for doubles.

1. discoverer	_____	2. carver	_____
3. sour	_____	4. pure	_____
5. circular	_____	6. scorer	_____
7. fewer	_____	8. tear-jerker	_____
9. another	_____	10. Percheron	_____
11. horror	_____	12. bearer	_____
13. harbor	_____	14. alligator	_____
15. conservation	_____		

One final bit of coaching! Words such as *wormier* or *thirstier* are best transcribed as [wɝmɪɚ] rather than [wɝmɪr], and [θɝstɪɚ] rather than [θɝstɪr]. Say the variations aloud.

Transcribe these words into general American speech.

REMEMBER

ðæt wi juz ɝ ɪn sɪləbl̩z hævɪŋ praɪ-mɛrɪ strɛs‖

ðæt ɝ ɪz juzd ɪn boθ ʌnstrɛst sɪləbl̩z ænd ðoz hævɪŋ sɛkəndɛrɪ strɛs‖

ðæt sɛntərɪŋ dɪfθɔŋz ɔlwɪz rɪkwaɪr ðə jus əv r wɪθ ðə vauəl‖

ðæt onlɪ wʌn ɝ wɪl bi faund ɪn ə wɝd‖ nɑt ɪnkludɪŋ kɑmpaund wɝdz laɪk ɝθwɝm‖

ðæt sɛvrəl ɚz me əkɝ ɪn ə wɝd‖

ðæt ɝ ənd ɚ ɑr vauəlz‖ ðe nɛvɚ ɑr juzd ɪn kɑnsənənt blɛndz sʌtʃ æz tr br kr‖

ðæt ðə prɪsidɪŋ rɪmaɪndɚ ɪz so ɪm-pɔrtənt pliz rid ɪt əgɛn ɔr‖ bɛtɚ jɛt‖ prɪnt ɪt ɪn kæpɪtəl lɛtɚz ɪn jur notbʊk‖

Do the last five words, using the eastern and southern [ɜ] and [ə], rather than in general American.

rɪmɛmbə ðət ði ɑː saundz ɑː kərɛktlɪ prənaunst əz ɜ ɪf ðe əkɜ ɪn sɪləblz hwɪtʃ ɑː strɛst‖ wi frəm ði istən ɔː sʌðən pɔːʃənz əv ðɪs kʌntrɪ prɪfɚ ðɪs sɔftə fɔːm əv ði ɑː‖

1. gallery _____

2. earlier _____

3. squirrel _____

4. emerge _____

5. murderer _____

6. searcher _____

7. surveyor _____

8. perversion _____

9. herbs _____

10. furrier _____

11. careful _____

12. carfare _____

13. further _____

14. circularity _____

15. lecturer _____

16. theater _____

17. courageous _____

18. restaurant _____

19. dirtier _____

20. armorer _____

21. firmer _____

22. persuader _____

23. farther _____

24. further _____

25. energy _____

Do these and you won't make the same error again.

ANSWERS

1. celery	——	elevate	——	1. gæləɪ	
2. wordier	——	worrier	——	2. ɝliɚ	
3. girl	——	whirled	——	3. skwɝəl	
4. submerge	——	returned	——	4. ɪmɝdʒ	
5. laborer	——	hamburger	——	5. mɝdɚɚ	
6. burner	——	worker	——	6. sɝtʃɚ	
7. conveyor	——	container	——	7. sɚveɚ	
8. conversion	——	dispersion	——	8. pɚvɝʒən	
9. heirs	——	hours	——	9. ɝbz	
10. curlier	——	thirstier	——	10. fɝɪɚ	
11. hair —— bear —— chair				11. kɛrfəl	
12. star —— fair —— bar				12. kɑrfɛr	
13. murder	——	sheep-herder	——	13. fɝðɚ	
14. popularity	——	scarcity	——	14. sɚkju/ɛrətɪ	
15. insurer	——	insecure	——	15. lɛktʃɚɚ	
16. mother	——	ant-eater	——	16. θiətɚ	
17. page	——	courage	——	17. kɚedʒəs	
18. pester	——	want	——	18. rɛstɚənt	
19. wormier	——	furrier	——	19. dɝtɪɚ	
20. stutterer	——	discoverer	——	20. ɑrmɚɚ	

On the next four use the [ɝ] and the [ə] vowels.

21. fɝmə

22. pervade	——	surround	——	22. pəswedə
23. garter	——	larder	——	23. fɑːðə
24. merger	——	earner	——	24. fɛðə
25. entering	——	winter	——	25. ɛnədʒɪ

Name _____ *Date* _____ *Score* _____

Hand this in to your instructor.

1. Transcribe

pervert (noun)	_____	pervert (verb)	_____
university	_____	handkerchief	_____
kerchief	_____	sailor	_____
butter	_____	limber	_____
earner	_____	polar	_____
squirrel	_____	urchin	_____
perhaps	_____	flustered	_____
Berlin	_____	western	_____
thirty	_____	thirstier	_____
virgin	_____	Virginia	_____

2.
cupboard	_____	unutterable	_____
succulent	_____	Buddha	_____
onions	_____	coupling	_____
subtle	_____	thumbs	_____
uglier	_____	buttons	_____
conduct (noun)	_____	conduct (verb)	_____
sufficient	_____	succumb	_____

3. applaud   _____   verve   _____

    luckier   _____   under   _____

    among   _____   burned   _____

    revert   _____   colonel   _____

    pumpkin   _____   pearls   _____

    occur   _____   mystery

4. Underline the errors in these sentences.

1. æt pɚdu junəvɜsɪtɪ ðə tɛləvɪʒən fʌsɪlətiz ɑr ɛksələnt‖
2. kəmjunəkeʃənz ɔfn̩ kænt bɪ dɪvɛlʌpt bɪtwin kəmjunətiz sɛpʌretɪd baɪ ə rɪvɚ‖
3. hɪz ʌŋkl̩ hɚid tʊ ðə gɚlz dɪfɛns‖

When we studied the [w] glide and the [j] glide, we saw that some of the sounds of English are not singles, but doubles. In these two sounds we find a shift from the position of one vowel into another, the [w] away from the [u] into the vowel in *we* [wi], and the [j] away from the [i] into the vowel in *you* [ju] or [iu]. In both of these glides the second vowel gets the most stress, so much so that we find it hard to recognize the vowels from which the shifts proceeded.

When we come to such sounds as the [ɔɪ] of *boy*, the [aʊ] of *cow* [kaʊ], and the [aɪ] of *sky*, we find the opposite kind of shift; instead of shifting away from the weaker and toward the stronger sound, we shift from the stronger to the weaker of the two vowels that make up these diphthongs. The two vowels are uttered so closely together that there is no syllable break between them. The [ɔɪ] sound in *boy* is an example. The [ɔ] and [ɪ] are blended together so quickly that the word *boy* [bɔɪ] is a single syllable. If you say the word *drawing* [drɔɪŋ], where the [ɔ] and [ɪ] are next to each other, you will notice that they do not merge with each other and are therefore in different syllables. As we said in Chapter 3, your ear will be your best guide for recognizing diphthongs.

We have three major diphthongs: [aɪ], [aʊ], and [ɔɪ], and seven others, called *centering diphthongs*. Remember, most of the diphthongs used in American English have the major stress on the first of the two dual vowels.

[aɪ]
The Sound [aɪ] as in *mine* [maɪn], *eye* [aɪ], *aye* [aɪ], *I* [aɪ]

This is the sound which we overwork when we are talking about ourselves. It occurs in isolation every time we use the perpendicular pronoun *I:* [aɪ]. Actually, the pronoun is not a single sound, as we explained above, but a diphthong. The two sounds follow each other so rapidly that there is no syllabic change between the two. One word of caution at the start: There are variations in the speed with which this diphthong is produced. An [aɪ] used at the end of a word may have a much less rapid shift between the [a] and the [ɪ] than when the [aɪ] is followed by a consonant. The diphthong in the word *hide* may sound shorter than the same sound in the word *high* [haɪd ænd haɪ]. Say these three words aloud; *sigh*, *side*, and *sight*. Which has the most rapid shift?

Some people find it difficult to believe that *I*, or *eye* is a combination of [a] and [ɪ]. Prove it to yourself by saying this aloud: [a:i la:ik pa:i‖] Naturally, the second vowel, being so much shorter, and unaccented, is transcribed as [ɪ].

The diphthong [aɪ] is represented in spelling most frequently by the letter *i: ice* [aɪs], *idea* [aɪdɪə]. It is also spelled in *i* combinations: *fight* [faɪt], *height* [haɪt], *pie* [paɪ], *aisle* [aɪl], and *guide* [gaɪd]. We find it often spelled *y: dry* [draɪ], *by* [baɪ], and *spy* [spaɪ]; or in various other ways: *dye* [daɪ], *guy* [gaɪ] and *eye* [aɪ]. It is an easy sound to recognize if you train yourself to listen for it.

Exercise 7.32.   See how many words you can get by combining one consonant in the initial position, with [aɪ] following. Write them in phonetic script. *Example:* [baɪ daɪ].

Exercise 7.33.   [rid ðiz wɜˈdz əlaud swɪftlɪ| ðen raɪt ðem ɪn ɪŋglɪʃ|||]

naɪs _____	saɪt _____	aɪret _____	taɪt _____
aɪl _____	saɪd _____	kaɪt _____	aɪlənd _____
traɪd _____	aɪrɪs _____	kwaɪət _____	baɪsɪkl̩ _____
waɪd _____	taɪmd _____	ɪmplaɪ _____	laɪvlɪ _____
laɪd _____	aɪsɪkl̩ _____	taɪdɪ _____	paɪl _____

Exercise 7.34.   [rid ðiz wɜˈdz n̩d put ə sɜˈkl̩ əraund ðə lɛtɚz hwɪtʃ ɑr saundɪd æz aɪ|| ðen raɪt onlɪ ðoz wɜˈdz ɪn fənɛtɪks||]

visit	rickets	timber	reign	psychiatry
invoke	ideal	split	gasoline	main
iodine	relative	spite	lion	buy
diamond	behind	bailed	oversight	tight

[aʊ]
The Sound [aʊ] as in *how* [haʊ]

This diphthong starts with the same symbol as the first one in [aɪ], but a change in the second vowel to [ʊ] produces an entirely new sound. A rapid glide from [a] to [ʊ] gives us the vowel sound in the word *cow* [kaʊ]. It is often spelled *ow*, as in *now* [naʊ], *prow* [praʊ], *owl* [aʊl], *down* [daʊn], and *row* [raʊ] (if the latter means a fight and not what you do with oars in a boat). [ðə læst wɜˈd ɪz ə gʊd rɪmaɪndɚ ðæt spɛlɪŋ ʃoz ʌs lɪtl̩ əbaut saund||] It is spelled as *ou*, as in *out* [aʊt], *count* [kaʊnt], *about* [əbaʊt], and *bough* [baʊ].

Exercise 7.35.   [bɪkɔz wi hæv ɔlrɛdɪ stʌdid boθ ðiz saundz ɪn aɪsəleʃən̩ ju ʃud bi ebl̩ tu tɛl ʌs ðə pəziʃən əv ðə lɪps| ðə tʌŋ| ænd ðə dʒɔ|| hau wʊd ju dɪskraɪb ðə prədʌkʃən əv ðɪs| dɪfθɔŋ]

Exercise 7.36.   Transcribe these word pairs.

1. mice _____	mouse _____	2. aisle _____	owl _____
3. thou _____	thy _____	4. buy _____	bow _____
5. sow _____	sigh _____	6. bought _____	bout _____
7. tan _____	town _____	8. who _____	how _____

Exercise 7.37.   Write these words in English.

saund _____	faulz _____	raɪt _____
vaʊl̩ _____	əlau _____	autɚ _____
laud _____	kwaɪt _____	fraɪ _____
haus _____	brau _____	əbaut _____
klaud _____	autsaɪd _____	aut _____

[ɔɪ]
The Sound [ɔɪ] as in *boy* [bɔɪ]

The third diphthong [ɔɪ] is one which seldom gives students any trouble. A very rapid glide is made from the [ɔ] to the [ɪ] and it is consistently represented in English spelling by the letters *oi* or *oy*. You see it in the words *moist* [mɔɪst], *oil* [ɔɪl], *noise* [nɔɪz], and *poison* [pɔɪzn̩], and as *oy* in *toy* [tɔɪ], *loyal* [lɔɪəl], and *coy* [kɔɪ].

When you say the sound, the [ɔ] receives more stress than the [ɪ]. The [ɪ] resembles the one used in a final unstressed syllable, as in the word [fænsɪ]. It is also like the second sound in the [aɪ] diphthong.

Exercise 7.38.   [rid ðiz wɝdz əlaʊd‖]

koɪl   nɔɪz   fɔɪl   ɪmplɔɪ   bɔɪlɚ   əhɔɪ   hɔɪst   rɔɪl   bɔɪlz   brɔɪl   sɔɪl
pɔɪzn̩   ɔɪlɪ   vɔɪs   vɔɪd   pɔɪnt   dɪkɔɪ   lɔɪɚ   ənɔɪ   lɔɪn   ənɔɪnt   ɔɪstɚ

Exercise 7.39.   Transcribe these sentences.

1. The boys in their rejoicing tried to avoid the scowl of their employers.

_____

2. Simon's voice annoyed the brown cow and she kicked over the pail adroitly.

_____

3. Roy appointed Mike to see that the sow wouldn't destroy the flowers.

_____

Exercise 7.40.   Transcribe these pairs of words.

1. Lloyd _____ loud _____   2. buys _____ boys _____
3. poise _____ pause _____   4. try _____ Troy _____
5. noise _____ gnaws _____   6. high _____ how _____

Centering diphthongs

Although there are only three primary diphthongs, [aɪ], [aʊ], and [ɔɪ], no study of diphthongs is complete without a discussion of the *centering diphthongs*. These are combinations of certain vowels with the terminal [r] sound: *chair* [tʃɛr], *car* [kɑr], *poor* [pʊr], *tore* [tɔr], *here* [hɪr], *fire* [faɪr], and *our* [aʊr]. Why do we use the consonantal form [r] instead of the [ɚ] to represent this second sound of the various combinations? Primarily because it seems to be weaker and more fricative in nature (less vowel-like) than the [ɚ] in such words as *mother*, and secondarily because this is the style used in most transcription today. We admit we find it hard to make a stronger case for writing [r] instead of [ɚ], and if you insist on using the latter style of transcription *consistently* you will be part of a large minority. In this text we shall transcribe the centering diphthongs with the final [r].

In the list of centering diphthongs you will note that we do not list [ær], [ir], [or], [er], or [ur]. This is due to the fact that these combinations are not heard frequently in standard general American speech although, as we shall see later, some of them may appear in British, New England, or deep southern speech. In general American speech we tend to say [ɔr] rather than [or] for the word *ore*, and [ɪr] rather than [ir] for *ear*.

If you use the stronger [o], [æ], [e], or [i], it will be coupled with the *er* vowel sound [oɚ æɚ eɚ iɚ] to form two syllables. In order to test this further for yourself, here are some pairs of words. Say them aloud.

mɔr	more	mower	moɚ
ʃur	sure	shoe-er	ʃuɚ
prɛr	prayer	pray-er	(one who prays) preɚ
lɔrd	lord	lowered	loɚd
mɛr	mare	mayor	meɚ
pɛr	pair	payer	peɚ
sɪr	seer	skier	skiɚ

As a general rule then, if we use a tense vowel followed by an *er* sound, we probably will be making a new syllable of *er*. All the words in the right-hand column above, for example, are two-syllable words, while those in the left-hand column have only one syllable. [hæv ju ɛvɚ sin ə kələm wɪθ ə raɪt n̩ lɛft hænd‖]

Exercise 7.41.   Transcribe these words.

1. barely _____   2. sheer _____
3. lawyer _____   4. lyre _____
5. pure _____   6. scored _____
7. third _____   8. jeer _____
9. skier _____   10. guard _____
11. flour _____   12. choir _____
13. hour _____   14. layer _____
15. beard _____   16. heard _____
17. adjourn _____   18. mayor _____
19. toward _____   20. sure _____

Exercise 7.42.   How many centering diphthongs can you put in the blanks below to make real words? *Example:* b _____ bɑr bɪr bɛr bɔr bur

$$\text{ɑr} \quad \text{ɪr} \quad \text{ɛr} \quad \text{ɔr} \quad \text{ur}$$

tʃ _____
p _____
st _____
m _____

Reading passage

bɪsaɪdz ði aɪ‖ aʊ‖ ɔr ɔɪ dɪfθɔŋz ænd ðoz juzɪŋ ðə [r] sʌtʃ æz [ɪr] [ɑr] [ɛr] wi wɪl nid sɚtn̩ ʌðɚ kɑmbəneʃənz əv vauəl saundz tu rɛprɪzɛnt ðə daɪəlɛktl̩ ænd fɔrɪn vɛrieʃənz ænd ɔlso ðoz əv dɪfɛktɪv spitʃ‖ ju wɪl rɪkɔl fɚst ðæt hwɛn wɚkɪŋ wɪð fɔrɪn spikɚz wi rɪgɑrd aur on [o] ænd [e] vauəlz æz ðə dɪfθɔŋz [ou] ænd [eɪ]‖ fɔrɪnɚz se ðiz saundz æz pjur vauəlz‖ wi dɪfθɔŋaɪz ðem‖

ɪn ʌðɚ rɪdʒənz əv ðɪs neʃən wi wɪl hɪr mɔr ʌnfəmɪljɚ dɪfθɔŋz‖ ɪn istɚn spitʃ wi kəmənli hɪr ɔl ðə sɛntɚɪŋ dɪfθɔŋz prənaunst wɪð ðə ʃwa ɛndɪŋ‖ ðiz spikɚz se tɛə fɔr tɛr‖ faɪə fɔr faɪr‖ ʃuə fɔr ʃur‖ doə ɔr dɒə fɔr dɔr‖

wɪðɪn nu jɔrk sɪti ɪtsɛlf wi faɪnd ʌðɚ ʌnfəmɪljɚ dɪfθɔŋz‖ ɪn bruklɪn wi hɪr ə dɪfθɔŋ hwɪtʃ saundz laɪk ɔɪ tu ʌntrend ɪrz‖ haʊɛvɚ most bruklɪnaɪts se tɚn ɪnstɛd əv tɔrn‖ ðə feməs bruklɪn besbɔl bɚd‖ klosli rɪletɪd tu ðə brɑŋks tʃɪr‖ ɪz prənaunst bɚɪd ræðɚ ðæn bɔɪd‖

138

ɪn mɛnɪ ridʒənz hwɛr dʒɛnɚəl əmɛrɪkən spitʃ ɪz juzd ðə dɪfθɔŋz [aɪ] ænd [aʊ]
ɑr mʌtʃ mɔr kɑmən ðæn [aɪ] ænd [aʊ]‖ wi ɔlso wɪl faɪnd spikɚz juzɪŋ [oɪ] ɔr [ɒɪ]
fɔr [ɔɪ]‖‖

ɪn sʌðɚn spitʃ wi faɪnd mɛnɪ ənjuʒʊəl kɑmbɪneʃənz əv vaʊəlz‖ ðə kɛrɪktɚɪstɪk
sʌðɚn drɔl ɪz lɑrdʒlɪ ðo nɑt ɪntaɪrlɪ du tu ðɪs fitʃɚ‖ ɪn ðə saʊθ ju wɪl ɔlso hɪr mɛnɪ
trɪfθɔŋz‖

Exercise 7.43.   Transcribe these sentences.

1. Arthur sure tore our chair apart merely to express his ire.

---

2. The poor Lord Mayor of the carnival in New Orleans was carried in our chariot
to the fire.

In the East and South the centering diphthongs have the schwa vowel [ə] instead
of the unstressed [ɚ]: [ɪə ɛə ɔə ʊə]. Just as they tend to say [mʌðə] instead of [mʌðɚ],
so they also say [fɛə] instead of [fɛr] or [fɛɚ]. The [ɑr] diphthong does not usually become
[ɑə], but the [ɑ] is merely prolonged; hence [kɑr] would be pronounced [kɑ:].

Even after people with incorrect articulation master the consonant r, the [ɝ], and
the [ɚ], they often have trouble with the centering diphthongs. These are usually the
most difficult sounds. Often these people distort the preceding vowel in addition to
having difficulty with the r.

Exercise 7.44.   Here is a transcription which will illustrate the faulty speech of a
college student. Read it aloud.

[ðə dɔktə kɪud maɪ ɪuek‖ ðə gɛul æt ðə dwʌg stɔ wɪfjuzd tu twaɪ tu ʌndəstænd
mi ivn̩ ðo aɪ twaɪd tu tɔk klɪulɪ so aɪ gɑt maɪ fwɛnd aθə tu tɔk fɔə mi‖ pəhæps
ɪt wʌz onlɪ æspuɪn bʌt ɪt wɜkt‖‖]

1. onlɪ faɪv sɪmbl̩z‖

2. ɪt raɪmz wɪθ æpl̩ p . . .‖

3. ðɛrz ə ʃwa hɪr‖

4. ə fulɚ‖

5. gɛt ðə dɪfθɔŋ raɪt‖

6. ju dont hæf tu no hwɑt ɪt minz‖

7. ðə tʃaɪniz dont it ɪt‖

8. dont lɛt ðə spɛlɪŋ θro ju ɔf‖

9. dɪto‖

10. ə fænsɪ sup bol‖

11. wʊd ju ræðɚ ðə wɝd wəz selɚ‖

12. ðɪs ɪz trɪkɪ‖

13. hwɑts ðə vaʊl‖

14. ðɪs wʌnz dɪfɚənt‖

15. bi ʃʊr tu ɪnklud ðə nɛkst tu ðə læst saʊnd‖

16. ə tʌf wʌn‖

17. baɪ naʊ ju no ðɪs wʌn‖

18. dont ju dɛr juz æn ɛs‖

19. bi ʃʊr ju juz æn ɛs‖

20. izɪ‖

21. faɪv sɪmbl̩z hɪr‖

22. ði ɛs ɪz ði onlɪ sɪmbl̩ ðæt mætʃɪz‖

23. hwɪtʃ lɛtɚ ɪz saɪlənt‖

24. hwɑts ðə dɪfθɔŋ‖

25. ðɪs ɪz trɪkɪ tu‖

1. foreign	_____
2. eye	_____
3. triumph	_____
4. synonym	_____
5. foul	_____
6. cloister	_____
7. chow mein	_____
8. hearty	_____
9. hyphen	_____
10. tureen	_____
11. mariner	_____
12. powerful	_____
13. fight	_____
14. freight	_____
15. argue	_____
16. joyous	_____
17. quarter	_____
18. noisy	_____
19. fierce	_____
20. ordain	_____
21. fury	_____
22. cautious	_____
23. aisle	_____
24. crowned	_____
25. acquire	_____

Do the penalty passages to the left for every word that you missed.

ANSWERS

1. bore	_____	roar	_____	four	_____	1. fɔrɪn
2. aye	_____	my	_____	high	_____	2. aɪ
3. riot	_____	phial	_____	diet	_____	3. traɪəmf
4. cinnamon	_____	hymn	_____	myth	_____	4. sɪnənɪm
5. towel	_____	rouse	_____	shower	_____	5. faʊl
6. oyster	_____	boister-ous	_____	Freud	_____	6. klɔɪstɚ
7. chowder	_____	brain	_____	ouch	_____	7. tʃaʊmen
8. bargain	_____	partly	_____	army	_____	8. hɑrtɪ
9. type	_____	Ivan	_____	philoso-phize	_____	9. haɪfən
10. poor bean	_____	seizure	_____	toured	_____	10. tʊrɪn
11. parent	_____	arid	_____	character	_____	11. mɛrɪnɚ
12. sorrowful	_____	sour	_____	shower	_____	12. paʊɚful
13. night	_____	write	_____	bright	_____	13. faɪt
14. afraid	_____	Braille	_____	crazy	_____	14. fret
15. you	_____	cute	_____	arduous	_____	15. ɑrgju
16. choice	_____	joyless	_____	join	_____	16. dʒɔɪəs
17. quorum	_____	quarrel	_____	quartz	_____	17. kwɔrtɚ
18. boys	_____	annoys	_____	destroys	_____	18. nɔɪzɪ
19. pierce	_____	hearsay	_____	fearsome	_____	19. fɪrs
20. orate	_____	ornate	_____	for sale	_____	20. ɔrden

ANSWERS

21. your _____ furious _____ Missouri _____ 21. fjʊrɪ

22. caught _____ anxious _____ audacious _____ 22. kɔʃəs

23. island _____ lisle _____ writhe _____ 23. aɪl

24. crowd _____ drowned _____ clowned _____ 24. kraʊnd

25. acquit _____ choir _____ desire _____ 25. əkwaɪr

Name _____ Date _____ Score _____

Hand this in to your instructor.

1. Transcribe these words.

career _____	bouquets _____	warrior _____
securing _____	liar _____	ointment _____
acorn _____	porches _____	hourly _____
blindfolded _____	carrier _____	clearer _____
rural _____	persevere _____	surround _____
aroused _____	aurora _____	allowed _____
rejoiced _____	purer _____	

2. Transcribe these sentences.

Our delegate drowned.

_____

Four lions roared loudly.

_____

Loyalty to the South.

_____

We'll raise your carfare.

_____

Shirley made a careless error.

_____

The armored car caught on fire.

_____

Tomorrow comes the terror.

_____

8 Transcribing Connected Speech

Thus far, in our effort to help you master the International Phonetic Alphabet, we have largely concentrated on individual words as the units to be transcribed. This has been helpful in the early stages of learning to discriminate the sequences of sounds that comprise our speech, but now it is time to recognize that we do not really talk by uttering a series of isolated words. Instead we link them together in a continuous flow. We speak in phrases and sentences, not in words. The pauses in our speech do not come after each separate word but occur as boundary markers for larger units of utterance. Let us illustrate. Were you to transcribe the sentence, "When is he coming to your house?" word by word, you would probably come up with this: [hwɛn ɪz hi kʌmɪŋ tʊ jʊr haʊs‖]. But we just don't talk that way. Instead, we would probably say it this way: [wɛnzikʌmn̩|təjɝhaʊs‖].

In our sample sentence of connected speech you will have noted the use of vertical bars to indicate the spots where the flow of connected speech becomes interrupted. The single bar [|] indicates the slight hesitation that marks the boundary of the phrase; the double bar [‖] marks a longer pause, in this case the end of the sentence. Yet often several sentences are strung together very closely in a larger utterance, and we need some marker to show when that speaker really stops speaking. The symbol for this terminal marker is #. Observe the use of these markers in the following utterance: [ɪtl̩biəlɔŋtaɪm| bɪfɔraɪmrɛdɪtətekðætɪgzæm‖ aɪmdʒʌsnɑrɛdɪ‖ hæd oʊnlɪfɔraʊrsliplæsnaɪt-kəzaɪhædəwɝklet#]

JUNCTURES IN CONNECTED SPEECH

There are some terms relating to these markers that you should know. *Juncture* refers to the manner in which the *words* (not the sounds) of connected speech are linked together. When they are run together, as in [wʌtʃəgɔnədu], they are said to show *close juncture*. When a pause occurs there is an *open juncture*. As we have said, open junctures are indicated by one vertical bar for a brief phrasal pause, by a double bar for a longer pause, and the end of an utterance is signified by the double cross [#].

You may wonder why you should now be asked to listen to silences as well as to sounds. Is this demand merely academic? No, for when you have to help deaf or severely hard-of-hearing children learn to speak intelligibly, you will find that one of their major problems lies in their misuse of junctures. They find it hard to master the rhythms and melody of speech. They break it in the wrong places. Research has shown that sentences spoken with appropriate junctures are four times more easily understood than those with inappropriate ones. We have to teach these children how to pause, and when to pause. Again, you may have to work with a person from a foreign land who is seeking to speak our language with more adequacy. He or she, too, will need to learn about the rhythms of our speech. We have even found that we gained in our ability to understand the almost unintelligible speech of language-impaired children by paying careful attention to the kinds of junctures they use. And there are the rare clutterers who will require training in juncturing if they are ever to overcome their unintelligible torrents of tumbling, stumbling, mumbled words.

ASSIMILATION

Besides the pauses, you will also have to learn to listen for the changes in the sounds of the words which occur in continuous speech rather than words in isolation. Compare the transcription of these two isolated words, [kʊd] and [ju], with the way that they are pronounced in the sentence, "Could you?" [kʊdʒu]. Of course, if you are very careful and speak very slowly, you might be able to ask the question this way: [kʊd ju]. But we just don't talk that way. Try to say [kʊd ju] over and over again as fast as possible, and you will find yourself slipping into [kʊdʒu]. This does not at all mean that you are speaking in a substandard way. It is how we talk, and if we are to transcribe conversational speech with fidelity, we must recognize these changes.

You have already come to recognize the basic phenomenon of assimilation in learning to transcribe individual words. You found out very early that when [n] precedes a [k] it changes into the [ŋ] sound, as in [sɪŋk]. It is too hard to shift from the front alveolar tongue tip contact of the [n] to the back velar contact required by the [k]. It's far easier to say [sɪŋk] than [sɪnk]. Indeed, the only way to say [sɪnk] is to say it slowly. The moment you speed it up, it becomes [sɪŋk]. In any sound sequence, each individual sound is influenced by its neighboring sounds and this influence is termed *assimilation*. Usually, a given sound is more influenced by the sound which immediately follows it (*regressive assimilation*) than by the sound which immediately precedes it (*progressive assimilation*.) Examples of the influence of regressive assimilation are found in the words [pʌŋkɪn] [ræzbɛrɪ], and examples of progressive assimilation in [bɝdz] [feɪkt].

Assimilation in connected speech

If, even within the boundaries of words, we find sounds being changed due to assimilation, it should be clear that the same changes would occur even more frequently in continuous speech, when words are linked together in close juncture. And this is what we find over and over again if we listen closely. As we mentioned earlier, you have been listening to individual words and saying them individually to yourself, when reading or writing phonemically. Now you should free yourself from this procedure and, instead, say the phrases and sentences as spoken in a conversational way. How, for instance, do most people say "Did you eat yet?" if they are talking swiftly? Most people will say, [dɪdʒiitjɛt], or even [dʒitjɛt], and they will be perfectly understood by the listener. Assimilation, then, does not simply change sounds; sometimes it can cause sounds to be omitted as well. Words may be compressed when we speak swiftly; combinations of sounds may be simplified by the substitution of a different single

146

sound in the interest of economy of effort. We follow the law of least effort in making transitions. Our tongues don't work any harder than they have to. We don't say "Is it not?" we say "Isn't it?" In transcribing connected speech, then, you should be alert to recognize contractions as well as the substitutions that are due to assimilation.

In the linking of words together, assimilation sometimes results in the omission of the final sound of the preceding word, as in [ðɪʃːɝt], the final *s* of *this* being lost. Or sometimes the final sound of the first word is simply prolonged, and the rest of the second word is blended with it. We rarely say [ðɪs sætɚdɪ]. Instead, we say [ðɪsːædɚdɪ]. You will find many instances where you will need to use the colon to show this prolongation. How would you transcribe "a lot of vegetables?"

In connected speech we also find many instances in which assimilation produces changes in the voicing or unvoicing of the final and initial sounds of words that are linked together. For example, we say [aɪhæftəgou] rather than [aɪhævtugou], the final [v] of [hæv] being changed to the [f] because of the influence of the unvoiced [t] in the word *to*. This would be evidence of the force of regressive assimilation.[1]

Progressive assimilation, in which the final sound of the preceding word influences the way that the subsequent word begins, is most evident when the second word begins with the [h] sound. Usually, the first sound of the second word is omitted. For example, in [ʃibæŋdɚfɪŋgɚ] or [hihædtuduɪzθɪŋ], the [h] of *her* and *his*, disappears.

ALTERED SYLLABICATION

At times you may have to pay attention to the altering of syllables that characterize some conversational speech. Suppose someone asks you for a cup of coffee, with only a little bit of sugar in it. The isolated words *cup* and *bit* are syllables of the consonant–vowel–consonant (CVC) variety. But when they are used in connected speech they may change to consonant–vowel (CV) syllables. The person says [kʌ-pə-kɔfɪ] and [bɪ-tə-ʃugɚ]. The syllables are not [kʌp] and [əv] or [bɪt] and [əv] but instead they are [kʌ] and [pə] and [bɪ] and [tə]. The final plosives of *cup* and *bit* do not arrest or stop the flow of speech but instead they release the following syllable. We omit the [v] in [əv], because we would have to slow down our speech; add a pause between the [v] and the [k] of coffee [kʌp əv|kɔfɪ] or the [ʃ] of sugar [bɪt əv|ʃugɚ]. We probably should not bedevil you with such a detailed explanation of how we say our syllables differently in conversational speech, but instead, merely ask you to listen more carefully. However, the example may help you to scrutinize connected speech with a keener ear.

THE INFLUENCE OF UNSTRESSING

We also must include in our description of the contrasts of isolated words versus connected speech some further discussion of the role of stress. Throughout this text you have found us using the schwa vowel [ə] in such words as *the* [ðə] and *a* [ə] rather than [ʌ], primarily because these words always introduce and are closely linked to the word that follows, and because they are so unstressed that they almost become a part of the following word.

---

[1] In narrow transcription we would use the little circle [̥] under the symbol to indicate its unvoicing [v̥].

Exercise 8.1.   Write the following passage in English script.

[strɛs ɪz ðə tɝm juzd tu ˈɪndɪˌket ðə ˌpɑrts əv ə ˈsɛntɪns ɔr frez ðæt hæv kəmˈpɛrətɪvlɪ ˈgretɚ ˈvaljum| ɪnˈtɛnsɪtɪ| ænd ˈhaɪɚ pɪtʃ|| strɛs ɛnˈkʌmpəsɪz ˈæksɛnt ɪn ðæt ðɪ ˈæksɛntɪd ˈsɪləbḷ əv ə ˌplurəsɪˈlæbɪk wɝd wɪl ˈɔlso bi ðə ˈstrɛst ˈsɪləbḷ| bʌt ˈɔlso ˈɪndɪkets hwɪtʃ ˈsɪŋgḷ ˈsɪləbḷ wɝdz ɪn ə frez maɪt rɪˈsiv ˈɛmfəsɪs|| ɪn ðə ˈsɛntɪns| ˌhi wəz ˈðɛr| nʌn əv ðə wɝdz hæz mɔr ðæn ˈwʌn ˈsɪləbḷ| bʌt ðɛr ɪz ˈvɛrɪɪŋ ɪnˈflɛkʃən|| ðə ˈlæst wɝd [ˈðɛr]| ɪz ðə ˈmost strɛst| ænd ðə ˈfɝst wɝd rɪˈsivz ˈsɛkənˌdɛrɪ strɛs| hwaɪl ðə wɝd [wəz] ˈɪzn̩t strɛst ət ɔl|| wi ʃo ðə læk əv strɛs ɪn [wəz] baɪ juzɪŋ ðə ˈʃwa|| strɛs ˈɔlmost ˈnɛvɚ ˈɔltɚz ðɪ æksɛnt ɪn ə ˌplurəsɪˈlæbɪk wɝd||

ˈmʌtʃ əv aur strɛs ɪz ˈɪndɪˌketɪd baɪ ə rɪˈvɝs ˌɪmplɪˈkeʃən|| æz jul ˈnotɪs ɪn ðə ˈprɪˈsidɪŋ ˈsɛntɪns| ðə wɝdz [əv] ænd [ə] ar kəmˈplit wɝdz ænd jɛt ˈkɔl fɔr ðɪ ʌnstrɛst ˈsɪmbḷ|| ðɛr ar ˈsɛvɚəl sʌtʃ wɝdz ðæt ar həˈbɪtʃuəlɪ ˌʌnˈstrɛst ɪn aur ˈæktʃuəl spitʃ|| ˈdʒɛnɚəlɪ ðɪ ˌɪnˈdɛfɪnɪt ˈartɪkḷz [ə] ænd [ən] rɪˈsiv ˈno strɛs ət ɔl|| ju wɪl ˈnotɪs tu ðæt əˈkeʒənəlɪ ˈlæk əv strɛs ˈtʃɛndʒɪz ðə ˈvauəl saund|| wi se [ən] fɔr [æn]| ænd [ət] fɔr æt||

In conversational speech we find that many more words are similarly unstressed, so many, in fact, that if anyone fails to speak English without showing a lot of unstressing, he will sound very foreign, or very stilted. We native speakers of American English have learned the rules that govern phrasal stress so well that we apply them unconsciously—until we start trying to transcribe connected speech, and keep thinking about how the words would sound were they spoken singly. Then we make mistakes.

Let us give an example. How would you transcribe, "He will do it," as spoken conversationally? The stressed words are *He* and *do*, the unstressed ones are *will* and *it*. The stressed words do not tend to change much in connected speech, but the unstressed ones sure do. They may become contracted or foreshortened, or the vowels tend to turn into the schwa. Thus, [wɪl] becomes [ɪl] or [əl] or [l̩] and [ɪ] in *it* may even turn into [ə]. So we hear the sentence as [hiɪlduət] or [hiəlduɪt] or [hil̩duət].

Perhaps one way you can learn to listen more carefully to these unstressed monosyllabic words is by thinking that they have both strong and weak forms. By strong, we mean stressed or spoken in isolation; by weak, we mean unstressed and as spoken conversationally. Indeed, most of these words have not one, but several unstressed forms and the one you will use will probably depend upon the phrase in which it is incorporated. In the following exercise we provide some, but not all, of the variants of the weak or unstressed froms of some common words. Put them in phrases, and speak the phrases swiftly and naturally, to determine which weak form you used.

Exercise 8.2.

STRONG FORM (STRESSED)	WEAK FORM (UNSTRESSED)
[hi]	[hɪ i ɪ]
[hɪz]	[ɪz z]
[ðæt]	[ðət æt]
[ðɛm]	[ðəm əm m̩]
[jur]	[jɚ jə]
[tu]	[tu tə]
[æt]	[ət]
[ʌv]	[əv v]
[ænd]	[ənd n̩d n̩]
[æm]	[əm m̩]
[kʊd]	[kəd kd]

148

STRONG FORM (STRESSED)	WEAK FORM (UNSTRESSED)
[hæd]	[həd əd d]
[hæz]	[həz əz z]
[ði]	[ðə ðɪ]
[æn]	[ən n̩]

Exercise 8.3.   Read this aloud, exactly as it is written.

[ə nu 'bɪldɪŋ| wəz 'goən ʌp| ɑn ðə 'graʊndz əv ðə stet 'hɑspɪtl̩| n̩ ðə 'fɔrmn̩ əv ðə 'prɑdʒɪkt| 'notɪst n̩ 'ɪnmet| 'hwɪln̩ ə 'hwɪlbɛro| 'ʌpsaɪd:aʊn|| 'wʌtʃə duɪn ðæt fɔ·| i sɛd tə ðɪ 'ɪnmet|| waɪ 'dontʃə tɝn ət 'ovɚ|| ɪtl̩ rol:ɑts bɛtɚ ɪf jə du||

aɪ traɪd ðæt| ænsɚd ðɪ'ɪnmet| bət 'ɛvrɪ taɪm aɪ dɪd| sʌm dæm ful pʊt brɪks ɪn ət||]

Exercise 8.4.   Now, transcribe the following into very informal, conversational speech. Include weak forms wherever appropriate, bars of juncture, and accent marks.

Three animals of the forest were arguing about which one was the most feared. The first, a hawk, claimed that since he could fly, he could attack anything repeatedly from above. The second, a lion, said that because of his strength nobody dared challenge him. The third, a skunk, insisted he needed neither strength nor flight to scare any creature. As the trio debated the issue, a grizzly bear came along and swallowed them all—hawk, lion, and stinker.

VOWEL SHIFTS IN CONNECTED SPEECH

Of course, it makes no sense to ask you to memorize all the weak forms of the host of words which are unstressed in our conversational speech. We have given some examples only to make you aware of the problem. A much better way is to hunt for the underlying principles.

One of these principles concerns the way that certain vowels and diphthongs shift from one sound to another when they are unstressed. You have already seen that in the word *above* the first "uh" is transcribed as the schwa [ə], while the second one is [ʌ], because the first is unstressed (weak) and the second is strong (stressed.) We find this same shift occurring in other central vowels. The first vowel of *murmur* is [ɝ] and the second is [ɚ]. You already know this, but you may not know that in continuous speech when one-syllable words containing these vowels are unstressed, the same shift occurs. This is why we hear [ən] and not [æn] in the phrase, *it's an awful thing* [ɪts ən 'ɔfl̩ θɪŋ], and we write the [ɚ] in *for instance* [fɚ'ɪnstəns]. The unstressing of the centering diphthongs [ɪr], [ɛr], [ɔr], and [ʊr] is very prevalent in continuous speech, and you must learn to recognize it when it occurs.

But we find the same shift in other vowels and diphthongs as well. In unstressed words as well as syllables, we often do not use the vowel [u] in swift conversation. Instead, it becomes [ʊ], or even [ə]. The words *to* and *you* are typical examples. "Are you going to the store?" becomes [ɑr jə goɪn tə ðə stɔr||]. The [æ] sound also lends itself to distortion: [kən] for [kæn], [kɛtʃ] for [kætʃ].

Exercise 8.5.   Write this in formalized English.

wɛr jə goɪn| sælɪz bɔs æst|| tə gɛt səm:ɔr:olz ə daɪmz fɚ ðə kæʃrɛdʒɪstɚ|| ɔraɪt| bət gɪmi olə ðɪ old:aɪmz fɚ maɪ kɔɪn kəlɛkʃn̩| ɚ bɔs:ɛd|||

149

THE SYLLABIC CONSONANTS

You also have already learned that, though most syllables must contain a vowel, there are times when the [l], [m], or [n] may serve as unstressed syllables by themselves, as in the words [tɝtl̩], [ædm̩], or [kɪtn̩]. Again, the reason for this is the law of least effort. Why put in a transitional vowel if the lateral [l] or the nasal sounds by themselves will serve well enough? Certainly in continuous speech we find these syllabic consonants being used over and over again. Remember to put the dot [.] under the symbol for the syllabic consonant. Though these syllabic consonants tend to be used most frequently after a preceding [t] or [d], as in [tɝtl̩] or [ædm̩], sometimes they follow a sibilant, as in [rɪzn̩] or [trækʃn̩] or [fæʃn̩]. It is because these special consonants can act as syllables by themselves that we find so many words being contracted into them. Why say [bekən] when we can say [bekn̩]; why say [endʒəl] when [endʒl̩] will suffice?

THE PROLONGATION OF SOUNDS IN CONTINUOUS SPEECH

As you transcribe snatches of conversational speech, you will find it necessary to use the [:] symbol frequently. As you have seen, it is the modifying mark we use to indicate that the sound which it follows was prolonged. In continuous speech, as we have said, we do not talk in words but in phrases, or in "meaning units." The speech unfolds in a continuous flow. It is (except for the stutterer) a smooth flow, not a series of staccato bits of speech. One of the ways that we achieve this fluent flow is by holding onto the tail of a preceding word until the next word comes along. How would you transcribe "It's half full?" The [f] is prolonged. "These zero's?" "This sermon?" [ɪts hæf:ʊl] [ðiz:ɪroz] [ðɪs:ɝmn̩]. In most cases, then, when a second word begins with the same *continuant* sound (or its cognate) as the last sound in the first word, that sound is merely prolonged, rather than reuttered.

When it comes to the same *stop* or *plosive* ending and beginning of contiguous words, a difficulty arises, since it is impossible to prolong a stop or plosive without distortion. Yet, we do not say [blæk kæts] or [old dɔgz]. If you try to do so, you will find yourself putting a tiny schwa between the words. What we actually do is prolong the *position* in the mouth of the "doubled" consonant, while uttering the sound only once. So, we say [blæk:æts] and [old:ɔgz].

Exercise 8.6.   Transcribe these phrases, using [:] whenever conversational speech requires it.

1. It's Sunday _____
2. He sits still _____
3. Matt takes some money _____
4. with this ring _____
5. dumb bunny _____
6. dumb Mable _____
7. dog gone _____
8. stop pushing _____

[wi hop jə notɪst ðət nʌmbɝ faɪv ʃudn̩t hæv :| ənd nʌmbɝ sɪks ʃud||]

This chapter has attempted to help you learn to analyze and transcribe continuous speech. We have pointed out some of the features that characterize it and have tried to smooth out your difficulties. Especially in the profession of speech pathology, you will find many occasions in which these new skills will be useful.

Here are some well-worn phrases to transcribe as they would be said in ordinary conversation.

1. What will you do   _____

2. Big gun   _____

3. Don't you know   _____

4. Did you   _____

5. With the   _____

6. Where is he   _____

7. Come here   _____

8. Give me   _____

9. All right   _____

10. He sat down   _____

11. Can you   _____

12. Thin knife   _____

13. Trick or treat   _____

14. An apple   _____

15. Yours and mine   _____

16. Black cow   _____

17. Here's mud in your eye   _____

18. Little Lucy   _____

19. Bigger ring   _____

20. Will he kiss her   _____

ɔl əv ðiz ɚ sʌbdʒɪkt tə ˈargjəmɪnt‖ lɪsṇ təjɚˈsɛlf| bət se ðə frez ˈnætʃɚəlɪ‖

1. wʌtḷjə du

2. bɪgːʌn

3. dontʃə no

4. dɪdʒə – dʒə – dɪdʒu

5. wɪðːə

6. wɛrɪzi

7. kəmːɪr–kəmɪr

8. gɪmːi

9. ɔraɪt

10. hi sætːaʊn

11. kṇjə – kɪnjə

12. θɪnːaɪf

13. trɪkɚtrit

14. ənæpḷ

15. jʊrzṇ maɪn

16. blækːaʊ

17. hɪrzmʌdṇjɚ aɪ

18. lɪtḷːusi

19. bɪgɚːɪŋ

20. wɪli kɪsɚ

Name _____ Date _____ Score _____

Hand this in to your instructor.

1. Here is a selection to transcribe into conversational speech. Use juncture marks, primary accent marks, prolongation marks, and assimilation, as needed.

   "Remember that progressive assimilation means that your mouth is already in a position and it doesn't change for the next sound."
   "Got you. But, could you give me an example?"
   "You just supplied two, on your own. Do you know what they are?"

2. Answer the question just asked.

3. Put in the appropriate juncture marks and primary accent marks in this selection.

   prəgrɛsɪv əsɪməleʃn̩ tʃendʒəz ðə falɔɪŋ saund n̩d rɪgrɛsɪv əsɪməleʃn̩ ɔltɚz ðə prɪsidɪŋ saund‖ ðɪ ŋ saund ɪn ɪŋkəm tæks ɪz n̩ ɪgzæmpl̩ əv hwɪtʃ kaɪnd əv əsɪməleʃn̩

4. Answer the question just asked.

5. Reduce the following words and phrases to the shortest possible utterances, while still maintaining coherence. Write them in phonetics.

   1. Aren't you
   2. Where are you going?
   3. Where did he go?
   4. When did her sister leave?
   5. For instance
   6. Maintenance
   7. Actually
   8. Give me her ring.

9 Narrow Transcription

In the last chapter we discussed conversational speech, and you had some practice in writing exactly what you *hear* someone saying rather than "correct" pronunciation of words. In this chapter we will go further in transcribing allophones, as opposed to phonemes. [wɪr ʃur ju rɪmɛmbɚ ðət ŋ æləfon rɛprɪzɛnts ði ɪgzækt saʊnd ðəts prədust| hwɛræz ðə sɪmbḷ fɚ ə fonim ɪndɪkeɪts ðə fæməlɪ tu hwɪtʃ ðə saʊnd bɪlɔŋz‖]

We have generally ignored the little details, the deviant forms and the allophones. But if we are to apply our newly acquired phonetic tools professionally, we must start paying attention to these variations. Our next two chapters deal with the analysis and transcription of dialects, substandard speech, and deviant speech. You could not possibly identify or record these behaviors by confining yourself solely to the *phonemic* symbols, used in broad (open) transcription. This chapter deals with narrow (closed) transcription (see Figure 7).

NONDISTINCTIVE FEATURES OF NARROW TRANSCRIPTION

In narrow, or closed, transcription we record not just the phonemically distinctive features which distinguish one family of sounds from another. Instead, we also symbolize the nondistinctive features, for we wish to put down *phonetically* just how a given person says those sounds in a given utterance. For example, thus far we have always transcribed the vowel of the word *show* as [o]. Actually, only foreigners tend to say it with this pure vowel. Most of us diphthongize it. We say [oʊ]. Say the word [ʃo], prolonging the pure [o] sound, then say [ʃoʊ], as you would in conversation. Both the [o] and the [oʊ] are members of the same phoneme, or sound family, for there are no two words such as [ʃo] and [ʃoʊ] in our language which have different meanings. The diphthongization of the [o] is therefore nondistinctive, and so we have used the phoneme [o] consistently heretofore, in our broad phonemic transcription. But now it is time to put down on paper exactly how we say *show*, and if we do that, we must use phonetic rather than phonemic transcription, and write [ʃoʊ]. This is not quibbling. If we say *obey*, however, we use the pure vowel [o]. Not all *o's* are said in the same way, and our job is to transcribe just how a speaker says them.

Similarly, from now on you must not automatically transcribe the vowel of the word *say* as [e] for it, too, is usually pronounced as the diphthong [eɪ], although occasionally we may need to use the pure vowel [e] in certain phonetic contexts just as we did with the [o]. Phonemically, [e] and [eɪ] are members of the same sound family, but phonetically they are different allophones that must be recorded.

THE INTERNATIONAL PHONETIC ALPHABET.
(Revised to 1932.)

	Bi-labial	Labio-dental	Dental and Alveolar	Retroflex	Palato-alveolar	Alveolo-palatal	Palatal	Velar	Uvular	Pharyngal	Glottal
Plosive	p b		t d	ʈ ɖ			c ɟ	k g	q ɢ		ʔ
Nasal	m	ɱ	n	ɳ			ɲ	ŋ	ɴ		
Lateral Fricative			ɬ ɮ								
Lateral Non-fricative			l	ɭ			ʎ				
Rolled			r						ʀ		
Flapped			ɾ	ɽ					ʀ		
Fricative	ɸ β	f v	θ ð s z	ʂ ʐ	ʃ ʒ	ɕ ʑ	ç ʝ	x ɣ	χ ʁ	ħ ʕ	h ɦ
Frictionless Continuants and Semi-vowels	w ɥ	ʋ	ɹ				j (ɥ)	(w)	ʁ		

	Front	*Central*	*Back*
Close	(y ʉ u)	i y ɨ ʉ ɯ u	
Half-close	(ø o)	e ø o	
Half-open	(œ ɔ)	ɛ œ ɜ ʌ ɔ	
Open	(ɒ)	æ a ɑ ɒ	

CONSONANTS

VOWELS

(Secondary articulations are shown by symbols in brackets.)

OTHER SOUNDS.—Palatalized consonants: ƫ, ɟ, etc. Velarized or pharyngalized consonants: ɫ, d̪, z̪, etc. Ejective consonants (plosives with simultaneous glottal stop): p', t', etc. Implosive voiced consonants: ɓ, ɗ, etc. ř fricative trill. ɔ, ʚ (labialized θ, ð, or s, z). ƪ, ƺ (labialized ʃ, ʒ). ƫ, ɕ, ʓ (clicks, Zulu c, q, x). l (a sound between r and l). ʍ (voiceless w). ɪ, ʏ, ʊ (lowered varieties of i, y, u). ə (a variety of ə). ɵ (a vowel between ø and o).

Affricates are normally represented by groups of two consonants (ts, tʃ, dʒ, etc.), but, when necessary, ligatures are used (ʦ, ʧ, ʤ, etc.), or the marks ‿ or ͡ (t͡s or t͡ʃ, etc.). c, ɟ may occasionally be used in place of tʃ, dʒ. Aspirated plosives: ph, th, etc.

LENGTH, STRESS, PITCH.—ː (full length). · (half length). ˈ (stress, placed at beginning of the stressed syllable). ˌ (secondary stress). ˉ (high level pitch); ˍ (low level); ˊ (high rising); ˏ (low rising); ˋ (high falling); ˎ (low falling); ˆ (rise-fall); ˇ (fall-rise). See *Écriture Phonétique Internationale*, p. 9.

MODIFIERS.— ̃ nasality. ̊ breath (l̥ = breathed l). ̬ voice (s̬ = z). ˌ slight aspiration following p, t, etc. ̩ specially close vowel (e̩ = a very close e). ̜ specially open vowel (e̞ = a rather open e). ̫ labialization (n̫ = labialized n). ̪ dental articulation (t̪ = dental t). ̓ palatalization (z̓ = ʑ). ˔ tongue slightly raised. ˕ tongue slightly lowered. ˒ lips more rounded. ˓ lips more spread. Central vowels ï (= ɨ), ü (= ʉ), ë (= ǝ), ̈ (= e), ö (= ө), ̈ . (e.g. n̩) syllabic consonant. ˘ consonantal vowel. ʃ variety of ʃ resembling s, etc.

FIGURE 7. From Louis H. Gray, *Foundations of Language.* New York: Macmillan, 1939. Reprinted with permission.

Exercise 9.1.   Say the following sentence exactly as written.

[oʊ meɪ aɪ goʊ tə ðə pɪktʃɚ ʃoʊ‖]

Now, attempt to say the same sentence, using "pure" sounds.

[o me aɪ go tu ði pɪktʃur ʃo‖]

The [o] and the [e] are the vowels most commonly diphthongized in this fashion. It is a function of our habit of using the least effort. We begin by saying the pure vowel, and then we tend to relax the lips, tongue, and jaw, and end up by producing the less tense vowel.

Exercise 9.2.   Which of these forms do you use in actual conversation?

o'ke	oʊ'keɪ	o'keɪ
'motɚˌbot	'moʊtɚˌboʊt	'motɚˌboʊt
'peˌde	'peɪˌdeɪ	'peˌdeɪ
'wɪndoˌpen	'wɪndoʊˌpeɪn	'wɪndoˌpeɪn

Exercise 9.3.   Transcribe the following into conversational speech. Listen carefully to the way you say these words before transcribing.

Most days we make overt attempts to overtake the ground we lost yesterday. We moan and groan but stay awake, for the sake of going toward our greatest goal.

This is one example of narrow transcription; the use of two symbols to represent the actual pronunciation of these vowels. There are other ways to indicate actual pronunciation, and these are the special diacritical markers or signs that you will find on Table 9.1, page 158. As we said before, using narrow or closed transcription is a skill that will come in handy when we need to analyze deviant speech.

Let us give an example. Once we were working with a very hard-of-hearing adult who kept putting [ə] after any final voiced plosive, saying *flag* as [flægə] and *need* as [nidə]. He even inserted this schwa after unvoiced plosives which began syllables, saying [kə:ip] and [pəleɪs] for *keep* and *place*. We suspect that these abnormalities were the result of tutors trying to teach him the plosives as isolated sounds, as [kʌ] [pʌ] [tʌ] [dʌ].

In helping him we had to teach him the difference between the aspirated and imploded allophones of these plosives. We had to show him, for instance, that the [g] in *flag* should not end in a puff of voiced air but that its final sound should be imploded ['] instead. We used the phonetic marker for this implosion ['], the apostrophe, to help him correct the errors on other final plosives. Then we used the same approach to show him that the initial plosives should be aspirated and without the schwa; that he could release the impounded air of the [k] in *keep* with an audible but voiceless airflow. In short, we had to show him that the first sound of *keep* was not just a [k] or [kə] but instead, it was [k'] or [kʰ].

SYMBOLS USED IN NARROW TRANSCRIPTION

When we try to record as exactly as possible the way that people speak, we will need some new symbols, some new modifying marks. Let us present these marks in tabular form first; and then gradually explain their application. Some of them are familiar, and you have already been using them. Others will be new. All are necessary if we are to record accurately how we speak.

Table 9.1

MODIFYING MARKS

1. [ː]   The preceding sound is markedly prolonged [ðə lifːɛl daʊn]
2. [.]   The sound is syllabic [itn̩]
3. [˜]   The sound is nasalized [kæ̃n]
4. [̥]   The sound is unvoiced [kw̥ɪk]
5. [͡]   Adjacent sounds are linked together [g͡rɪn]
6. [͆]   The sound is labialized, as in an articulation error [r̫eɪdɪo]
7. [̪]   The sound is dentalized [ɪn̪ ðə stɔr]
8. [']   The sound is imploded, as in final plosives [sæk']
9. [ʻ]   The sound is aspirated, as in initial plosives [t'æm]
10. [ʰ]   The sound is strongly aspirated [kʰip]
11. [̬]   The sound is partly voiced [bɪt̬ɚ]
12. [-]   The plosive is unreleased [aɪ hædə bæd-eɪ]
13. [']   The lips are rounded, as in an articulation error [l'eɪdɪ]
14. [ˈ]   Primary accented syllable [ðə ˈvɪln̩ daɪd]
15. [ˌ]   Secondary accented syllable [sɪˌlæbɪfəˈkeɪʃn̩]
16. [|]   Pause after phrase [ðæt' æftɚnun| aɪ wɛnt hoʊm]
17. [||]   Pause after sentence [ðɪs ɪz ðɪ ɛnd||]
18. [#]   Pause after utterance is ended

All of these modifying signs refer to phenomena that are to be found in our normal everyday speech; they do not necessarily refer to abnormal or deviant speech, though we will certainly be using them when it is time to transcribe it.

ASSIMILATION NASALITY

The [˜] sign is placed over vowels, or more rarely over continuant consonants, when they are nasalized. This nasalization is much more common than one might think unless one listens closely for it. Remembering that assimilation refers to the way neighboring sounds tend to influence each other in the interest of economy of articulation, we can readily see that in words like *mine*, *men*, or *mangle*, the nasal sounds which both precede and follow the vowel would tend to cause that vowel to become nasalized too. The more swiftly we say such words, the more likely that the nasality will be heard throughout the sequence of sounds. In those cases we would transcribe them as follows: [mãɪn] [mɛ̃n] [mæ̃ŋgl]·

It is not only these nasal sound-sandwich words that show assimilation nasality. All some persons need is any nasal sound in the near vicinity, and some of their vowels and diphthongs will be nasalized. Can you swiftly say "thanks" three times in a row without having the [æ] become [æ̃]? Most people cannot. Vowels which often show assimilation nasality are the [æ], [ɛ], and [i]. The diphthongs [aɪ] and [aʊ] are also highly vulnerable. In a continuous utterance, the more frequently nasal sounds are used, the more likely you will have to remember to use the [˜] marker. But do not use it unless you hear the nasality. Certain persons are said to speak with "a nasal twang" when actually they are simply more prone than others to this assimilation nasality. As to the use of the nasal marker over consonants, try saying *haven't*, to see if you nasalize the [v].

Exercise 9.4.   Here is a passage for you to say out loud, with as much nasality as possible. Read each phrase, transcribe what you say, go on to the next phrase, and so on. If you do this exercise in class, pair off with someone, and take turns transcribing each other's speech. Be sure to use the [~] sign over the sounds on which excessive nasality is produced.

Fancy Nancy managed to anger the men with what they considered her mangled meaning of the word "chauvinism." She singled them out in savage derision as adhering to a fanatical unreasoning attachment to their own superiority.

DENTALIZATION

In most foreign languages we find a pronounced tendency to produce the [t], [d], and [n] sounds with the tongue tip against the teeth rather than on the gum ridge, and so we will need the dentalization symbol [ ] to transcribe the speech of persons with such foreign accent problems. We will also need it to show how children with pronounced tongue-thrust habits say these, and even other sounds. But, this same dentalization occurs in our normal speech, too. Notice how you say the [t] and [d] sounds in the phrases, *bit the bone* and *five inches in width*. You will observe that the contact of the tongue tip is on the teeth, not on the alveolar process. You say [bɪt̪ ðə boʊn] and [faɪv ɪntʃɪz ɪn wɪd̪θ]. Once again we find here a special kind of assimilation; the dental sounds [θ] and [ð] influencing their preceding sounds, to be articulated similarly. It is easier to make the shifts if we lower the tongue tip to the teeth in producing such particular consonant clusters as [dθ], [tθ], [nθ]. How do you say the [n] in *tenth?* Where is your tongue tip?

Exercise 9.5.   Here are some paired phrases. Decide which phrase in each pair has dentalization in it.

1. I went with Terry   I married Terry
2. Win two games   Win the game
3. First things first   The first day
4. Breadth and brawn   Breath and song
5. At the theater   In the theater

[fɔrgɪv ʌs ɪn nʌmbɚ faɪv fɚ hævɪŋ boʊθ freɪzɪz juz ðə dɛnt̪lɪzeɪʃn̩ mɑrk‖]

NARROW TRANSCRIPTION OF THE PLOSIVE SOUNDS

The modifying marks [ʰ], ['], ['], [-], [̥], and [ ] describe the specific ways that the plosive consonants are variously uttered. Earlier in this chapter we demonstrated that the same plosive sound may be pronounced differently in the initial and final positions of a single-syllabled word; that when it begins the word it is released with an audible puff of air, but when it terminates that word we do not hear that puff.

Aspiration and plosion

All the plosive sounds [p], [b], [t], [d], [k], and [g] are created by closing the oral cavity at one location or another, then by building up some air pressure behind that barrier (implosion), and then by releasing the dammed up air (plosion). Our new set of modifying marks refers primarily to the manner of release. Again let us say that we are not just being academic in presenting this material. Stutterers frequently have trouble attempting a word beginning with a plosive, because they fail to release it in the appropriate way. For example, they start the word *pipe* with the imploded allophone [p‘], rather than with the aspirated [p‘], and then they tend to go into tremor. They must be taught to begin *pipe* with a [p‘] or [pʰ] (loose contact) if they are to prevent tremor or recoil. Hard-of-hearing children may not only partially voice the two plosives in this word pipe and say [paɪp] or [baɪb], but they also release the final [p] into a schwa vowel, saying [paɪbə]. Persons with cleft palate, foreign accent, or substandard speech often make errors of plosive release. So it is important that we study this material.

We have two modifying marks to indicate that an audible puff of air occurs in the release of a plosive. The [ʰ] is used when the forceful flow of air is strong and very noticeable; the [‘] (reversed apostrophe) sign is used to indicate a less forceful flow. At first you may have trouble distinguishing between these two degrees of force; either sign will indicate the aspiration which is the important thing to record. As you begin to listen to the way plosives are released you will notice that the voiced plosives [b], [d], and [g] at the beginning of a syllable do not show much audible airflow, but that the unvoiced plosives [p], [t], and [k] do. Compare how you say these word-pairs aloud: pat–bat, tin–din, came–game. If you say them as most people do, you would say [p‘æt–bæt], [t‘ɪn–dɪn], and [k‘eɪm–geɪm]. Or you might say [tʰɪn]. Hold your hand before your mouth as you say words beginning with the voiceless plosives. If the airflow is short, use the [‘] mark, if it lasts longer, use the [ʰ]. But do not worry about it. Just be sure that if the plosive is aspirated, that aspiration is recorded. And *remember to place the reversed apostrophes above and to the right of the plosive.*

Exercise 9.6.   Remembering that the [ʰ] represents the more forceful flow of released air of an unvoiced plosive and the [‘] the less forceful flow, read the following aloud, as it is written. This exercise will be more helpful if you practice with a fellow student.

[pʰæt‘ɪ kʰeɪk| pʰætɪ kʰeɪk| beɪk‘ɚz mæ̃n||
beɪk mi ə k‘eɪk əz fæst‘ əz jə kʰæn||]

Unaspiration

The unvoiced plosives are not always aspirated. Compare the way that the [t] is released in the words *top* and *stop*. In *top* you can easily hear the air puff; in *stop* you cannot. So we need a modifying sign to indicate this lack of aspiration and that sign is the true apostrophe [’], which is placed above and to the right of the unaspirated plosive It has also been called the implosion sign. This implosive sign [’] does not mean that no air at all is released, but merely that it is not very audible. The air which is in the mouth leaks out; it is not forced out. Compare the [k] sounds in the word pairs *cat–tack* or *kiss–sick*. You will notice that those in which the [k] occurs in the final position have very little forced air flow, and that what there is of it is very short in duration. We would therefore transcribe them thus: [k‘æt’–t‘æk’] and [k‘ɪs–sɪk’].

Over and over again you will find that when a voiceless plosive starts the syllable it is aspirated, and when it ends the syllable it is not. Moreover, voiced plosives, when they end the last word of an utterance (i.e., come just before the single bar, double bar, or double cross markers) are usually imploded and should be recorded with the [’] sign, as in [aɪ geɪv ɪt tʊ ðə dɔg’||].

Exercise 9.7.   Write the following in phonetics, using the ['] and ['] wherever they belong; then read aloud what you have written.

1. The cat sat on a tack.
2. Stop the tops.
3. Pass the tag to the sick sap.
4. The chain gang became chaotic.
5. A cow and a pig can't dance a jig.

You will soon find that when a voiceless plosive comes before a syllabic consonant it will be unaspirated, as in the words *title* [taɪtʼl̩] *spoken* [spoukʼn̩], or *totem* [tʼoutʼm̩]. Also, in the consonant clusters involving the *s*-blends *sp̀*, *st*, and *sk*, the plosives will be released without any forceful airflow. Compare *key* [kʼi] and *ski* [ski]. And, remember that when connected speech is being transcribed these blends occur in the linking of words, as well as within words.

Exercise 9.8.   Add the appropriate modifying marks to all plosives in the following utterance.

[ðə lɪtl̩ skæmp tuk ə mɪljn̩ spɪlz ɑn hɪz æŋkl̩ hwɛn i traɪd kɪkn̩ hɪz ʌŋkl̩ ɑn ðə pɔrtʃ‖]

Unreleased plosives

The modifying mark [-], a hyphen, is used to indicate still another characteristic of the unvoiced plosives. When two plosives are linked together, as in *swept* or *walked*, the first plosive's air puff is inhibited or not released as it is usually. You will hear no air flow on the [p] in *swept* [swɛp-tʼ] or on the [k] in *walked* [wɔk-t]. This holds true both for individual words as in *worked* [wɝk-t] and also in connected speech, as in the phrase *not down there* [nɑt-daʊn ðɛr]. Note that this [-] sign is used even when one of the two plosives is voiced. This inhibition of the air puff becomes obvious when you try to say [nɑt̩ daʊn ðɛr], giving the [t̩] its full [tʰ] sound.

Exercise 9.9.   Try saying these pairs of words and phrases as they are written. Which do you really say?

1. nɑkʰ daʊn faɪt   nɑk-daʊn faɪt
2. dip-pɝpʼl̩   dipʼ pɝpl̩
3. tɔkʼt   tɔk-t

The partial voicing of unvoiced plosives

We now introduce a new phonetic marker, the [ˌ]. It is used to indicate that a sound which is usually unvoiced is instead actually voiced or partly voiced. As such, it performs a function opposite to that of the little circle [̥] which, as you know, is placed under a sound to show that a voiced sound has become unvoiced, as in the common pronunciation of *three* [θr̥i]. In certain phonetic environments the voiceless plosives become partially voiced. By this we mean that some voice comes in before the vowel begins. Observe how you say *bread and butter* swiftly or casually. The [t] in *butter* is not aspirated at all even though it begins a syllable, an unstressed syllable. Instead it has some vocalization in it. Not much. Not enough to turn it into the phoneme

[d], but enough to distinguish it phonetically from the aspirated [tʻ] which usually begins a syllable. The [t̬] is an allophone of [t] and we use the [̬] marker to show how it is really spoken. You should not find it difficult to remember the marker for it is a tiny *v* (for *voice*), and it is placed directly under the sound that has become voiced. How do you usually say *battery* in the phrase, *assault and battery?* [bæt'ɚɪ] or [bæt̬ɚɪ]? If you are careless, perhaps you may voice the [t] too much or too soon, and say [bædɚɪ]. Voiceless plosives that come before unstressed vowels often lose their aspiration, their little air puffs, and instead become partially voiced. We also find the same voicing of an unvoiced plosive in words or stressed syllables which begin with the *s*-blends. We say [sp̬un], [sk̬ul], and [st̬ænd]. Watch for this voicing of the unvoiced plosives.

Exercise 9.10. Remember: [̥] indicates unvoicing of a voiced sound, and [̬] indicates voicing of an unvoiced sound. Transcribe these words the way you ordinarily say them.

1. quit
2. pitter patter
3. throw
4. special
5. aspen
6. Seattle
7. shriek
8. tree
9. school

THE GLOTTAL STOP

[ʔ] is a voiceless, glottal plosive. This new symbol represents a sound which occurs occasionally in normal speech where it is nondistinctive and hence not phonemic, but we find it often in the abnormal speech of stutterers and persons with cleft palates. Some children with severe articulatory disorders also use it as a substitution for any of the other plosive sounds. It sounds something like a brief, miniature cough, and is produced by closing the vocal folds tightly, then suddenly releasing them to produce a brief clicking puff of air. In normal speakers we frequently find it appearing in place of the [t] before a syllabic consonant, as in the words *kitten* [kɪʔn̩], *little* [lɪʔl̩], or *mountain* [mãʊʔn̩]. It also occurs in the initiation of a vowel, especially when the first word of an utterance begins with a vowel as in [ʔɑbviəslɪ ɪts ɪnkɚɛkt‖]. When it is followed by [:], the symbol and mark refer to the prolongation of the glottal closure, a common feature in stuttering, and the more colons that follow the [ʔ], the longer the blocking lasts. Note that the symbol is an *undotted* question mark. When [ʔ] is turned upside down, it represents the glottal click [ʕ], and we find it frequently in the glottal or vocal try which can be transcribed as [ʕʕʕʕʕ: ɑr ju goɪŋ] when uttered by a stutterer.

Exercise 9.11. Transcribe this passage, using the symbol for the glottal stop wherever it could possibly be used by a normal speaker.

The little kitten settled in a certain position in the maintenance of his dignity.

162

So far we have discussed in detail these modifying marks. We present them, each with their label or definition. You supply a word or phrase illustrating each. Reread the last few pages if you get stuck.

1. [~] Assimilation nasality   _____

2. [ˌ] Dentalization   _____

3. [ʰ] Strong aspiration of a plosive   _____

4. ['] Less forceful aspiration of a plosive _____

5. ['] Implosion of plosives   _____

6. [-] Unreleased plosive   _____

7. [ˬ] Partial voicing of unvoiced plosive _____

8. [˳] Partial unvoicing of a voiced plosive _____

9. [ʔ] The voiceless glottal stop   _____

See if your word or phrase follows the principle as stated for each sound. We give only one example of the many choices for each.

1. The presence of the nasals [m], [n], and [ŋ] usually evokes nasality on the vowels which follow or precede them: [mãɪ æ̃ŋkl].

2. The dental sounds [θ] and [ð] often make us dentalize the [t], [d], and [n] when the two come together: [aɪv bɪn̪ ðɛr].

3. The voiceless plosives [p], [k], and [t], when they begin a syllable, are often blown forcefully out of the mouth: [pʰitɚ].

4. The same as #3, except the force of the expelled air is not so great: [kʻeɪm].

5. The voiceless plosives [p], [k], and [t], when they come at the end of a word or just before a syllabic consonant, do not have a rush of air accompanying them; they are imploded: [stɑp' ðə pip'l].

6. When two plosives are linked together, the first plosive's air puff is inhibited: [spæ̃ŋk-t].

7. In unvoiced plosives, and especially if they are preceded by [s], we sometimes let some voicing creep in: [spik stɚⁿlɪ].

8. The voiced plosives [b], [g], and [d] become unvoiced: [θ̥rɪftɪ kw̥in].

9. A brief clicking puff of air, often found substituting for a [t] before a syllabic consonant: [brɪʔn̩].

Now, to a bit of extra practice. Go backwards, up this page, trying to label each of these modifying marks, then refer to the Self-Checking Test, to see if you were correct.

Prove to yourself that you really have mastered these modifying marks. Write each of the following words or phrases in the right-hand column, using the appropriate symbol. Say them naturally.

1. Make a syllable of a consonant.   countenance

2. See that the plosive in the middle of the word is
   unreleased.   countenance

3. Nazalize.   meander

4. Dentalize.   10,003

5. Simulate a person aspirating as he speaks.   Can Polly tango?

6. Now, simulate a stutterer blocking, then say,   Can Polly tango?

7. Remember how we really pronounce our
   vowels.   Oh, say, can you see?

8. Use ['] and [']'.   Put ink in it.

1. jʊr just-ə ðɪs baɪ naʊ

   kaʊntn̩əns

2. Listen to the way you say "I don't know."
   aɪ doʊnt-noʊ aɪ doʊnˀnoʊ

   kaʊnt-n̩əns ɔr
   kaʊnˀn̩əns

3. frɛntʃmən wəd faɪnd ðɪs ə snæp

   mĩænd˞

4. It's hard to keep your tongue from
   anticipating the following sound.

   tɛn̩ θaʊzn̩d ənd θri
   ɔr tɛn̩ θaʊzn̩d θr̥i̥

5. The ['] and [ʰ] denote the strength of the
   plosion.

   kʻən pʰalɪ tʻæŋgoʊ

6. Remember the glottal click and the
   prolongation.

   ʕʕʕ::kʰn̩ ʕʕ pʻalɪ tʻæŋgoʊ

7. Our lazy mouths relax the vowels.

   oʊ| seɪ| kʻn̩ jʊ si||

8. [']pushes the sound out, and ['] holds
   the sound in.

   pʻʊtʼ ɪŋkʼ ɪn ət||

THE NARROW TRANSCRIPTION OF CONTINUANTS

Apart from the matters of voicing and unvoicing, as indicated by the modifying marks [͜] and [͜], or their nasalization, as signified by [˜], the major differences that we describe in the narrow transcription of continuants are those of duration. We have two signs for this: [·] and [:]. The latter, the colon, indicates that the sound has been held at least twice as long as it is normally, that is, its duration has been doubled or more than doubled. The former, [·], the centered dot, or one dot, means that the preceding sound is held longer than it usually is, but not long enough to merit the colon sign [:]. Now, of course, none of us has ears sharp enough to do these precise measurements with accuracy, so you should just guess. If the [v] in the phrase *we have very few* seems to be held noticeably longer than it normally is in the isolated word *have*, you should use either [:] or [·] after it. In the speech of the authors of this book, the [v] in that phrase is just long enough to cause us to transcribe it as [wi hæv·ɛrɪfju].

How do *you* say it? You decide.

THE NARROW TRANSCRIPTION OF THE GLIDES

Unlike the continuants, the glides require some careful listening and analysis to transcribe them with some fidelity. You doubtlessly remember which sounds they are (the [w], [j], and [r]), and that they are produced while gliding or shifting from one vowel position into another vowel in producing a syllable. Only one of these glides, the [j], has no normal allophones; the others have several to watch for.

The allophones of [w]

By now you will have no trouble with the symbol for the first sound of such words as *wind* and *water*, the [w], and you will, of course, be using it often in your narrow transcription. But now you may have to listen a bit more alertly to the way people say *queer* or *quack*. In broad phonetic transcription we would write them as [kwɪr] and [kwæk], but the [w] in these words is not a voiced sound; it is unvoiced. Some few modern phoneticians use the [ʍ] (upside down *w*) to indicate this unvoicing. But figuring that you already have had more than enough symbols to learn, we suggest that you simply use the little circle under the [w̥] which signifies the same thing. Thus, we would transcribe *queer* and *quack* as [kw̥ɪr] and [kw̥æk]. Notice that the unvoiced allophone follows an unvoiced plosive in both these words.

But suppose the [w] follows a voiced plosive, such as [d], as in the word *dwell?* Would it tend to be voiced or unvoiced? It is voiced, and so we would write *dwell* [dwɛl]. Yes, you have to listen and ask yourself if the sound you hear is the [w] or the [w̥].

And there is a third allophone, too, the [hw], though scholars argue a bit about whether it consists of one phoneme or two. There is also some confusion engendered by English spelling *wh*, when we actually say [hw]. Try it for yourself; attempt to say [whɛn], then [hwɛn]. Many speakers confuse the [hw] with the [w] or use them interchangeably in words such as *what* or *when* or *why*. Say the following word-pairs and see if they need different symbols for their first sounds: *watt–what; wine–whine; why–Y*. Though our usage seems to be trending toward using the [w] indiscriminately, most of us who are educated seem to employ all three forms of the [w] phoneme in different words or phonetic contexts. In your narrow transcription of a speaker's utterance, you are to put it down as it is said, not how it *should* be said.

One more pointer: Be careful to note the use of [w] in words like *going* or *showing*, for some speakers use this glide in linking the two vowels together. Does your roommate say [duwɪŋ] and [ʃouwɪŋ], or [duɪŋ] and [ʃouɪŋ]?

Something of the same sort occurs with the glide [j] in words such as *being* [bijɪŋ] and *freeing* [frijɪŋ]. Otherwise you should have no difficulty with the [j] for, as we said earlier, it has no other allophones, but is a phoneme in itself, a sound family with only one member.

The allophones of [r]

There are many members in the phonemic family of [r], and we shall need more than our set of modifying marks to identify all of them. However, only four of the *r*-glide allophones occur in ordinary general American English: the [r] and the [r̥], which are most common, and the [ɹ] and [ɹ̥]. The others we shall consider in later chapters on abnormal, foreign, or dialectal speech.

As consonantal glides, all of these four allophones begin from the position of the stressed vowel [ɝ], then shift into the mouth formation of the following vowel to form syllables. By so doing, they modify the transitional characteristics of vowel's onset, thereby achieving their identity. The [r] is commonly heard at the beginning of a stressed syllable as in *run* [rʌn], *rasp* [ræsp], and *red* [rɛd], but it can also begin unstressed syllables, especially when they begin a word as in *review* [rɪ'vju] or *return* [rɪ'tɝn]. These should give you no trouble.

But there is also an unvoiced *r*-allophone [r̥] which you will observe when it follows an unvoiced consonant to make a [pr], [kr], [fr], or [θr] blend. Listen to the [r]'s in the word-pairs *ray–pray*, *throw–row*, *read–freed*. In the blends beginning with an unvoiced sound, the [r] is unvoiced; it seems whispered. And so again we use the little circle under the sound to indicate its unvoicing. [r̥], then, is a second allophone of the phoneme [r]. Why bother with such a detail? Were you to try to help a child with his *r*-blends, a very common problem in speech therapy, by the way, he might end up saying *furry* instead of *free* unless you teach him to unvoice that [r] and say [r̥]. Besides, our job is to record how people speak. They don't say [fraɪ]; they say [fr̥aɪ].

We hate to mention the other two allophones of [r] in our ordinary speech because they occur mainly in the blends *dr* and *tr*, when these blends begin a syllable. You write them by turning the *r*-symbol upside down, as in the words *dry* [dɹaɪ], *drip* [dɹɪp], *tree* [tɹi], or *trick* [tɹɪk]. They differ from the [r] and the [r̥] only in that they are much more fricative. In the [ɹ] you can hear the buzzing noise you characteristically also find in [v]; and in [ɹ̥] you can hear something of the same rushing airflow you hear in the [f].

CLOSE TRANSCRIPTION OF THE LATERAL ALLOPHONES

The phoneme [l] has several allophones. The first of these is the familiar [l], and we use the usual phonemic symbol in brackets to represent its role in beginning syllables as in the words *luck* [lʌk], *lope* [loup], or length [lɛŋkθ]. Here the sound serves as a voiced continuant or glide. When it is voiced as in such words as *blame* or *glee*, we write [bleɪm] and [gli]. This allophone [l] is called the *clear l*.

It also has an unvoiced twin, the [l̥], which will be heard when the [l] follows an unvoiced consonant to produce a blend. Listen to these word triplets and notice how they are transcribed: *lays–blaze–plays* [leɪz–bleɪz–pl̥eɪz], *lack–black–plaque* [læk–blæk–pl̥æk]. In these triplets, the first word uses the clear *l*, in the second we find it also used in the blend, and in the third, the *l* is unvoiced, so there are only two allophones in these triplets. The [l̥] allophone occurs only in unvoiced blends; the [l] occurs either as a simple continuant sound or as a glide.

The third allophone is called the *dark l*. It is represented by the symbol [ɫ] which consists of the ordinary [l] with a single crossbar [-] intersecting it. This crossbar [-] is the modifying mark used to indicate that the sound is centralized in the mouth, and we shall see it again when we consider the allophones of certain vowels. In the production of the dark *l* the center and back of the tongue bulges upward, even though its tip remains in contact with the upper gum ridge, and it is the effect of this new tongue contour which distinguishes the dark *l* from the clear *l*. You will hear the dark *l* most often in the final position of syllables where it follows one of the back vowels as in the words *bowl* [boʊɫ], *pool* [puɫ], or *bull* [bʊɫ].

Listen to the [l] sounds in these pairs of syllables and seek to identify the special features which distinguish the dark *l* from the clear *l*. Do they really sound the same, and are they made in the same way? Which has the longer duration? Say them in slow motion. Is there any difference in pitch? *Lute–tool* and *loaf–foal*. We would transcribe them thus: [lut–tʻuɫ] and [louf–fouɫ].

We also find the dark *l* when it is syllabic and follows sounds in which the rear of the tongue is elevated, for example, [ʌŋkɫ̩], [tʻɪkɫ̩], and [æŋgɫ̩]. On the other hand, when the [l] precedes the [j] in the middle of a word like *bullion*, the dark *l* of *bull* [bʊɫ] becomes clearer, and we hear [bʊljən].

Exercise 9.12.   Arrange the following words under the appropriate mark for the [l] sound. Some words may go under more than one heading.

lilt	lull	frill	million	salmon	angle	angler	spool
eel	glue	towel	play	fiddle	scalp	baloon	cruel
[l]			[ɫ]		[l̥]		[l̩]

Name or identify the following.

1. A single sound you can continue without distortion. _____

2. Sounds produced while shifting from one vowel position to another. _____

3. The modifying mark to indicate voicing of an unvoiced continuant. _____

4. The modifying mark to indicate unvoicing of a voiced continuant. _____

5. Show a slight prolongation of a continuant. _____

6. Show a marked prolongation of a continuant. _____

7. How do the [r] sounds differ in the words *rue* and *through?* _____

8. How do you indicate the dark *l* sound? _____

9. A lateral phoneme. _____

1.   continuant

2.   glide

3. bɛt̬ɚ st̬ap ðæt   [̬]

4. kw̥inlı kw̥ɝks   [̥]

5. əv·æst dɪmɛnʃn̩z   [·]

6. əvːɛrı lɔŋ dʊreɪʃn̩   [ː]

7. The [r] assimilates the unvoiced quality of the [θ].   [ru] [θr̥u]

8. boul̥ ful̥ pul̥   [l̥]

9.   [l]

Name _____ Date _____ Score _____

Hand this in to your instructor.

1. What is the difference between the pronunciation of these two utterances: [kʼʌpʼ] [kʰʌp]?

_____

2. What is the difference between the pronunciation of these two utterances: [drʌm:eɪdʒɚ] [drʌm·eɪdʒɚ]?

_____

3. What usually happens to the [w] when it follows an unvoiced plosive, such as in the word *twinkle?*

_____

4. Transcribe these words as they "should" be said: who what where when

_____

5. Transcribe this, using modifying marks.

At Last Count

One billion seconds ago—the bombing of Pearl Harbor.
One billion minutes ago—Christ was living on Earth.
One billion hours ago—man had not yet appeared on Earth.
One billion dollars ago—was only yesterday.

NARROW TRANSCRIPTION OF THE VOWELS

We confess that we approach the writing of this section with some ambivalence, as well as reluctance. While we wish to provide you with the tools you need, we do not want to overwhelm you with too many of them, or to belabor you with too fine discriminations. Some vowels, unlike the consonants, have many variant forms if you scrutinize them very carefully. They change in vocalic quality even as they are being spoken, for the tongue is in continuous motion. They vary with the speed of utterance, stress, and, of course, with the phonetic environment in which they are embedded. Dialectal variations affect the vowels more than the consonants, and since our culture generally seems to tolerate more deviance in vowel production than in consonant production, we show more variation in our use of vowels. The best solution seems to be to boil down the sap into the syrup, point out the major variations in vowel utterance, show you how to transcribe them, and let it go at that.

Narrow transcription of [i] and [ɪ]

You doubtless remember your earlier bewilderment, frustration, or even irritation, when we insisted that you transcribe *city* and *pretty* as [sɪtɪ] and [prɪtɪ] rather than [sɪti] and [prɪti]. We have had many students protest that the final sound of these words was not [ɪ] but [i], and they were half right and half wrong. But that final sound, though we can cram it, with some creaking, into the phonemic box for [ɪ], is really neither [ɪ] nor [i] phonetically, but something in between both. By using our diacritical marks we can give the sound a clearer identity, and this is what we do in narrow transcription.

Our problem is to find an appropriate symbol to represent a sound that is about midway between [i] and [ɪ]. Some phoneticians, in their narrow transcription, have used the crossbar [ɨ] or the "horizontal colon" [ï] (which are equivalent and serve the same purpose) and write *pity* as either [pɪtɨ] or [pɪtï], or, if they hear more of the [ɪ] in the unstressed vowel, they may write them as [pɪtɨ] or [pɪtï]. Other phoneticians prefer to use the directional modifying marks, and place [ᴛ] or [⊢] after the [i] to show that it has been produced by lowering [ᴛ] or retracting [⊢] the tongue from the usual [i] position. Neither procedure has won universal acceptance, so, since we have to choose one or the other, we shall use the crossbar. When the sound resembles [i] more than [ɪ] we shall write [ɨ]. [ænd meɪ ðə lɔrd-hæv mɝsɨ an ʌs‖]

Exercise 9.13.   Read this as written.

ðɪs simz prɪtɨ sɪlɨ tʰə ɛmfəsaɪz sʌtʃ ə maɪnɚ‖ pɔltrɨ pɔint‖ bət ðɨ ounlɨ rizn̩ fɚ hævɪŋ ə founɛtɪk ælfəbɛt' ɪz fɚ prɨsɪʒn̩‖ ə wulf an ə strit kɔrnɚ maɪt seɪ‖ prɪtʰi‖ æz ə gɝl pæsəz baɪ‖ n̩ ðɪs‖ saund: ɪfrənt frəm ðə weɪ ə pɛrət' sɛz prɪtɨ pɑlɨ‖

In choosing between [ɪ] and [i] or [ɨ] and [ɨ], you cannot conclude that if the sound comes at the end of a polysyllabic word, it would never be [i]. How would you write *employee* [ɪmplɔii], or *guarantee* [gɛrənt'i]? If the final syllable has some stress on it you will hear either [i] or [ɨ] but not [ɪ] or [ɨ]. And since there are such word-pairs as *branded–brandied* and *taxis–taxes*, where the difference is phonemic, you must select your vowel symbol with care. How would you transcribe *the stories* and *the store is?*

Sometimes students have difficulty with words like *pitying* or *studying* when using broad transcription. Now that you have ways of recording the intermediate sounds between [i] and [ɪ] you should have little trouble. [wi ɑr pˈɪtɨɪŋ ju fɔr stˈʌdɨɪŋ ðɪs: tʌf‖]

173

Exercise 9.14.   Say the following aloud, then transcribe it.

He was fleeing the country on a recent Sunday, to keep from marrying the seedy employee of an indecent film company.

Narrow transcription of the other vowels

Except for the diphthongization of the [e] and [o] as in [seɪ] and [ʃou], you should have no more difficulty in the narrow transcription of the other vowels than you did when you were using broad transcription. No more, perhaps, but still plenty. Your main problems will center about deciding whether the speaker is saying [æ] or [a] (he may have come from Boston, or had a mother from Maine), or deciding whether he is saying [ɑ] or [ɔ] or [ɒ]. If the speaker uses general American speech, your task should be easy, for there are few important variations in the utterance of [ɑ], [ɛ], [æ], [u], [ʊ], [ʌ], or [ɝ]. You will have to watch for the presence of undue nasality and listen sharply to distinguish between the [ə] and [ɪ] in unstressed syllables. You may fail to recognize how vowels shift when they are unstressed, for example, that there is no [u] in *gradual*, that it has shifted to [ʊ]. But these problems require no new symbols or modifying marks for their solution; they merely need a keener ear so that the right symbol can be chosen.

In so saying, we are highly conscious that we are omitting information that a professional phonetician should possess. We could discuss how the [æ] is often raised or fronted when some speakers say *ask* in this way [æ˷sk] or this [æ˰sk], but [wɨ æ˷sk jə tə tʃɛk' ə mɔr ədvæ˰nst tɛkst]. Or, we could expatiate on the use of the [ʉ], but [tʉ hɛl wɪð ɪt].

Reading passage

   [æ˷sk' nat ʍət jɪu: k'ʌntɹɨ kn̩ dʉ fə jɪʉ| bət' raðə| hwət' jɪʉ kæ˷n dʉ fɔ: jɪu: k'ʌntɹɨ||]

NARROW TRANSCRIPTION OF THE DIPHTHONGS

Again, as with the vowels, you will not need any new modifying marks or symbols. However, you may need to combine them in new ways. The diphthongs that you have previously recorded phonemically, the [aɪ], [au], and [ɔɪ], will all be used, but there are others too. For example, the speaker you are transcribing may say the perpendicular pronoun *I* not as [aɪ], but as [ɑɪ], and he may also say [ɑu] instead of [au]. These new diphthongs are not uncommon in general American speech, though the standard diphthongs are, of course, much more frequently heard. Even though there is no phonemic difference between [au] and ɑu], there is a phonetic difference, and we must record the speech that is emitted. If the gentleman from Indiana says [kæʊ] for *cow*, we must change the first member of the usual diphthong. If the gracious lady from Mobile, Alabama, observes that you have a lovely [feɪəs], she is using a *triphthong*, and if you return the compliment but use the diphthong, and say [feɪs], she'll know that you're a [mɪzɚəbl̩ lou dæun jæŋkɨ||].

There are many new diphthongal vowel combinations to be found in pathological or foreign or dialectal speech: [ɛɪ], [ʊə], [ɪi], [ɜɪ], etc., but there are only a few others we should now call to your attention. First, there are the diphthongs where the final member is the schwa vowel, and which occur mainly before the dark *l*. In the phrase *it's really good*, the word *really* has the diphthong [ɨə] in the speech of many persons (and they probably would also say [sprɔəl] for *sprawl*, or [fɔəl] for *fall*). And there will be times when you might hear [ɔəf] and [kʻæət]. Speech which is drawled tends to be full of these schwa (or *falling*) diphthongs.

There also are some *rising* diphthongs in which the diphthong's second vowel is stressed, the most common of which is the [ɪu], as in the perhaps overly precise pronunciation of *June* [dʒɪun] or *due* [dɨu]. Falling diphthongs, then, are those in which the stress falls or declines from the first to the second vowel of the diphthong; and the rising diphthongs are those where the second vowel has more stress than the first, and the tongue has to rise in the mouth to produce it.

For a long time you have been writing the centering diphthongs, the [ɛr], [ɪr], [ar], [ɔr], [ur], [aur], and [air]. Until now we have been using the [r] as the last member of these diphthongs because we have been transcribing phonemically. However, from now on, since we are using narrow transcription, we will use the symbol [ɚ] for the second part of these diphthongs, and write them [ɛɚ], [ɪɚ], [aɚ], [ɔɚ], [uɚ], [auɚ], and [aɪɚ]. This may seem an unreasonable imposition, but it makes sense. These are diphthongs, not combinations of a vowel and a consonant. You can hear the vocalic quality in the final sound. They terminate in the unstressed vowel [ɚ]. In broad transcription it is all right to use the [r] in these diphthongs. In narrow transcription, you had better use the [ɚ]. Some argument exists on this matter, and a case can certainly be made for considering the [r] as an off glide, but most phoneticians (as opposed to linguists) seem to prefer using the [ɚ] as the second member of the centering diphthongs. It will help you when you try to code certain dialects.

Besides the usual centering diphthongs listed above, there are others; but the only ones that you may be likely to hear in general American speech are the [æɚ] in the pronunciation of *carry*, [kʻæɚɪ] instead of [kɛɚɪ], or the [uɚ] in *poor*, as [puɚ] rather than [puɚ]. And so, [sela]. Enough!

Reading passage

[ɪf| hwɛn juɚ ɪn ˈbɪznəz| n̩ jə riəlɨ nid-tə faɪɚ sʌmwn̩| ænd juɚ stʌmək eɪks æt ðə vɛɚɪ θɔt| rɪmɛmbɚ ðət ɪts bɛtɚ tu hæv ə ˈhɔɚəbl̩ ɛndɪŋ ðæn ˈhɔɚɚz wɪðˈaut ɛnd||]

Here are the modifying marks and symbols that we have discussed in this chapter. We provide one example for each, and you are to provide another. When you finish, check with the appropriate page in the chapter to make sure you are correct.

SYMBOL	DESCRIPTION	EXAMPLE	YOUR EXAMPLE
[oʊ]	Americans diphthongize the [o]	hoʊm	————
[eɪ]	Americans diphthongize the [e]	meɪbɪ	————
[~]	Assimilation nasality	mãɪn	————
[̪]	Dentalization	naɪn̪θ	————
[']	Implosion, or unaspirated plosive	trɪk'ɚ trit'	————
[ʻ]	Aspiration of a plosive	tʻɛn pʻaʊndz	————
[ʰ]	Strong aspiration	ˌkʰəmˈɪɚ	————
[-]	Unreleased plosive when followed by a plosive	beɪk-t	————
[◡]	Partial voicing of unvoiced plosive	skɑtʃn̩ wɔtɚ	————
[◦]	Partial unvoicing of a voiced plosive	bɪtwin frɛndz	————
[ʔ]	Glottal stop	faʊʔn̩	————
[:]	Marked prolongation of a continuant	kɪs:uzɪ	————
[·]	Slight prolongation of a continuant	hæf·ʊl	————
[ɹ]	The fricative, buzzing [r]	dɹim	————
[ɹ̥]	The noiseless airflow of [r]	θɹ̥etn̩	————
[ɫ]	Dark 1	fʊɫ	————
[ɨ]	Closer to the [i] than the [ɪ]	prɨsaɪs	————

SYMBOL	DESCRIPTION	EXAMPLE	YOUR EXAMPLE
[ɨ]	Closer to the [ɪ] than the [i]	mɛnɨ	_____
[ɑɪ]	A slightly higher position of the tongue for [a]	nɑɪt	_____
[ɑʊ]	Same as above	krɑʊn	_____
[ɚ]	The [r] symbol to use in centering diphthongs	aʊɚ pʊɚ kɑɚ	_____

Name _____ *Date* _____ *Score* _____

Hand this in to your instructor.

1. Transcribe the following, using as many modifying marks as are appropriate.

   There was a young lady named Jeanie,
   Who wore an outrageous bikini.
   Two wisps light as air,
   One here and one there
   With nothing but Jeanie betweenie.

2. Describe each of the modifying marks in these words:

   [kɪʔn̩] _____
   [kætl̩] _____
   [pɚˈhæps] _____
   [dauɳðə hætʃ] _____
   [mæ̃n] _____
   [kɑː] _____

3. True or false:

   A. mɛnɪ pipl̩ trɪfθɒŋgaɪz dɪfθɒŋz‖ _____
   B. əv grædʒuəl grædʒuəl‖ ðə fɚst trænskrɪpʃn̩ ɪz kərɛkt‖ _____
   C. ðə saɪn fɚ neɪzælɪtɪ əv ə vauəl ɪz ‿‖ _____
   D. oupn̩ trænskrɪpʃn̩ ɪz nɛɹou trænskrɪpʃn̩‖ _____
   E. ðə tu vaulz moust ɔfn̩ dɪfθɒŋgaɪzd ɚ ðɨ o ænd ðɨ i‖ _____
   F. ðɪ æspɚeɪʃn̩ maɚk ɪz ∘‖ _____
   G. ə lɪtl̩ sɚkl̩ bəlou ə kansənənt minz ənvɔɪsɪŋ‖ _____
   H. ɪmplouʒn̩ minz houldɪŋ ðə saund ɪn‖ _____
   I. ðə maɚk ðət-ɛlz əs tu dɛntl̩aɪz ɪz ⌐‖ _____
   J. ðə [ˈ] ɪz juzd moust ɔfn̩ ɑn ðə læst saund əv ə sɪləbl̩‖‖ _____

10 American Dialects and Standards of Pronunciation

In the United States we recognize at least three major speech areas where people show differences in their manner of speaking, one from the other. Much linguistic and phonetic research has been and is being carried out to define the boundaries of these regions and the sub-areas within each.

The variety of American speech usually termed *eastern* is spoken in Maine, New Hampshire, the eastern parts of Vermont, Massachusetts, and Connecticut. It is also termed *eastern New England speech*. New York City has dialectal variations all its own. Charles K. Thomas[1] outlines nine major speech areas in the United States, and Hans Kurath[2] has made a strong case for a Midland dialectal area between the speech of eastern New England and that of the southern Atlantic states. The speech of the people living in the southern mountains also has its own identifiable features.

Exercise 10.1.   Read the sentences below as they might be spoken by an individual from the various speech areas mentioned.

1. Eastern New England: mɛrɪ askt ðə faməz gɜl hwaɪ hi fɛd ðə naɪs arɪndʒɪz tə ðə hɒgz‖
2. New York City: mɛːɪ æskt də faməz gɜɪl waɪ hi fɛd də naɪs aɚɪndʒəz tə də hɑgz‖
3. South: meːɪ æskt ðə faməz gɜl waɪ hi fɛd ðə naɪs aəɪndʒəz tu ðə hɑgz‖
4. General American: mɛrɪ æskt ðə farməz gɜl waɪ hi fɛd ðə naɪs ɔrɪndʒɪz tə ðə hɒgz‖

In this elementary text we shall deal generally with the more obvious differences between general American, eastern American, and southern American speech.

Each of these speech regions has speech which is acceptable and speech which is nonstandard. Before we describe the characteristic variations of eastern and southern American English, we should say something about substandard speech of the general American variety. The person who says [ðe wʌz] for *there was, or* [aɪ sid] for [aɪ sɔ] is certainly using substandard speech, but the error is one of grammar rather than pronunciation. However, there are plenty of phonetic errors prevalent in substandard general American speech. If you say [tɝbəl] for *terrible*, [ɔftɪn] for *often*, or [kɑlm] for *calm*, you are not using standard speech.

[1] Charles K. Thomas, *An Introduction to the Phonetics of American English*, 2nd ed., New York, Ronald, 1958.

[2] Hans Kurath, *A Word Geography of the Eastern United States*, Ann Arbor, University of Michigan Press, 1949.

So far we have been speaking about single words. Much substandard speech occurs in the utterance of phrases or sentences. Consider these and transcribe them into standard speech.

Exercise 10.2.

1. dontʃəduət

_____

2. haʃədaɪno

_____

3. snaɪsde

_____

4. waɪntʃəwatʃwɛrjugoɪn

_____

5. watʃəgɔnədutənaɪ

_____

The student of phonetics is always confronted by the question, "Which pronunciation is correct?" John Samuel Kenyon in *American Pronunciation* declares that another question must be answered first, namely, "Correct for what occasion and under what circumstances?" He continues:

Good spoken English, even in the same dialect, is not all alike. Omitting considerations of natural local dialect of the uneducated, which is "good" in its place, there is, first, the kind of speech appropriate to the most informal and personal occasions, the most informal colloquial style.

Then there is that colloquial style which has been aptly called, "the speech of well-bred ease." Both styles use such contractions as I'm, he's, it's, doesn't, don't, can't, shan't, won't, etc., the chief difference being in vocabulary and speed of utterance. Next there is a more formal colloquial speech, which cannot be sharply distinguished from the more familiar colloquial, differing somewhat in the vocabulary called forth by more formal circumstances and less familiar acquaintance, but also making considerable use of the contractions mentioned.

More formal still is the public speaking style, In this, the need of being understood by large audiences calls forth more careful sentence structure and more deliberate and careful enunciation, especially of the consonant sounds and the accented vowel sounds.

Most formal of all is the public reading style, used in declamation, literary reading, and church services. For practical purposes we may then designate four principal styles of good spoken English as (1) familiar colloquial, (2) formal colloquial, (3) public speaking style, and (4) public reading style.

Reading passage

[studn̩ts frikwəntlɪ mɪstrʌst ðer on pronʌnsɪeʃən əv sɝtn̩ wɝdz ænd ðe prabəblɪ ɛvɪdəns wɪzdəm hwɛn ðe du so‖ bʌt hwat ar ðe tu du‖ ðɪ ævɚɪdʒ dɪkʃəneriz ar ɔfn̩ ʌnrɪlaɪəbl̩ ænd ðoz hwɪtʃ du ɛmplɔɪ ðə fonɛtɪk ælfəbɛt ænd bes ðer jusɪdʒ əpan rɪsɝtʃ ar sɛldəm əveləbl̩ ðerfɔr ðə bɛst ædvaɪs wi kæn gɪv sʌtʃ ə studn̩t ɪz tu kʌltɪvet ə kin ænd dɪskrɪmɪnetɪŋ fonɛtɪk ɪr‖ lɪsn̩ tu ðə spitʃ əv ɛdʒu-

180

ketɪd pipl̩ əbaut ju‖ kəmpɛr ðɛr ʌtɚənts wɪð jur ʌðɚ əkwentənsɪz‖ əbzɚv ðə
dɪkʃən əv ðə bɛtɚ redɪo ænd tɛləvɪʒən ənaunsɚz‖ rɪkɔrd ɔltɚnətɪv prənʌnsɪeʃənz
ɪn fonɛtɪk skrɪpt‖ præktɪs jur on ɛrɚz dəlɪbɚətlɪ ɪn ɔrdɚ tu brɪŋ ðɛm tu kanʃəsnəs
ænd ðɛn kænsəl ðɛm bɪfɔr fɪnɪʃɪŋ jur sɛntɪns‖ spik ɪn rom æz ðə romənz du‖ ðɪ
onlɪ ædɪkwət gaɪd tu kərɛkt prənʌnsɪeʃən ɪz ðə jusɪdʒ əv ðoz pipl̩ hu ar goɪŋ tu
pæs dʒʌdʒmənt an ju‖ juz ðə spitʃ əproprɪət tu ðə rol ju ple ɪn ðə grups ɪn hwɪtʃ
ju faɪnd jurɛlf‖‖

Transcription passage

Every speaker is judged in part by his pronunciation. John Ruskin once said, "A false accent or a mistaken syllable is enough, in the parliament of any civilized nation, to assign to a man a certain degree of inferior standing forever." Throughout our life we are acquiring new words. We find ourselves embarrassed by the social penalities we receive for mispronunciation. Phonetic training aids greatly in the prevention of this distress. Once you have written out an unfamiliar word in phonetic script you can be pretty sure that future errors will be rare. However, it would be wise for all of us to take inventory of our pronouncing skills occasionally.

Reading passage

[æz wi hæv sɛd bɪfɔr sʌm prənʌnsɪeʃənz ar pɚmɪsəbl̩ æt wʌn lɛvl̩ əv fɔrmælɪtɪ
hwɛn ðe wud bi pinəlaɪzd æt ənʌðɚ‖ mɔrovɚ sɚtn jusɪdʒɪz ar æksɛptəbl̩ ɪn wʌn
ɛrɪə hwɪtʃ wud bi rɪdʒɛktɪd ɪn ənʌðɚ‖ sʌm əv aur wɚdz hæv nat æz jɛt ətend ɛnɪ
kəmplit æksɛptəns bʌt hæv vɛrɪənt fɔrmz‖ ɛnɪ əv hwɪtʃ ɪz sætɪsfæktɔrɪ‖ ʌðɚ wɚdz
ar ɪn ðə prasɛs əv tʃendʒ‖ bʌt dʒɛnɚəlɪ ðə most kamən fɔlts ar θri ɪn nʌmbɚ‖
æksɛntɪŋ ðə rɔŋ sɪləbl̩ slɚɪŋ ðə wɚd so ðæt sʌm ɪsɛnʃəl saund ɪz lɔst‖ ænd ɛmplɔɪɪŋ
ðə rɔŋ fonɪm‖ sʌm pipl̩ mek mɪstɛks bɪkɔz ðe ar tu kɛrfəl ænd gɪv sɚtn saundz
strɛs hwɛn ðe ʃudnt‖ ɔfn̩ ðɪs ɪz du tu ðə spɛlɪŋ əv ðə wɚd ɪnvalvd‖ ʌðɚ rizənz
fɔr ɛrɚz ar ʃir kɛrlɪsnəs‖ pur madl̩z‖ plen ɪgnɚəns‖ ɔr no motɪveʃən fɔr bɛtɚ spitʃ‖‖]

Exercise 10.3.   Here are some commonly mispronounced familiar words. Transcribe them correctly and incorrectly. *Example:* again [əgɛn][əgɪn]

been	————	————	catch	————	————
get	————	————	for	————	————
ate	————	————	sure	————	————
just	————	————	poor	————	————
can	————	————	your	————	————
kept	————	————	figure	————	————
picture	————	————	singer	————	————
had	————	————	when	————	————
something	————	————	such	————	————
what	————	————	nothing	————	————
why	————	————	fellow	————	————
where	————	————	pretty	————	————
next	————	————	once	————	————
umbrella	————	————	film	————	————
asked	————	————	always	————	————
last	————	————	best	————	————
belong	————	————	recognize	————	————
theatre	————	————			

Exercise 10.4.   Which word of these pairs of words would be appropriate in formal speaking? Underline the appropriate one.

1. maʊntən   maʊən   6. əgɛnst   əgɪnst
2. tɝəbl̩   tɛrɪbl̩   7. numrəs   numɚəs
3. ɪnsɪs: ɪnsɪsts   8. hɪstɚɪ   hɪstrɪ
4. ɔrdnɚɪ   ɔrdɪnɛrɪ   9. pɚhæps   præps
5. kʊdʒə   kʊd ju   10. spoz   səpoz

Exercise 10.5.   Transcribe these words, using pronunciations for formal speech.

1. leisure _____	2. serious _____
3. policeman _____	4. probably _____
5. regular _____	6. research _____
7. revenue _____	8. picture _____
9. violence _____	10. poor _____
11. wrestle _____	12. accurate _____
13. suggest _____	14. capital _____
15. such _____	16. chocolate _____
17. somebody _____	18. data _____
19. secretary _____	20. elite _____

The people of the United States speak more uniformly than those of almost any other foreign country. Most of our children go to public schools. With millions of automobiles and many miles of good roads, we travel widely and frequently, visiting every corner of the nation. The radio, movies, television, and telephone link each community with every other one. Dialects are the product of isolation and there is little of it here. In Great Britain small communities are closely knit and they cling tenaciously to the speech peculiarities and variations which a thousand years have fostered. America is a melting pot and the speech which is spoken here is unusually homogeneous.

haʊɛvɚ æt ðə prɛznt̩ taɪm ðɛr ɛgzɪst θri medʒɚ ɛriəz wɪθ rɪdʒənəl spitʃ dɪfrənsɪz| ði ist| ðə saʊθ| ænd ðə dʒɛnɚəl əmɛrɪkən|| əbaut ɪlɛvən mɪljən pipl juz ði istɚn spitʃ əv nu ɪŋglənd ænd mɛtrəpalɪtən nu jɔrk|| twɛntɪsɪks mɪljən juz ðə sʌðɚn daɪəlɛkt ænd mɔr ðæn naɪntɪ mɪljən ðə dʒɛnɚəl əmɛrɪkən|| wi ɔl kæn ʌndɚstænd itʃ ʌðɚ bʌt wi rɛkəgnaɪz ði əpraksɪmət lokælɪtɪ frəm hwɪtʃ ɛni pɚsən kʌmz baɪ lɪsnɪŋ tu hɪz prənʌnsieʃən|| ɪn ðɪs ɛlɪmɛntɚɪ tɛkst wi du nat ɪntɛnd tu dɪskʌs ðə diteld spitʃ kɛrɪktɚɪstɪks əv itʃ rɪdʒən ɔr ðə sʌb daɪəlɛkts faund ðɛrɪn|| nɛvɚðəlɛs ə fju dɪstɪŋgwɪʃɪŋ fitʃɚz me bi notɪd||

ɪn istɚn spitʃ ðə brɔd ɑ saund ɪz ɔfn̩ juzd ɪn wɝdz hwɛr ə spikɚ əv dʒɛnɚəl əmɛrɪkən wʊd juz æ|| ðə nu ɪŋglɛndɚ tɛndz tu se past fɔr pæst ænd dans fɔr dæns|| hi ɔlso ɔfn̩ drɑps hɪz faɪnəl ɚ saundz ænd juzɪz ðə ʃwa vauəl ə ɪnstɛd| seɪŋ mʌðə| tɛə| ænd foə|| ði æksɛntɪd ɝ ɪz dʒɛnɚəli ɜ æz ɪn bɜd| θɜd| ænd fɜðɚ|| ə gud dil əv əsɪmɪleʃən nezælɪtɪ ɪz hɝd ɪn ðɪs spitʃ|| ðə vauəlz a ænd ɒ ar prevələnt||

ɪn sʌðɚn spitʃ ðɛr ar junik dɪfrənsɪz ɪn ðə mænɚ əv artɪkjuleʃən|| sʌðɚnɚz lɛŋkθən sɝtn̩ vauəlz ænd dɪfθɔŋz|| ðe mek ðə sɪŋgl̩ vauəlz əv dʒɛnɚəl əmɛrɪkən ɪntu dɪfθɔŋz ænd ðə dɪfθɔŋz ɪntu trɪfθɔŋz|| ði artɪkjuleʃən ɪz mɔr læks ænd ʌnprisaɪs ænd ɪt ɪz ðɪs ræðɚ ðæn ðə ret ɔr spid əv spitʃ hwɪtʃ kɛrɪktɚaɪzɪz ðə sʌðɚn drɔl|| laɪk ði istɚnɚz ðe ɔfn̩ juz ðə ʃwa ə fɔr ði ʌnæksɛntɪd vauəl ɚ æz ɪn sɪstə|| ði ɜ ɪn ði æksɛntɪd saund æz ɪn wɝd|| ðə sɛntɚɪ dɪfθɔŋz [ar] [ɔr] [ɛr] ar juzʊəli prədust baɪ prolɔŋɪŋ ðə fɝst saund ɔr baɪ ʃwaɪŋ ðə sɛkənd|| ə gud dil əv nezælɪtɪ ɪz hɝd ɑn ðɪ æ fonim ænd sʌmtaɪmz ðə dɪfθɔŋz [eə] ɔr [ɛə] ɑr juzd ɪnstɛd|| ðɪ [ɔ] saʊnd ɪn wɝdz laɪk gɔn tʃendʒɪz tu æn [oʊ] so ðæt wi hɪr sɛntənsɪz sʌtʃ æz hi ɪz goʊn oʊn rɪliəf| mʌtʃ mɔr frikwəntlɪ ðæn ɪn dʒɛnɝəl əmɛrɪkən|| ðə spikɝ frəm bɪlo ðə mesən dɪksən laɪn juzɪz ə [j] saʊnd bɪfɔr [u]||| ðɛr ɑr mɛnɪ ʌðɝ vɛrɪeʃənz hwɪtʃ kʊd bi mɛnʃənd bʌt ju kæn faɪnd ðɪs ɪnfɝmeʃən ɪn ʌðɝ tɛksts||

Exercise 10.6.   Reading passage. Substandard general American speech.

A. hi dʒɪs kʊnt rɛkənaɪz də pɪtʃɝ əv ɪz pɛrnts kəz hi hænt sin əm fɝ twɛnɪ jɪr|| sə gʊd pɪtʃɝ tu|| ðə ditel ɪn ɪt wʌz pətɪkɝlɪ klɪr|| jə kən si ðə mʌðɝ n̩ fadɝ ɝ stænɪn ðɛr ɪn də opm̩ dɔrwel|| smoks kʌmən aʊdədə tʃɪmblɪ| əkrɔst də bækədə pɪtʃɝ sʌmənz rɪtn̩ dɪs lɪl sʌdʒɛstn̩ ɛf jə don mɛmbɝ jɝ fæmblɪ jent no dʒɛnjuaɪn kɪnfok nohaʊ||

B. də rɛglɝ kɑlətʃ stu:nts dɪnt laɪk ðə nuz fɪləm de so læs sædəde|| ʃod ɑr krul plis juzɪn ðə far hoz tə bʌst ʌp də pardɪ ɪn frʌnədə θietɝ|| ðə tɛmpətʃɝ wʌz rɪlɪ frizn̩ dæ naɪ n̩ ðə pɔr stu:nts ʃor ga sokt wɪ wadɝ|| bɛt mɪnɪ əv əm kɛtʃ ə kol|| de ʃʊnədʌndæ||

Although we Americans are tending to speak more and more alike, a great deal of attention is now being focused on helping blacks and chicanos alter their speech patterns to a closer approximation to "standard" English. Below are transcriptions from tape recordings of black and chicano speakers.

Black English

[ɑ 'dɪtn̩ wɔn tə si freɪd leɪd aʊt kol̩ n̩ deɪd|| ðə kiɪd hi seɪ freɪd 'barə dʒɛf kɑ: n̩| wæəl| hi dɪtn̩ æks hɪm fʌ:s|| naʊ hi deɪd|||]

I didn't want to see Fred laid out cold and dead. The kid (he) said Fred borrowed Jeff's car and, well, he didn't ask him first. Now he's dead.

Chicano

[ma'ɹia no is hɪr|| ʃi is mɔɹ lɛt ðan 'xɔɹge|| hi go tu bi mad̩ kəz hi hɔŋgrɪ|||]

Maria is not here. She is later than George. He is going to be mad because he is hungry.

(The [x] is a voiced fricative [h] sound produced by humping the back of the tonque against the soft palate.)

Here are some words which are often given substandard mispronunciations. Transcribe how they would be mispronounced. The answers to all of them will be found on the next page.

1. apron	____	21. family	____	41. since	____
2. fifths	____	22. genuine	____	42. sound	____
3. couldn't	____	23. history	____	43. dirty	____
4. recognize	____	24. yes	____	44. strength	____
5. coming	____	25. just	____	45. such	____
6. regular	____	26. kept	____	46. suggest	____
7. across	____	27. little	____	47. temperature	____
8. adult	____	28. open	____	48. theater	____
9. burst	____	29. our	____	49. this	____
10. catch	____	30. chorus	____	50. toward	____
11. chimney	____	31. party	____	51. thirty	____
12. clothes	____	32. poem	____	52. water	____
13. college	____	33. police	____	53. yellow	____
14. cruel	____	34. picture	____	54. casual	____
15. data	____	35. positively	____	55. often	____
16. deaf	____	36. really	____	56. poor	____
17. details	____	37. once	____	57. again	____
18. eighths	____	38. Saturday	____	58. won't	____
19. film	____	39. route	____	59. another	____
20. finally	____	40. secretary	____	60. didn't	____

1. epən
2. fiθs
3. kʊnt
4. rɛkənaɪz
5. kʌmɪn
6. rɛglɚ
7. əkrɔst
8. 'ædəlt
9. bʌst
10. kɛtʃ
11. tʃɪmlɪ
12. kloz
13. kɔlətʃ
14. krʊl
15. dætə
16. dif
17. 'ditelz
18. ets
19. fɪləm
20. faɪnlɪ

21. fæmblɪ
22. dʒɛnjuaɪn
23. hɪstrɪ
24. jis
25. dʒɪst
26. kɛp
27. lɪl
28. opm̩
29. ɑr
30. kɔrs
31. pɑrdɪ
32. pom
33. plis
34. pɪtʃɚ
35. pɑztɪvlɪ
36. rilɪ
37. wʌnst
38. sædədɪ
39. raʊt
40. sɛkətɛrɪ

41. sɛns
42. saʊn
43. dɚdɪ
44. strɛnθ
45. sɪtʃ sɛtʃ
46. sədʒɛst
47. tɛmpətsʊr
48. θietɚ
49. dɪs
50. tʊward
51. θɚdɪ
52. wadɚ
53. jɛlə
54. kæʒəl
55. ɔftən
56. pɔr
57. əgɪn
58. won
59. nʌdɚ
60. dɪnt

It is difficult to generalize about eastern American English, since within the region where it is spoken there are many differing pronunciations. We recognize immediately the distinctive Yankee flavor of coastal New England, the twang of the Vermonter. Perhaps this is due to the fact that it has more local tradition and insularity of standards than the remainder of the country. Perhaps, too, it is due to the fact that the "Cabots speak only to God," and doubtless in His language. But we are primarily concerned with the ability to read and write these dialectal variations.

The use of [ɑ] for [æ] in such words as *class* or *laugh* is one of the major characteristics of Eastern speech. Regarding this, Mark Twain is quoted as saying, "When I say *ass* with a broad *a*, I feel like an ass with a flat *a*." Many speakers of Eastern English, however, use the vowel [a] in such contexts. In turn the [ɑ] becomes [ɔ] or [ɒ] in such words as *warm* and *horrible*. The schwa [ə] is used regularly instead of the [ɚ] in centering diphthongs and unstressed syllables, and [ɜ] is used instead of [ɝ] in the accented ones. Some of the twang characteristic of New England is due to the use of the nasalized [æ̃ɪ] for the [aɪ] diphthong.

Let us review these key sounds a bit before proceeding to examples of the speech of Eastern New England.

[a]

This vowel [a], often called the broad *a* sound, is the lowest of the front vowels. Many of our midwestern students seem to be able to produce it most easily by assuming the mouth posture for an [æ] and then attempting to produce an [ɑ] through this [æ] shaped cavity. The best key words for native Yankee speakers seem to be *ask*—not [æsk] but [ask], and *park*—not [pɑrk] but [paːk]. Many Southerners use this vowel in such words as *five* [faːv].

[ɜ]

This is the nonretroflexed vowel used only in stressed syllables. It is used in the same way as we use the [ɝ] in general American speech. The front part of the tongue for [ɜ] remains almost flat in the mouth.

[ɒ]

This is the back vowel, about midway between [ɑ] and [ɔ]. By placing the mouth in the proper formation to make the one and then uttering the other, an approximation to the sound can be had by speakers to whom it is foreign. It is used, as we shall see, in such words as *frog*, *bomb*, and *lot*.

While these contrasting vowels constitute major characteristics of eastern American speech, there are many other variants as well. Indeed, in an introductory text like this it would be unwise to attempt to describe them all, and it would probably be an impossible task for not only are there subdialects within a region, but also individual differences in usage. All we should do here is to point out some of the variations from general American speech which you should look for. There will be others.

Watch for the presence of diphthongs as [ɪu] in *do* [dɪu], [æʊ] or [ãʊ] in *cow* or *now* [k'æʊ], [nãʊ], and such unusual vowels as [ö] or [ʌ'] in words like *home* [höm] [hʌ'm].

Note the frequent use of the intervocalic consonantal [r] in such words as *carry* [ka·rɨ], *very* [vɛ·rɪ], tourist [tʼʊ·rɪst]. These speakers often break up the centering diphthongs and begin the final syllable of a two-syllable word not with a vowel, but with the [r]. They say [flatərɨ], not [flætəˑi]. This will be especially noticeable in connected speech.

You will also discover what is known as the *intrusive r*. It is used to link a word ending in the schwa [ə] with a following word beginning with another vowel. President Kennedy's speech, like that of many educated New Englanders, had many of these intrusive [r]'s in it. Here is one example: [ðɪ aɪdɨ (ɚ, ɜ, ɪr) ɪz ðɪs‖]. The intrusive sound may be any one of those in the parenthesis.

Samples of eastern American speech

1. ðə hwaɪt-tʼɜkɪ med sʌtʃ ə nɒɪz ðɪ fɑ·mə ləft‖ hɪ ɒlmoʊst skɛɪd hɪz hɔ·s haf aʊt əv hɪz wɪts‖ gis n̩ tɜkʼɪz mɛ·k mɒ·nɒɪz| ðen ðe ɑ ɪntaɪtɫd tu‖
The white turkey made such a noise the farmer laughed. He almost scared his horse half out of his wits. Geese and turkeys make more noise than they are entitled to.

2. aʊə pastʼə| oʊvəˈkʌm baɪ hɪz oʊn ɛlokwɪnts| bɪgan tu wip'‖ ju hav ðɪ ʃɒ·tʼ ɪst mɛmərɨz fɔ ðɪ wɜd əv gɒd ɣ ɛnɪ pipɫ sɪnts sɒdm̩ n̩ gomɒ·rə‖ wə·ɫ| sɛd old man bɛ·kɪt| ɛz hi lɛft ðə tʃɜtʃ‖ aʊə rɛvrɪnd ʃʊə kʌvəd ə lɒt əv hɪstərɪ ɪn hɪz hɪstɛ·rɪks ðɪs mɒ·nɪn‖
Our pastor, overcome by his own eloquence, began to weep. "You have the shortest memories for the Word of God of any people since Sodom and Gomorra!" "Well," said old man Becket as he left the church, "Our reverend sure covered a lot of history in his hysterics this morning."

3. hi hʊ sʌps wɪ·ðɪ dɛvɪl ʃʊd hɛv ə lɒŋ spʼun‖
He who sups with the devil should have a long spoon.

4. at na·t ɒl kats ɑ· greɪ| ɪksɛp fɔ· ðɪ tɒmz‖
At night all cats are gray—except for the toms.

5. ɪts ə lɒŋ rod ðət hɛz noʊ tɜnɪn| and n̩ ʌld wa·ɪf huz tʌŋz stɒpt bɜnɪn‖
It's a long road that has no turning, and an old wife whose tongue's stopped burning.

6. la·tnɪn·ɛvə stɹaɪks twa·ɪs ɪn ðɪ sɛɪm ples| wʌnts ɪz ɪnʌf‖
Lightning never strikes twice in the same place. Once is enough.

7. ðɪ wʊdz ʃɪməd ɪn ðɪ·ivnɪn briz| ðɪ stɒ·z glimd n̩ old man kɑ·tə snɒ·d z̩ jʊʒl‖
The woods shimmered in the evening breeze; the stars gleamed, and old man Carter snored as usual.

8. ðə bʊtʃə kʌt ðə mɨt so kɹʊkɪd aɪ kʊd hɑ·dlɪ tɛɫ hwɛə tə sta·t ɒn ɪt‖
The butcher cut the meat so crooked I could hardly tell where to start on it.

More samples of eastern speech[3]

1. if ə pr̥ɪtʃə z̩ mɒə ɪntʼrəstʼɪd ɪn·ɪnkwãɪərɪŋ əbæut maɪ sɪnz ðn̩ ɪn maɪ hɛlθ| hiːz fẽɪlɪn ɪn hɪz wɛkʼ| and aɪ·m̩ nɒt goʊɪn tə hɪz tʃɜtʃ‖

---

[3] For other reading passages showing the eastern dialect, see the old book by Avery, Dorsey, and Sickels, *First Principles of Speech Training*, Englewood Cliffs, N.J.: Prentice Hall, 1928.

2. aɪ θɔt ju sɛd jə sɪstə wɒznt‘ ət houm‖ aɪl bɪliv ə sɪlɪ dʒaka:s bɪfoə aɪl bɪliv ju frəm næʊ ɒn‖

3. ɛz ə nju:lɪ əlɛktɪd rɛprɪzɛntətɪv tu kɒŋgrɪs‖ aɪ prɒmɪs tu ansə ðə lɛtə:z ju sɛn:tə mi‖ nou matə hæʊ stɪupɪd ðe: ɒə‖

Exercise 10.7.   Transcribe this into general American dialect. It is the way a Boston actor read a poem by Matthew Arnold. The poem is, "Shakespeare."

ʌðəz əbaɪd aʊə kwɛstʃn̩‖ ðaʊ ɑ:t fri
wi ask ənd ask‖ ðaʊ smaɪlist ənd ɑ: stɪl‖
aʊtɑpɪŋ nɒlɪdʒ‖ fɔ ðɪ lɒftɪɪst hɪl‖
hu tu ðɪ stɑ:z ənkɪɑʊnz hɪz madʒɪstɪ‖
plantɪŋ hɪz stɛdfast fʊtstɛps ɪn ðə si‖
meɪkɪŋ ðɪ hɛvn̩ əv hɛvn̩ hɪz dwɛlɪŋ pleɪs‖
spɛ:əz bʌt ðə klaʊdɪ bɔ:də əv hɪz beɪs
tu ðə fɔɪld sɜtʃɪŋ əv mɒʰtælɪtɪ‖

Eastern American English seems to be a bit closer to the standard British of the upper classes. We submit samples of both for comparison.

istən əmɛrɪkən stedʒ spitʃ
tu bi‖ ɔ nɒt tu bi‖ ðat ɪz ðə kwɛstʃɪn‖ hwɛðə tɪz noublə ɪn ðə maɪnd‖ tu sʌfə slɪŋz n̩d ærouz əv aʊtredʒɪs fɔtʃən‖ ɔ tu teɪk ɑmz əgenst ə si əv trʌblz‖ n̩d baɪ əpouzɪŋ ɛnd ðɛm‖

ʃeɪkspɪə

brɪtɪʃ spitʃ
ðə kwɛst‖ fə ðɪ əbɒmɪnəbl̩ snomən wi həd wɒtʃt wɪð kənsɪdrəbl̩ ɪntrɪst‖ sɪmɪlə ɪlju:ʒənz həv hɒntɪd mɛn θru ɛvrɪ steɪdʒ əv sɪvɪlaɪzeʃn̩‖ ɪt simz wi mʌst rɛzəljutlɪ tʃeɪs sʌm fæbjələs mɪrɑ:ʒ ouvə ðə maʊntɪnz ənd fɑ: əweɪ‖ ðɪs dʌz nɒt ɪmplaɪ ðat mɪstərɪ ɪz nɪsɛsɪtɪ‖ ɪt ɪz mɪəlɪ aʊə dɪzaɪə fɔ wɪŋz‖

As in general American or any other dialect, it is possible to speak substandardly in New England. In the following exercise are given some of the substandard pronunciations heard in rural New England by one of the authors.

Exercise 10.8.   Word matching. In the space following each numbered word place the letter which corresponds to the proper pronunciation of the word. Number one is solved for you.

a. point	b. scarce	c. skinned	d. just	e. well
f. drew	g. haven't	h. broom	i. can	j. potatoes
k. whole	l. borrowed	m. calculate	n. rather	o. been
p. pretty	q. scared	r. get	s. hold	t. you
u. asked	v. boil	w. had	x. from	y. boy
z. ideas				

1. hɛd __w__   2. teɪtɪz _____   3. skun _____
4. hʌl _____   5. fʌm _____   6. skeɪt _____
7. rʌðə _____   8. æst _____   9. bɛn _____
10. gɪt _____   11. dʒɛst _____   12. kɪn _____
13. wæəl _____   14. brum _____   15. paɪnt _____
16. hoult _____   17. baɪ _____   18. aɪdɪəz _____

19. jɪ _____   20. drɔd _____   21. skeɪs _____
22. heɪnt _____   23. bɒrɚd _____   24. pʊtɪ _____
25. kælet _____   26. bəɪl _____

SOUTHERN SPEECH

Southern speech seems to be concentrated in the area below Maryland that borders on the Atlantic and the Gulf of Mexico, but because we Americans are highly mobile people it can be heard anywhere. Even more than in New England, many subdialects exist. The speech of the mountaineers in southern Appalachia is very different from those who live in the lowlands, and there is a small inland island area in South Carolina and Georgia where a Gullah dialect is spoken that is almost completely unintelligible to those of us who use general American English. Indeed, there are so many local variations that it is hard to generalize about the characteristic features of southern speech and, moreover, the influence of television and radio seems to be modifying those characteristics in the direction of general American usage. In this book we are mainly interested in helping students to recognize and transcribe varieties of speech rather than to identify them geographically.

Most of us, however, seem to be able to know from his or her speech if a person was raised or has lived in the South. We say that he has a "southern drawl" which may mean a slower rate of utterance, or a greater use of diphthongs or triphthongs, both of which do seem to occur. But there are other contrasts too. Let us provide some samples first, then discuss them.

1. aːv goən foːə wɔək ɛn ði wuədz iɫtʃ moːnɪn| sɪɛnts aːsoud mə lɪːɫ kɑː‖ aːfiɪl kæɪndə sɪːlɪ tə bi sou badlɪ ɔgɪnæɪzd| bʌt aːswɛːə aːm hɛəl̥θɪ̶ə ðɪn aːv bɪn foː jiəz‖
I've gone for a walk in the woods each morning since I sold my little car. I feel kind of silly to be so badly organized but I swear I'm healthier than I've been for years.

2. hwʌtʃɪu skɛəd əbæut ðɛt lɪːl̩ ouɫ gɒːdɪn sneɪk‖ eːɪn gonə hɜtʃə nʌn‖ dountʃə bɪ sou sɪːlɪ‖
What are you scared about that little garden snake? (It) aint going to hurt you none. Don't you be so silly.

3. mɑ kɪɑ dʒɪs wõ stɑːt ðɪs mounɪn no weɪ‖
My car just won't start this morning—no way.

4. aː geɪs aːəɫ dʒɪs hɛv tə woək tə ði stoː| ənlɛs aː kɪn kɪtʃ mɪ ə raəd wɪ ðə mɪn hwʌts goːwɪn tə wɜk‖
I guess I'll just have to walk to the store unless I can catch me a ride with the men what's going to work.

5. wɛn ɪz waːf daːd jo mæmɪ tuk ouvə n̩ rejɪzd juːənz læk hɜ ouən kɪn‖ aːspɛks hɪt wɜkt æut dʒɪs faːn| kəz ʃɫ gɒt moː tʃɪlən n̩ ðɛt sæsɪfaːd hɜ dʒɪs fæɪn| mɪnɪ tʃɪlən n̩ nou mæːɪdʒ‖ dɪdn̩ hɛv tu gɪt mɛːrɪd noːweɪ‖
When his wife died your mother took over and raised "you-uns" like her own kin. I expect it worked out just fine, because she got more children and that satisfied her just fine—many children and no marriage. Didn't have to get married, no way.

We are pretty certain that many southerners would insist that they would never have spoken as these speakers did and we are sure that they would be speaking the truth, for again let us call attention to the tremendous variation in pronunciation which exists in this southern dialect at this time. In defense, we can say that the samples were recorded on audiotapes, and that we played them repeatedly before doing our transcription. But let us examine the ways that this speech contrasts with the general American dialect.

First of all we note, especially in the centering diphthongs, that many of them are monothongal, the second sound dropping out after the first vowel is prolonged. Southerners tend to say the words *farm* and *pork* as [fɑːm] and [poːk] or [pɔːək]. You will need to use the colon frequently when transcribing southern speech.

Secondly, we find the substitution of the [ɜ] for the [ɝ] and the [ə] for [ɚ] to be pretty consistent (though an occasional [ɝ] can sometimes be heard). These speakers say [aː prɪfɜ bʌtə raðə ŏṇ mɑːdʒɝɪn]. The centering diphthongs often end in the schwa but you may find some other unusual ones such as (ʊɔ) in *you-all* [juːɔl], [ɜə] in *third* [θɜəd], [ɔə] or [ɑə] in *hawk*, [oə] in *order* [oədə] or *poke* [poək], and [æʊ] as in *thousand* [θæʊzɪnd].

The intrusive *r* is not found in southern speech as it is in that of the Northeast, but we often hear the same breaking of the centering diphthong in which the [r] is used to begin a new syllable, for example, *Florida* [flɑːrɪdə], sorry [sɑːrɪ] or [sɒːrɪ], and *oranges*, pronounced as [ɒːrɪndʒɪz].

We find triphthongs, too, as in *made* [meɪəd] or *head* [heɪəd] or *fail* [feɪəl]. In the very deep South, and especially in substandard speech, many sentences will have a triphthong in them of one form or another. Sometimes these triphthongs are broken up by the glide [j] as in the word *bale*, to turn the monosyllabic word into a bisyllabic one [beɪjəl].

The final sound in *city* and all other similar words should be recorded either as [ɪ] or [ɨ] and not as [i], for it belongs to the [ɪ] phoneme in southern speech. We hear [sɪtɪ] and [pr̩ɪtɪ] and [ɛɪkstʼɪsɪ]. There are other vowel changes, too, so many that we will not attempt to list more than a few. Our general American [ɛ] is often replaced with [a] or [ɪ] or even [e]. *Mary* may become [meɪrɪ], *carry* becomes [kærɪ], and *tense* becomes [tʼɪns] or [tɛɪns]. We hear *many* pronounced as [mɪnɪ mɪnɪ taːmz]. *Hog* and *dog*, often spelled *hawg* and *dawg* to indicate a special vowel sound, should probably be transcribed as [hɔʼg] or [dɔ˞gʼ], using the [ʼ] mark to indicate the pronounced lip rounding of the vowel, or using the [˞] to show that the tongue is more retracted than usual. But information, like all things, is subject to the law of diminishing returns, and you have probably learned more for the moment than you need or desire. So we will proceed with some reading and transcription exercises, and call it quits.

[gəˈbaɪ mɪz dʒoənz| jɪu goːɪn tə mɨɪs mɪ| aːhoʊp|| dõ bɪ skeəd næʊ| dʒɪs kɔəl mɪ ɛf jɪu wɔːnt mɪ|| ɛvɪθɪnz hwɛə jɪu kɪn fæɪnd ɪt|| gəˈbaɪ næʊ| aːv gɒtə hʌrɪ||]
Goodbye, Mrs. Jones. You're going to miss me, I hope. Don't be scared now. Just call me if you want me. Everything's where you can find it. Goodbye now. I've got to hurry.

[ðeᴛəz sʌmpɪn əbæʊt əˈfɑːəpleɪs ðɛt dʒɪs kɔəlz fə bɜːbɪn ṇ breɪəntʃ wɔːtə| tʊ hɑːtɪn ðɪ spɪːrɪt| ṇ tə koəz ðɪ mɪzrɨz tə dɪsɪpɪə|| tʃɪəfl̩nɪs kɪn bɪ fæundʼ ɪvṇ on ə mɪzr̩ɪbl̩ deɪ ɛf ðeːəz ə fɑːəpleɪs||]
There's something about a fireplace that just calls for bourbon and branch water to hearten the spirit and to cause the miseries to disappear. Cheerfulness can be found even on a miserable day if there's a fireplace.

[əv koəs a læɪk lɪlɪz əv ðɪ vælɪ| bʌt aːdʒɪs ədoː tjulɪps iɪvṇ moːə|| ðeəz sʌmθɪn əbæʊt siːɪn ðɪm ɛn ðɪ jɒəd on ə naːs sprɪŋ deɪ| ðɛt meːɪks mɨ woʊnt-tʊ læɪjəf|| aː dʒɪs keɪnt hɛp woʊntɪn tə sɪŋ ṇ dæːɪnts||]

Of course I like lilies of the valley, but I just adore tulips even more. There's something about seeing them in the yard on a nice spring day that makes me want to laugh. I just want to sing and dance.

[mɪrændɪ ʃʌt ðɛt doː| ɪts bǽʊt-tǽɪm foˑ joˑ poˑoʊld pæpɪ tʊ goʊ dǽʊn tǽʊn| bʌt fɜst hiːz goːntə hɛv tʊ kɛtʃ ɪz bɹɛf‖]

Miranda, shut that door! It's about time for your poor old father to go down town, but first he's going to have to catch his breath.

(The above samples of southern speech were tape recorded in a small town in Alabama.)

Below are three sentences, each written in a different dialect. Read them aloud, then label each general American, eastern, or southern.

1. [tɒm tɜnd fɜst tə ðə kɒːnə əv ðə rum bifɔː askɪŋ|
   dɪu ju θɪŋk ɪts ə gʊd aɪdɨ˞ tə go wɒkɪŋ ɪn ðə paːk||] _____

2. [dɪdʒə nou ðət kɚɛkt spitʃ z̩ mɪrlɪ ðæt
   hwitʃ ɪz æksɛptɪd baɪ ðə klæs əv pipl̩ wi ədmaɪr ðə most||] _____

3. [aː keɪnt bɛː tə si sæ̃lɪ flɜːtɪn wɪð ɔəl ðouz
   bɔːɪz| ʃiz goːnə gɪt-tɜːrɪblɨ hɜt hwɪn ðeːɪ læːɪf ət hɜː||] _____

Transcribe the following words.

1. As a southerner would say them.   forever   _____

    mercy   _____

    can't   _____

    my aunt   _____

2. As an easterner would say them.   murder   _____

    anchor   _____

    desire   _____

    laugh   _____

1. eastern

2. general American

3. southern

aː keɪnt si maːaːɪnt
fɔːɛvə æɪt jɔː mɜːsɪ

maɪ dɪːə| ðɪ aɪdɪər əv
mɜːdə wɪð ŋ aŋkə ʃəd nɒt
fɪl jɪu wɪð ə dɪzaɪə
tə laːf

1. fɔːɛvə
   mɜːsɪ
   keɪnt
   maːaːɪnt
2. mɜːdə
   aŋkə
   dɪzaɪə
   laːf

Name ——————— *Date* ——————— *Score* ———————

Hand this in to your instructor.

1. Transcribe this into general American, informal speech.

   Experts now think that when we say something, the brain selects the grammatical framework for the thought, and then it chooses specific words to express it.

2. Now, try to put this into eastern New England speech.

   Proof that grammatical structure comes first can be found in slips of the tongue. The Reverand Dr. William Spooner once said, "the queer old dean," when he meant to say, "the dear old queen." He also is the one who said, "you have tasted the whole worm," when he thought he was saying, "you have wasted the whole term."

3. Try your hand at what is often slanderously called "New York cabdriver" language.

   When I say, "the early bird," I don't mean that black stuff you put in your crankcase. I'm saying that he gets up before Mervin who lives in Long Island.

4. Transcribe into some facsimile of southern speech.

Northern papers never weary of making merry over the southern style of sounding the letter *r*. All the same, the southern pronunciation is correct. The Yankee habit of walloping the letter around before turning it loose is just Yankee and nothing else. There is no reason why the letter should be pronounced in capital in the middle of a word, nor for turning it over and over in the mouth, nor for delaying the conversation in order to elaborate the sound thereof. The southerner sounds the letter *r* and then lets it go. He has no more use for it. He dismisses it promptly but politely. The Yankee lingers with it at the door, shakes it by both hands, weeps on its neck, kisses it goodbye, and watches it around the corner as though the two should never meet again. Every letter in the alphabet and every sound in the language must be kept waiting while the Yankee is slavering and licking his favorite letter as though he were a mother cow and the letter *r* his new born calf.[4]

[4] Edward Ward Camack, *Memphis Commercial*, July 9, 1893.

11 Abnormal Speech and Foreign Dialect

DISORDERS OF ARTICULATION

One of the first tasks that confronts the student in speech pathology as he begins his practicum is to administer and score articulation tests. Without any background in phonetics it would be almost impossible to understand or analyze the results of such testing, but by now you should have no trouble. Certainly, you will be able to identify the abnormally produced phonemes. However, to be a skillful clinician you should also be able to recognize the features of those allophones of the sound which may indicate the direction that therapy should take. Clients with articulation errors do not always make the same replacement for the standard sound in all contexts. Some come closer than others, and often in certain phonetic contexts we can get the person to produce the sound immediately. Again, since the desired sound is often acquired gradually through a series of approximations, it is important that you are able to identify them and to know when the person is progressing toward its mastery.

In our first illustration, we present a transcription of some of the responses made by a client as he was given the Templin–Darley test.[1] His main difficulty lay in the production of the [r] phoneme, but please note and summarize not only the correct production of these sounds in certain phonetic contexts, but also the different kinds of errors.

Exercise 11.1.   Analysis of [r] errors.

rabbit [r̠ˈæbət]   paper [peɪpə]   horn [hoən]
bread [bwɛd]   rubber [wʌbə]   sharp [ʃɑːp]
tree [t̠ɹi]   doctor [dɑktə]   curb [kɝb]
dress [dwɛs]   ladder [wædə]   heart [hɑːt]
crayons [k̠ɹeɪjənz]   cracker [kɹækə]   card [kɑːd]
grass [gwæs]   tiger [taɪgʊ]   fork [foək]
frog [fʊɔg]   gopher [goufɚ]   scarf [skɑːf]
three [θri]   mother [mʌðɚ]   fourth [foəθ]
shredded wheat [fwɛdɪd wit]   washer [waʃu]   porch [poətʃ]
hammer [hæmə]   arm [ɑːm]   large [lɑːdʒ]

---

[1] The Templin-Darley Tests of Articulation can be procured from the Bureau of Educational Research and Service, University of Iowa, Iowa City, Iowa 52242. Reprinted with permission.

The Templin–Darley Test also contains sentences to be spoken, as the clinician analyzes the errors. Here are four responses.

Ruth was horrified. [wuθ wʌ hɔːfaɪdʻ]
The president enjoyed his breakfast. [ðə pwɛzdənd ɪndʒɔɪd hɪz bwɛkfəst]
Is it true that she has a new dress? [ɪz ɪt twu ðæt ʃi hæz ə nu dɹɛs]
The crayons were blue and green. [ðə kɹejənz wɜ blu n̩ gwin]

Exercise 11.2.   What inconsistencies do you find in comparing the client's responses on individual words with those in connected speech? Be sure to check the phonetic contexts in which some allophones of [r] occur, for only when they are the same can we be sure that the error is consistent.

Another much used instrument for assessing deviant phonemic ability is the McDonald Deep Test of Articulation.[2] It consists of stimulus materials which present each phoneme so that it either precedes or follows each of the other phonemes. When this deep test is given to most persons with articulation disorders, it usually reveals that they can already say the sound correctly—though only in certain phonetic contexts. Primarily, it is based upon the deliberate use of assimilation to facilitate correct phonemic production. We gave this test to the same person whose responses on the Templin–Darley Test were given earlier, and found the following responses. (The word-pairs are to be blended together without pause.)

car–pipe	[ɚp]	[kɑːpaɪp]	cup–rake	[pr]	[kʌpweɪk]
car–bell	[ɚb]	[kɑːbɛl]	tub–rake	[br]	[tʌbweɪk]
car–tie	[ɚt]	[kɑɚtaɪ]	kite–rake	[tr]	[kaɪtreɪk]
car–dog	[ɚd]	[kɑɚdɔg]	bed–rake	[dr]	[bɛdɹeɪk]
car–cow	[ɚk]	[kɑəkaʊ]	duck–rake	[kr]	[dʌkweɪk]
car–gun	[ɚg]	[kɑːgʌn]	pig–rake	[gr]	[pɪgweɪk]
car–moon	[ɚm]	[kɑːmun]	comb–rake	[mr]	[koʊmweɪk]
car–fork	[ɚf]	[kɑəfɔːk]	pin–rake	[nr]	[pɪnreɪk]

Exercise 11.3.   Identify the consonant clusters which showed the correct utterance of the [r] sound.

We also often have to analyze spontaneous speech, as well as isolated words, in order to identify errors. Oral reading passages are not spontaneous enough to give a true picture. Here is the transcription of another client with multiple articulation errors.

[maɪ twʌboʊ ɪ dæt aɪ tænat pwənaʊnt tʌm əb maɪ pit' taʊnd‖ aɪ tæn teɪ tʌm kəwɛkwɪ bʌt nat ʌðʊ‖ ɪt ɪ dɪfɪkut fɔ mɛni pipoʊ tu ʌndətænd mi‖ aː jut tu fɪŋk dæt aɪ wʌ tʌŋ taɪd bʌt ə dɑktə tɛd aɪ wʌʔn̩t‖ aɪ hoʊp maɪ teɪ æt ðə pit kwɪnɪk wɪo kjuə mi‖ aɪ hæ tʊ gɛt ə dɑb n̩ meɪk fwɛnd‖]

Exercise 11.4.   From the above passage, make an analysis of the defective phonemes and the types of error for each.

[2] The McDonald Deep Test of Articulation can be procured from Stanwix House, Inc., 3020 Chartiers Ave., Pittsburgh 4, Pa. Reprinted with permission.

We asked a sixteen-year-old lisper to read this passage, and this is what she said:

[lɪŋgwəl ɔr ɪntɚdɛntl̩ lɪsp]

[ðɪθ θpitʃ dɪfɛkt ɪð du tu ðə θʌbθɪtɪtuʃən əv ðɪ ʌnvɔɪθt θ fɔr ðɪ ɛθ θaʊnd æð ɪn θup| θætɚde| ænd θɪkθtin|| ðə ðɪ θaʊnd ɪð ɔlθo mɪθprənaʊnθt|| ðə pɚθən hu hæð ðɪθ trʌbl̩ θʌbθɪtɪtutθ ðə vɔɪθt ð θaʊnd fɔr ðə ði|| hi θɛð θɪðɚð ænd ðɪpɚð ænd ʌðɚ θʌtʃ wɚdð ɪn ə θɪmɪlɚ fæʃən| əkeʒənl̩ı ðɪ ɛθetʃ ænd ðə [ʒ] θaʊndð ɑr ɔlθo dɪfɛktɪv|| hwɛn ðɪθ əkɚð wi kæn hɪr wɚdð laɪk fæɪθən fiθ ænd meðjur| θʌmtaɪmð ivn̩ ðɪ əfrɪkətɪvð [tʃ] ænd [dʒ] ɑr prəduθt ɪnkərɛktlɪ ænd ju wɪl hɪr θʌtθ θɛntənθɪð æð kætθ ðə pɪtθɚð fæθt bɔl| θʌmtaɪmð ðɪθ lɪθp ɪð trænðɪθənəl ɪn fɔrm|| hwɛn ðɪθ ɪð ðə keθ ju wɪl hɪr θɛntənθɪð laɪk θsælɪ θsold θsʌm səpeʃəlɪ praɪθst səop||]

Some of these interdental lisps are not so consistent. There are also words in which the [θ] or [ð] substitution precedes or follows an acoustically adequate [s] or [z] sound. Omissions of a silibant are not infrequent, and there are times when the [t] or other sound are substituted. And there are usually key words where no sibilant error occurs.

Exercise 11.5.   Analyze the following passage to determine all the different errors or key words.

lɪŋgwəl lɪθpθ me əraɪð æz ə rɪðʌlt əv ædɪnɔɪdð ɔlðo nɑt mɛnɪ səpɪtʃ θerəpɪθt no ðɪs|| ɪt ɪð bɪkʌd ə pɚθsən wɪð ædnɔɪdð bɪkʌmð ə maʊθ briðɚ θɪnθ hi kænt brið aʊt əv hɪz noð|| maʊθ briðɚð het tu kloðz ðer maʊθ ænd so ðə tið ɑr ɔlwɪð pɑrtəd|| ðə tʌŋ tɛndð ðɚrfɔr tu θrʌθt ɪtself bɪtwin ðə tið ænd ən ɪntɚdɛntl̩ lɪθsp ɪðz prəduθt||

List the words in the above passage which fit these patterns.

1. The [θ] is substituted for the [s] or the [ð] for the [z].

_____

2. A transitional [θ] or [ð] *precedes* the [s] or [z].

_____

3. A transitional [θ] or [ð] *follows* the [s] or [z].

_____

4. The [s] and [z] is omitted.

_____

5. A sound other than [θ] or [ð] is used as a substitution for [s] or [z].

_____

There are many other types of lisps; the one most frequently encountered is called the *lateral lisp*. There are two chief varieties of this disorder. In the first, the person produces an unvoiced but fricative *l* sound instead of the *s*, the tongue being placed in contact with the alveolar or upper gum ridge, thus directing the airflow about the sides of the tongue. The modifying mark to indicate this nonvoicing is the tiny circle placed under the symbol. Thus, this type of error would be shown as [l̥]. Such a lateral lisper would say [l̥u l̥old ðə ledɪ ə gul] for "Sue sold the lady a goose." Another variety of this lisp closely akin to [l̥] is represented by the symbol [ɬ]. It is termed an *unvoiced lateral fricative*. It tends to have a bubble of saliva in it. In some instances the person with one of these occluded lateral lisps plugs the airway so that the airstream can emerge on only one side of the tongue. This can be ascertained by tapping the cheeks, first one, then the other, with a forefinger during the utterance of the sound. Some linguists have suggested that the symbol [ɫ] be used for a unilaterally emitted lateral lisp. For the [z] sounds in this latter type of lateral lisp, the person usually substitutes either the [ʃ] or the voiced alveolar fricative [ʒ]. There is a slushy bubbly buzz in it.

      Exercise 11.6.   Read this material as spoken by a lateral lisper who occludes the tongue against the upper gum and forces the air stream out laterally.

> ʌm əv ʌç laɪk tu li fɔɚɪn muvɨz‖ ɛçpɛʃəlɪ ðouʒ meɪd ɪn frǣç‖ ðə gɚlß ɪn ðouʒ
> p̥ɪktjɚ̃ʒ dount wɛɚ ɛnɪ klouʒ‖

(See Fig. 7, page 156, for any unfamiliar symbols.)

The second variety of lateral lisp has no tongue tip contact with the upper gum. The error is due to the presence of a much wider tongue groove down which the air stream must flow. A narrow groove produces a high-frequency sibilant; a broad one creates a lower pitched mushy sound. The teeth are usually parted much too far, and the resulting sibilant is midway between the [s] and the [ʃ]. The modifying marks commonly used to indicate this type of lateral emission are hyphens preceding and following the sibilant; thus: -s- and -z-. Some cases show both types of lateral lisps.

> [wʌn vɛɚɪ kamən fɔɚm əv lætɚəl lɪlp ɪʒ ðə jul əv æn ʌnvɔɪlt ɚ brɛθɪ ɛl laʊnd
> fɔɚ ðɪ ɛl‖ ɪf ju wɪl proulɔŋ ə hwɪlpɚd l ju wɪl əpraklɪmeɪt ðɪl lɪlp‖ laɪk ðə lɪŋgwəl
> frʌntl lɪlp ðə moʊlt kamən mɪlprənʌnlɪɛʃənʒ əkɚ an ðɪ ɛl ænd ʒ laʊndʒ‖ pip̩l
> wɪð ɪl fɪtɪŋ dɛntʃɚ̃ʒ ɔfn dɛmənl̩treɪt ðɪʒ ɛɚɚʒ‖ ʃʌmtaɪmʒ ðə ʃ ænd ʒ ʃaʊndʒ aɚ
> juʒd ɪnʃtɛd‖ ðə tʃ ænd dʒ -s-aʊnd-z- kæn ɔl̥loʊ bi ɨmɪtəd lætɚəlɪ‖]

SPEECH RETARDATION

The speech therapist frequently encounters children who simply have never learned to talk. Some of them are mute, using signs and pantomime to express the desires they cannot communicate orally. Others have a lot of vocalization with which they support their gestures, but the omissions, substitutions, and distortions are so bizarre as to approximate jargon or gibberish. Here are some samples of one such child's speech. Try to interpret for him. Other children could understand what he said. Practice until you can read it swiftly and naturally.

> [dɪ mi ʌm aɪtito‖ aɪ wɑ i ɪ‖ aɪti ɔpu dud‖ danɪ no i teto‖ wa aɪti‖ aɪ wa ɪ na‖
> pi dɪ mi ɪ na‖ u bæ dædə‖ u hʌt danɪ‖ aɪ 'wo ɪt dau‖ danɪ do aɪ dædə ɪ danɪ do
> dɛ aɪ tim na‖ mə mʌmə dɪ mi tʌm‖ aɪ do paɪ hʌ‖ mʌmə‖ mʌmə‖ dɪ mi aɪtito‖ dædə
> no dɪmi ɪ‖]

This is how he should have said it:

> [gɪv mi ən aɪs krim koun‖ aɪ wɑnt tu it ɪt‖ aɪs krim ɪz ɔf̩ gud‖ d͡ʒanɪ dʌz̩nt
> wɑnt tu it pəteɪtoʊz‖ hi wɑnts aɪs krim‖ aɪ wɑnt aɪs krim nau‖ ju aɚ ə bæd dædɪ‖
> ju hɚt d͡ʒanɪ‖ aɪ woʊnt sɪt daun‖ d͡ʒanɪ woʊnt laɪk [hɪz] dædɪ ɪf d͡ʒanɪ dount
> gɛt aɪs krim nau‖ maɪ mamə [wɪl] gɪv mi sʌm‖ aɪ gou faɪnd hɚ‖ mamə‖ mamə‖
> gɪv mi aɪs krim koun‖ dædɪ woʊnt gɪv mi ɪt‖]

Let us illustrate how useful phonetics is in the diagnosis of stuttering. One of the problems concerns the differentiation of normal disfluency from the abnormal kinds, and what we look for besides the frequency of the interruptions is their essential character. The research has shown pretty clearly that the stuttering child shows more part-word repetitions (syllabic or phonemic repetitions) rather than the whole word or phrase repetitions shown by the normal child. Compare these two samples of the same utterance:

[mʌmɨ-| kæn kæn kn̥ːaɪ| kɪn aɪ gou aʊt tu| aʊt tʊ pleɪ naʊ‖]
[mːːmʌmɪ| kʌkəkə kɪ kæn aɪ gʌgugou aʊt-tʊ pʌpleɪ naʊ‖]

Moreover, the speech pathologist also becomes concerned when he finds a child unduly prolonging some of his sounds. Here are some samples of a child's speech which have dangerous features:

[dʌ dʌ dædɪ| aɪ sːːːsə sɪ si b̥ːːbɪg bɚbɚdɪ ouːː//vɚ ðɛːː//ɚ‖]
[ʌgˈ ʌgə əgɪ gɪmɨ mːːː//aɪ əgˈː gʌm‖]

Generally, the longer a sound or silent articulatory posture is maintained, the more likely will it be that the child is in real trouble and needs help. The more colons after a sound, the more the danger. Note, too, in the above sample, the use of the double diagonal bar//.[3] When this appears in the transcription, it indicates that the preceding sound has been produced with a marked pitch rise and it signifies that the child is beginning to feel frustrated and beginning to struggle. There are other ways of showing this pitch rise, but the double diagonal is probably most convenient and we shall use it here.

Also, in the above samples we find the unvoicing sign [̥] on some of the [b̥] and [g] sounds. These sounds are therefore articulated, but not phonated. Many silent articulatory postures on the voiced consonants are shown by certain stutterers, and so we use the [̥] marker to point out this feature. At times we may even need to use it below a vowel. This stutterer had long silent fixations of the articulatory posture of the vowel sounds he feared. How did he stutter? Demonstrate. [ʌʌ aɪ æ̥ːːːːːəæm e̥ːːːɪːɛːeɪtin jɚz o̥ːːould‖]

Stutterers often have trouble with plosion. Instead of starting the word *take* with the aspirate [ˈ] they instead squeeze the tongue against the gum ridge to make a complete seal and then they build up air pressure behind that occlusion. We will therefore use the implosion marker [ˈ] to show this kind of blocking. Again, some stutterers build up tongue thrust behaviors to make the blockade with the tongue against the teeth. Here we would use the dentalization marker [̪]. Can you duplicate this stutterer's abnormality?

[k̪ˈːːkˈʌ kˈæn jʌ jʌ jɪju tˈːːː ət̪ˈɪ ət̪ˈɛl tɛl mi| haʊ tʊ gˈːː gə əget tʊ ðə spˈːːtʃ klɪnɪkˈ‖]

There is another behavior which, in young stutterers, is a danger sign; the difficulty in initiating phonation. Phonetically, we can represent this with the symbol for the glottal stop [ʔ]. A few beginning stutterers show this at onset, but most of them develop it later. They have trouble "getting started." The vocal folds are closed tight

---

[3] In the IPA the sign for an upward inflection is the slanted single quotation mark [ˊ] but it is so easily confused with the mark for primary accent [ˈ] that we have found it wiser to use the double diagonal//.

and the stutterer tries and tries again to blow them open with a blast of air. The experience for the child is a devastating one. All speech clinicians should be able to recognize it. Here is a sample: [ʔʔʔwʌ wʌ ʔ wʌns| ə lɔŋg t'ʔʔaɪm əgou|||].

Speech pathologists should also know something of the way that stuttering usually grows. Is the child getting worse? It is not enough merely to count moments of stuttering; we must also examine the changes in the behaviors shown when disfluency occurs. Are the syllabic repetitions regular or irregular? How fast are they? Do they end with the inappropriate schwa vowel? If so, the disorder is becoming more severe. Here are two sample sentences of the speech of a six year old taken two months apart, and it is obvious that he is getting worse.

First Sample: [ə: hwaɪ də də du aɪ hæhæ hæv tʊ tʊ rɪsaɪt|||]
Second Sample: [ʌdə əd'-də| d'ʌ dɪ| d':u aɪ hʌʔʔæv tu ɝ::: rɪsaɪt|||]

Fearing that they will have trouble on certain words or sounds, many stutterers resort to postponing the speech attempt, for sometimes if they can wait until their fear ebbs they can say the word they dread. Often these pauses are disguised to hide the abnormality. This stutterer has two major strategies which he uses frequently, at times in vain, and both contribute to the abnormality of his speech. What are they?

[ʌm ɑ: ʌm ɝ hwat tʌtʌ taɪm ɪz ɪt|||]
[d': dʌ du ju- du ju| du ju n:::ou hwɛ ʔ| du ju nou hwɛn ðə ge ʔ| hwɛn ðə geɪm stʌ staɝts|||]

The tragedy of using these postponement tricks is that they soon become automatized and become an integral part of his stuttering.

Confirmed stutterers also use various strategies to time the moment of speech attempt. Some of them are gestures, gasps, facial tics, and the like, but others are verbal and can be recorded phonetically. This stutterer had never developed any fear of the [z] sound, and so he used it to start the words on which he anticipated stuttering: [z:::maɪ neɪm ɪz:::tʌtʌtounɨ| ænd aɪ z:ʌz: zlɪv ɪn ðə z:dɔɝm|||]. Here is another sample in which a whole word is used as a timing starter device: [wɛl:ɪts əbaut| wɛl wɛl wɛltaɪm fɔɝ m:i tu ɑ: wɛl:lɪv fɔɝ houm|||].

Your knowledge of the modifying diacritical marks will also be useful in transcribing the speech of severe stutterers, for many of them attempt the first sounds of the words they are trying to say in highly inappropriate ways. One of them squeezed his lips together, not only on the [p] and [b], but also on all the other stop consonants, and even on some of his vowels. Using the modifying mark [̫] to indicate this labilization, here is how he stuttered: [b̫ d̥'u ju hæv ɛ: ɛnɨ mtʃʌ tʃuɪŋ g̫':gʌ gʌm|||].

The voicing and unvoicing marks [̬] and [̥] will find plenty of use in the speech of some stutterers. Often they will start a voiced sound with its unvoiced cognate, then stop and revise again and again until finally the necessary phonation is achieved, concurrent with the articulation: [k'kʌ g: gəgɪv mi m::aɪ ʌʌʌd'ə ʌt'ə d̥a daɪm b̥'bæk|||].

Some stutterers, when they find the oral airway blocked, may turn to the nasal opening and snort some portion of their utterance, or nasalize all of their speech. Here is a sample: [h̃aɪv g ̃: ŋgatə ŋgou nau| ĩts ŋgẽʔĩŋ lẽɪt|||].

Since many severe stutterers show a lip rounding, or lip protruding posture, as they initiate certain sounds, we will need to use the ['] mark to show this: [p'itɝ wɨl b̥':bˈɪ bˈi hɪɝ| əp ʌ p'rɪtɨ sun|||].

These are but a few of the sorts of behaviors which can be identified phonetically. There are many others. Indeed, in the tortured vocalization of very severe stutterers, we hear sounds that are very strange to our ears. There are lip, tongue, and palatal clicks that normally occur only in the languages of the Zulus or aboriginals, and even the International Phonetic Alphabet's more exotic symbols hardly come close to identifying them. See if you can imitate this stutterer, using the IPA table on page 156 to know what the unfamiliar symbols mean.

[β'vɛˤɪ ɸːfju ʬtɪ tə timz ɔːʃ.x:k'kud ʌbit ɔə jæŋkɨz ɪn ðə d̥ɔɔɔd̥ɔɔʌdeɪz əv ɔeɪb ruθ‖]

This stutterer was trying to say, "Very few teams could beat the Yankees in the days of Babe Ruth." When he first came for therapy, his speech was almost unintelligible, and you can see why. Often, he would resort to paper and pencil to get his message across.

But, you may object, what is the point to all this? Has it any utility? Our answer is yes. The stutterer must unlearn these habitual and inappropriate behaviors, and to do so, he must identify them. Of course, he will not need to master phonetics in order to do so, but you will need to analyze what he does if you are to help him. It is not enough just to recognize that he has had a moment of stuttering, for research has shown that a molecular, rather than a molar, analysis, is required. But this is no place to describe the intricacies of stuttering therapy. It should be enough to say that you will find the analytical transcription of abnormal speech a valuable tool if you intend to become a speech pathologist.

CLEFT PALATE SPEECH

Persons born with cleft palates or lips, of course, require surgery or prosthedontia to give them a chance to acquire fairly normal speech, and many of them do. However, many of these individuals show residual articulatory errors, even after these services have been completed, and the speech pathologist must be able to analyze their speech. A narrow transcription of their verbal output can reveal the errors which exist.

While perhaps the major perceptual feature of cleft palate speech is the excessive nasality, which can be indicated by the [˜] symbol over the vowels and voiced consonant sounds, the clinician must also recognize denasalization. This is frequently shown in the articulation of the nasal sounds themselves. To record it, we insert the oral cognate of the nasal sound in this fashion: *me* [mᵇi]; *no* [nᵈoʊ]; *wing* [wɪŋᵍ]. Often when such a client attempts syllables beginning with the voiced plosives, we can hear their nasal cognates preceding them, as in *go* [ⁿgoʊ], *do* [ⁿdu], *bee* [ᵐbi]. These transitional sounds are usually placed a little bit above the line.

Cleft palate speech is also characterized by the substitution of glottal stops [ʔ] or clicks [ʗ] for the normal plosives. The client says [ãɪ ʔæn ⁿdu ɪt‖] or [ʗɪu ɪt ʈu mᵇi‖]. Similarly we may hear glottal, velar, or pharyngeal fricative substitutions, when, for example, the person is saying, "Show me how far you can jump." [xoʊ mĩ ʔãʊ çã˞ hju ʔæ̃ː ʌmp̃‖]

Nasal snorting, or nasal leaking is evident on many consonants, and when this occurs, we simply place the [˜] marker above the sounds so emitted. Or, if a snort occurs on a nasal sound, place the unvoicing marker under it, as in *snow* [n̥ːo] and *me* [m̥i].

Here is a sample of the speech of a very handicapped child who first came to us for speech therapy at the age of six.

m̥ãɪ ndãŋɨ ɪ mbɪʔ‖   hĩ ĩ mbwæ̃ n̥ wãɪ‖   wæ̃ʔɨ ɪ hĩ
My doggie is big. . . He is black and white. . . Randy is his

nẽm‖   h̃ĩ x̃ĩm ɪ maɪ m̥bɛ̃ xʌm ʔãɪm‖   aɪ h̃æ̃ m̥ʌn m̥õːn.
name. . . He sleeps in my bed sometimes. . . I have fun throwing
mãɪ m̥bã æ̃ ĩ‖   æ hi ʔæ̃ ʔæ̃ ɛ̃ ĩ ĩ mãu‖   m̥bʌ hi
my ball at him. . . and he can catch them in his mouth. . . but he
wõ mbwĩŋ m̥ mbæ̃ ʔu mi‖   aɪ ŋã ŋõ ŋɛ̃ ɪ‖
won't bring them back to me. . . I got to go get it.

HEARING PROBLEMS

The phonetic transcription of the speech of persons with severe hearing problems is often difficult when using live, rather than recorded, samples. These individuals show many distortions of vowels, as well as consonant sounds, partial omissions, and unusual substitutions, and there are inflectional and intensity problems as well. The following sample was spoken by a high school girl who had been intensively trained by the oral method, and who had been totally deaf since the age of two and a half years. As the errors indicate, her speech was frequently unintelligible.

wʌ̃ de lõ tãɪ əgo‖ ə lɪtõ pɜɪ‖ wʌ ʃɛ̃ ə tão
One day, a long time ago, a little boy was sent to town
tə ʃɛə pɛʔɪ ə eːk‖ hi mʌ̃ðə sɛ̃ gɪu‖ ʃəːʔ
to sell a basket of eggs. His mother said, "Go straight
tə tãu‖ deːo tɑp ɑn ði we‖ ðːi pɜɪ ʔɛ̃ tə wɪəvə‖
to town. Don't stop on the way." The boy came to a river.
bɪtʌ̃ hi ‖ tɪnɑ wã:tə ʔɛ̃ hɪ fi wɛ̃‖ hi ʃæ dãu ã
Because he did not want to get his feet wet, he sat down on
ði bɛ̃ʔ‖ wɑ sæ a dɪu ʃɛ ði pɜɪ‖ ði wɪəvə ɪ
the bank. "What shall I do?" said the boy. "The river is
vɛ̃ ɪ waɪ‖ ãɪ wɪ wɛ̃ fo ĩ tə peə bɛ̃ɪ‖
very wide. I will wait for it to pass by."

In reading this sample aloud, be sure to use her nasalization of vowels, the use of the glottal stop, and say all words in a monotone, except those followed by the double diagonal ‖. These should be spoken at a pitch level about five semitones higher than the rest of her speech.

FOREIGN ACCENT

This term is probably a misnomer since it usually refers to more than accent, and in the samples we provide of the speech of foreigners speaking English, we are concentrating on the speech sounds rather than the stress and melody patterns. It is difficult to get typical samples, since such speakers are inconsistent. Often they have been taught their first English by a teacher to whom that language was not a native tongue. However, these selections should provide some of the flavor of several different varieties of foreigners speaking our language.

FINNISH: just no gɛdt anɪtrɑuts ɪn dæ krɪkʲ‖ fɪs dæ plɛs mɛɪnɪ tɛɪm‖ no bɛɪdts‖ ju vɑn go gɪud plɛs kɛts fɪs justə go dɑn də rodᵗ tu mɛɪls pɛɪ də swɑump‖

FRENCH: õ zi wɪn ʃi blo fram zi noːɚ‖ æ zi wɪn ʃi blo sam moːɚ bat ju wõ gɛ̃ drãũ õ læk ʃæ̃mplã so lõŋ ju ste ã zi ʃoːɚ‖

204

GERMAN: ɣaɪ hæf ju nɛfə lift ɪn ɪŋgləndt‖ aɪ dʰɪŋk ɪt: zo pjudɪfʊl ə blezs ɛvtə ɪt renz‖

ITALIAN: no mɛkə də mistɛkə tæl ju go dʒampa də lekᵊ‖ mɛkə mi də pitsɑ an spægæt‖

SPANISH: ðat ɛstɹit iz no so aɪd tu fain‖ ju ʃud go ɹid dˤɪ inskɹipsiən on ᵈðɪ ɛstɹit ɛsain‖ aᵈðɪos‖

Here are some selections from the speech of foreign-speaking people using their own language.

BENGALI (India):   tumi‖ bari jə onə‖
Translation: hwaɪ dont ju go hom‖

FINNISH: minulə eɪ ɑlek keŋkiə mutə sukət on‖
Translation: aɪ dont hæv ɛnɪ ʃuz bʌt aɪv gɑt ə pɛr əv saks‖

RUSSIAN: njɛt‖ spaˈsiˌbɑ‖
Translation: no‖ θæŋk ju‖

GAELIC: bi:ʌn fu:ər ən gi:e:rə‖
Translation: ðə wɪntɚ ɪz juʒʊəlɪ kold‖

SALISH (American Indian):   Mother ꞌtee
                          Father mɑmɑ
                          Stuttering sɪtsɪts

FIJIANS (Fiji Islands):   Stutter βɑkɑ

SPANISH: lɑ kukɑɹatʃɑ lɑ kukɑɹatʒɑ jɑ no pweᵈðe kɑminɑd pɔᵈɹke no tiene‖ pɔᵈɹke le fɑltɑ
          mɑᵈɹihwɑnɑ ke fumɑᵈɹ
Translation: The cockroach, the cockroach, can no longer go on, For he doesn't have, he lacks,
          marihuana to smoke.

FRENCH: ʒe vʊ un vaʃ monte un ɑɹb‖
          pɛɹsʌn ɑ vʊ sɛt vaʃ sof mwɑ‖
Translation: I saw a cow climb up a tree.
          Nobody saw that cow but me.

GERMAN: ɪç kan mɪç nɪçt beɹeden lasɛn
          makt mɪɹ den tɔɪfʊl nuɹ nɪçt klaɪn
          aɪn kɛɹl‖ dən ale mɛnʃɛn hasɛn
          dɛɪ mʊs vʌs saɪn‖
                          —Goethe, *Faust*

Translation: aɪ stɪl ɹɪmen kwaɪt ənkənvɪnst
          ðæt ɪts gʊd sɛns tu pent ðə dɛvɪl smɔl‖
          ðɛr mʌst bi sʌmθɪŋ in ə tʃæp
          huz hetɪd so baɪ ɔl‖

And, finally, a Welsh baseball fan: ɑˈgɔɹwɛk ɚ dɹɪz‖
Translation: Kill the umpire!

12 Exercises for Practice and Review

Some teachers of courses in phonetics and some students of that subject have complained that they never have enough practice material.

The purpose of this chapter is to provide reading of phonetic script, materials for transcription, and various phonetic puzzles and games so that those students who welcome such challenges or who need extra work may be given such opportunity.

1. Which of these words is spelled with the letter *a* in ordinary English? Write them out in English.

pel	lip	mit	fes	kɑntɛnt	drek
dɛl	lek	fel	min	prɪzɛnt	drɛd
fil	sek	fil	mɛn	prɛzɑn	pel
rek	sim	fɛl	rid	lɛmɑned	krip
fem	rik	bel	red	hid	krep
fet	rɛk	pil	rɛd	hɛd	wet
fit	met	sik	het	kɑnten	hel

2. Finish these words by putting appropriate symbols in the spaces to make real words.

sɪkj__   θrɔ__   tʃɛr__
tændʒ__l   i__ɪ__t   g__r__ʒ
θ__gz   dʒ__nt   __kn__

3. Circle the correct transcriptions of these words.

surgeons: sɚtʃʌns   sɚtʃəns   sɚdʒənz   sɚdʒʌns
exactly: ɪgzæktlɪ   ɛgzæklɪ   ɛgzæktli   ɛgzæktlɪ
heiresses: hɛrɛsɪs   ɛrɪsɪz   hɛrɪsɪs   ɛrɪsɪs

4. Opposite some of the words below there are blanks. Write one word in which the italicized symbol is silent in the phonetic spelling, just as the *b* is silent in the word *debt*.

b as in *boy*, but not as in de*b*t

d as in *d*oll

f as in *f*all

g as in *g*oat, but not as in ——————

h as in *h*ouse, but not as in ——————

k as in *k*ing, but not as in ——————

l as in *l*arge, but not as in ——————

m as in *m*eat, but not as in *m*nemonics

n as in *n*ose, but not as in hym*n*

p as in *p*ap*e*r, but not as in ——————

r as in *r*ed

s as in *s*and, but not as in ——————

t as in *t*able

v as in *v*inegar

w as in *w*alk, but not as in ——————

z as in *z*ebra

du ju rımɛmbɚ duıŋ ðıs bıfɔr‖]

5. In the following list of words, tell whether or not the italicized consonants are sounded as they are spelled. Answer yes or no.

licke*d* _____	cau*t*ion _____	remain*s* _____
cla*s*p _____	*c*innamon _____	spea*k* _____
rou*g*e _____	trie*d* _____	mu*t*ual _____
wi*s*dom _____		

6. Translate this sentence.

dʌbl̩ ju etʃ e ti‖ di o i ɛs‖ aı ti‖ ɛs e waı‖ e ti‖ ti etʃ i‖ bi o ti ti o ɛm‖ o ɛf‖ pi e dʒi i‖ ɛs aı ɛks ti waı‖ ɛs i vi i ɛn‖

7. Make up some phonetic crosswords to fit into these spaces as in the example.

ı	n
t	u

8. Which of these are not true English words? Underline.

pot	mɛt	mug	dɛk	now	dov
hub	nuz	ʃıne	θınk	aızık	kɔm
dul	pukɚ	θɛr	kuk	ret	brıŋ

9. Cross out all the wrong transcriptions.

Once	upon	a	time	there	was	a	young	rat	named	Arthur.
wons	ʌpon	ʌ	tım	θɛr	wʌz	a	yʌŋ	ӡæt	nemd	arθɚ
wʌns	əpan	ɑ	teım	ðer	was	e	yʌng	ræt	naımd	ærðɚ
wonce	əpon	ə	taım	θer	wʌs	ə	jʌng	ɚæt	nemed	ɑrθɚ
wʌnce	ʌpan	ı	tɔım	ðer	wəz	ɑ	jʌŋ	ӡɛt	named	arθur

10. pliz falo ðiz dırɛkʃənz‖ fɚst raıt ðə fɚst nem əv ðə fɚst ɔθɚ əv ðıs tɛkst ın fənɛtıks ın ðə læst blæŋk spes əv ðoz gıvn̩ bılo‖ ðɛn raıt ðə wɝd ‖ænd‖ ın ðə spes ımidıətlı prısidıŋ ıt‖ ðæt ız tu se ın ðə nɛkst tu ðə læst spes gıvn̩ bılo‖ nau fıl ın ðə θɝd frʌm ðə læst spes wıθ ðı ʌðɚ ɔθɚz fɚst nem‖ stıl wɝkıŋ frʌm raıt tu lɛft fıl ın ðə faınəl θri spesız wıð ðız wɝdz‖ het‖ aı‖ sʌmtaımz‖

—————— —————— —————— —————— ——————

11. Read aloud as swiftly as possible.

əkɔrdɪŋ tu ən ɪtæljən skɑlɚ nemd pænkəntʃɛlɪ əz lɔŋ əgo æz naɪn hʌndrɪd bi si sænskrɪt tɪtʃɚz hæd klæsɪfaɪd ðə saundz əv ðæt læŋgwɪdʒ fonɛtɪklɪ‖

12. Transcribe these words.

cute _____	thin _____	clang _____
choke _____	rouge _____	yes _____
rage _____	knees _____	toil _____
wrong _____	flute _____	right _____
cooks _____	perch _____	father _____

13. Find and transcribe words which include these combinations. Do not separate the phonemes within each group, but the group may occur anywhere in the word.

[ntθ] _____	[skw] _____	[skr] _____
[mpt] _____	[kst] _____	[spl] _____
[mps] _____	[str] _____	[spr] _____
[kt] _____	[ft] _____	[mp] _____
[pt] _____	[nt] _____	[nd] _____
[dʒd] _____	[zm] _____	[ŋk] _____
[tw] _____	[kw] _____	[lfθ] _____
[ŋkl̩] _____	[ŋgl̩] _____	[ɚst] _____

14. Transcription passage (with emphasis on consonant symbols).

choke _____	jest _____	thing _____
strength _____	chews _____	yellow _____
fresh _____	shows _____	throne _____
use _____	though _____	threw _____
jokes _____	whetstone _____	eggs _____
length _____	huge _____	muse _____
cubes _____	breath _____	breathe _____
six _____	edge _____	leisure _____
know _____	new _____	gnome _____
wretch _____	mesh _____	clothes _____
measure _____	whose _____	cello _____
tooth _____	sweet _____	etching _____
coach _____	seethe _____	school _____
fusion _____	knell _____	juice _____
hex _____	wring _____	

15. Read these words as rapidly as you can.

brɪtʃɪz	ʃɛlvz	kotʃ	hɛks	buθ
skjud	huz	ɛtʃɪŋ	ʃuz	nɛl
lɛdʒɚ	goɪŋ	jɛs	tʃuz	ɛdʒ
hwɛn	strændz	dʒus	tʃokt	hop
θrʌʃ	brɪð	jus	hu	stol
pætʃ	skiz	sɪks	uz	pil
sɛlf	lɛŋkθ	loʒ	rɛntʃ	lip

209

16. rid fɔr plɛʒur æt jur lɛʒur‖

   sɪŋɪŋ ɪz swit bʌt bi ʃur əv ðɪs
   lɪps onlɪ sɪŋ hwɛn ðe kænat kɪs‖

   —dʒemz tɑmpsən

   fɔr aɪv bɪn bɔrn ænd aɪv bɪn wɛd
   ænd ɔl əv maɪ trʌbḷ stɑrtɪd ɪn bɛd‖

   —tʃɑrlz wɛb

   so taɪbɪrɪəs maɪt hæv sæt
   hæd taɪbɪrɪəs bɪn ə kæt‖

   —mæθju arnəld

   kæləməzu ænd kæŋkəki
   kokəmo ænd kɪtʃɪtəkəpi
   ɪf ðɪs ent kuksvɪl hwɛr ar wi‖

   —di i smɪθ

   si ðə hæpɪ mɔran‖ hi dʌzṇt gɪv ə dæm‖
   aɪ wɪʃ aɪ wɚ ə mɔran‖ maɪ gɔd pɚhæps aɪ æm‖

   —ənɔnəməs

   wumən wud bi mɔr tʃɑrmɪŋ ɪf ju kud fɔl ɪntu hɚ armz
   wɪðaut ɔlso fɔlɪŋ ɪntu hɚ hændz‖

   —æmbros bɪrs

   hɪz mæmɪ hɪrd hɪm hɔlɚ ṇ hɪz dædɪ hɪrd hɪm bɔl
   æn hwɛn ðe tɚnd ðə kɪvɚ daun hi wʌznt ðɛr ət ɔl‖

   —dʒemz hwɪtkəm raɪlɪ

17. How many of these phonetically transcribed words represent more than one common English word?

   [lo]   [no]   [ro]   [to]   [do]   [flo]

18. Underline the consonants which when combined with the vowels on the left, will create a real word. *Example:* underline the *d* in the [o] column because it makes the word *dough*, or *owed*, or *ode*, or *doe*. Do not underline the *v* because there is no such English word as *vo*.

o	b	p	w	m	n	t	d	k	g	f	v	s	z	r	l	h
e	b	p	v	m	n	t	d	k	g	f	v	s	z	r	l	h
ɪ	b	p	v	m	n	t	d	k	g	f	v	s	z	r	l	h

19. Reading passage. These are names of cities. Write them in English.

   a. sænhwan _____
   b. kwɪbɛk _____
   c. tokɪo _____
   d. bwenosaires _____
   e. æŋkɚɪdʒ _____
   f. kaɪro _____
   g. akapulko _____
   h. tɔmsk _____
   i. kito _____
   j. marsejə _____
   k. berut _____
   l. æmstɚdæm _____
   m. hɔŋkɔŋ _____
   n. lɛnɪngrad _____
   o. glæsgau _____

20. Read for speed and content.

   ɪn ðə fənetɪk ælfəbɛt ðɛr ar twɛntɪ fɔr kɑmən kansənənt sɪmbḷz‖ tu θɚdz əv ðiz ar fəmɪljɚ tu ju sɪns ðe ar aɪdɛntɪkəl wɪð lɛtɚz əv ði ɔrdɪnɛrɪ ælfəbɛt‖ et əv ðə sɪmbḷz ar ə bɪt strendʒ æt fɚst bʌt sun ðe bɪkʌm fəmɪljɚ tu‖

ðə strendʒ sımbḷz hæv ən ıntrıstıŋ hıstərı‖ aur [ð] sımbḷ fɔr ıgzæmpḷ kem frʌm ðə fækt ðæt ðə romən ælfəbɛt hæd no sımbḷ fɔr ðə ti etʃ saund so ði entʃənt skraıbz ṇ skoləz əv ðæt taım krɔst ðə lɛtər d tu mek ð ænd ðʌs ə nu sımbḷ wʌz bɔrn‖ ıt sımz tu bæd ðæt wi feld tu kip ıt‖ ʃurlı ðɛrz no sɛns ın spɛlıŋ ðə [ð] ænd [θ] saundz wıð ðə kambıneʃən ti etʃ‖ bʌt ladʒık luzəz mɛnı ə bætḷ wıð ði ælfəbɛt‖

21. Underline the proper transcription of each of these words.

locate	loɔet	lokɑt	loket	loɔɑt
prays	prez	preyz	praz	pres
quaked	qwekd	kekt	kwekt	kwɑkt
wastes	wests	hwests	hwesdz	wasts
sachet	sætʃıt	səʃe	sæʃe	sætʃe
bathes	bethz	beθs	beθz	beðz
vacation	vəketʃən	vəkeʃən	vʌkeʃən	vekeʃən
razor	razɚ	rezɚ	rezʒɚ	resɚ

22. Unscramble these words.

dʒɑrl _____ piʃ _____ lɔʃ _____

prıd _____ onıl _____ raıθs _____

skıs _____ sıre _____ glıŋs _____

ræɚð _____ nɛvəs _____ gʌlı _____

23. faınd hwat hæpənd tu klıopetrəz lʌvɚz‖ bıgın æt ðə ð sımbḷ an ðə lɛft wʌn əv ðə kɔrnɚz ænd æd ən ədʒesənt sımbḷ ın ɛnı dırɛkʃən tu mek ðə wɚdz əv ðə sɛntəns ðæt ænsɚ aur kwɛstʃən‖ ju nid nat juz ɔl ðə sımbḷz‖

i
szo
ınmθɔ
ðourlɛd
eandı
mop
3

24. Make two other words out of each of the following, using all the symbols in each. Write them phonetically.

Scot _____ _____

claps _____ _____

crisp _____ _____

pits _____ _____

25. Fill in the blanks with the obvious phonemes. Write them in phonetic script.

__ __ __dıd ju se‖ aı et ə dʒusı p__ __‖

__ ıs bʊk ız m____n‖ ðə __ı__ seld ovɚ ði __ʃ__‖ ðə bɔı ız tu jʌŋ tu__ev‖

m__nı br__v h__rts__r __sl__p ın ðə d__p‖

__ __ __hwɛr jur goıŋ‖ __ __ __ __ __jur on bıznız‖

26. Write the silent letters of these words as spelled in English. When a word may be spelled two different ways, choose the one which contains silent letters.

nat _____ nom _____ riθ _____ ni _____ raıt _____

rıŋɚ _____ nab _____ hu _____ nıt _____ maıt _____

27. æn old rul fɔr spɛlɪŋ ðə dɪfɪkəlt aɪ i kɑmbɪneʃən rʌnz laɪk ðɪs‖ juz aɪ bɪfɔr i ɪksɛpt æftɚ si ænd ɪn sʌtʃ wɝdz æz we n̩ ne‖

ə dɪfθɔŋ ɪz ə blɛnd əv tu vauəl saundz əkɝɪŋ ɪn wʌn sɪləbl̩‖ ə daɪgræf kənsɪsts əv tu ədʒesənt lɛtɚz hævɪŋ ðə sem saund‖

spɛl aut ɪn ɪŋglɪʃ ə wɝd kəntenɪŋ ə daɪgræf ænd ənʌðɚ hwɪtʃ ɪnkludz ə dɪfθɔŋ ænd faɪnəli raɪt ðə wɝd rɪsiv so ðæt ɪts spɛld kɚektli‖

a. _____

b. _____

c. _____

28. Read swiftly. If you falter go back and start over.

pʊt	bɑm	ðɪz	pɝl	klʌŋ
frut	θʌm	ðaɪ	tʃæp	dʒæz
ʃʌt	bʌm	θaɪ	tʃɪp	dʒæg
əmjuz	bum	pjur	tʃɑp	dʒɪg
buʃəl	rʊf	pʊl	tʃɪp	dʒʌg
trulɪ	rum	pol	tʃʌmp	dʒɔg
rʊkɪ	rʌm	pɪl	tʃuz	θri
pʊlpɪt	rom	pɪl	ʃep	θro
kju	ðɛn	pel	ʃɪp	θru
pʊlɪ	θɪn	paɪl	ʃɑp	θrʌst
krud	ðæn	pʊl	klæŋ	θrɔŋ
fju	θɪŋk	pæl	klɪŋ	mɛʒɚ
buʃɪz	ðɪs	pɔl	ʃɪp	trɛʒɚ
kom				

29. Say these nonsense words aloud without faltering or error. Increase your speed until you can say them all in one breath.

tʃo	ðɛdʒ	uŋgo	rotɛp	oŋkɛt
θɛt	vuʃ	tʃɛʃ	vuno	sladʒ
boŋ	oʒu	muθ	uðob	frʌp

30. hɪr ar sʌm kɑmənli mɪspɛld wɝdz‖ kæn ju spɛl ðɛm kɚektli ɪn ɪŋglɪʃ‖

laɪbrɛrɪ	_____	pɚhæps	_____	muvəbl̩	_____
kəmɪtɪ	_____	præktɪs	_____	nɛsəsɛrɪ	_____
vækjuəm	_____	riəlaɪz	_____	əkɝəns	_____
mɪstʃɪvəs	_____	kənvɪnjəns	_____	numonjə	_____
fɝlo	_____	ɛriəl	_____	prabəblɪ	_____
ɔlwɪz	_____	dɛrɪ	_____	rɛkəgnaɪz	_____
brɪð	_____	ɔtəm	_____	rɪlif	_____
ɔfəl	_____	rɪsit	_____	sɪzɚz	_____
sɛmətɛrɪ	_____	æθlɛtɪks	_____	sɛpɚət	_____
kaləm	_____	bɪskɪt	_____	sɪmələ	_____
dɪsəpɔɪnt	_____	bɪgɪnɪŋ	_____	θɝəlɪ	_____
ɪmbɛrəs	_____	kɝnəl	_____	wɪrd	_____
fɔrɪn	_____	dɪfrənt	_____	rɪðm̩	_____
hæŋkɚtʃɪf	_____	etθ	_____	siz	_____
laɪsəns	_____	ɪgzædʒɚet	_____	sardʒənt	_____

luzıŋ _____ gɑrd _____ səˈpraɪzd _____

mɪsəl _____ ɪntɛlədʒɪns _____ trædʒədɪ _____

naɪntɪ _____ nɑlɪdʒ _____ frɛnd _____

naɪnθ _____ mɛdəsɪn _____

31. There are two English spellings for each of these words. Write them in the blank spaces.

[brek] _____ _____   [ɔltɚ] _____ _____

[əsɛnt] _____ _____   [kæpɪtəl] _____ _____

[kɔrs] _____ _____   [dɪzɚt] _____ _____

[lɛd] _____ _____   [maɪnɚ] _____ _____

[pis] _____ _____   [plen] _____ _____

[ðɛr] _____ _____   [west] _____ _____

32. Analogies. Fill in the gaps from the words on the right.

intʃ ɪz tu maɪl æz aʊns ɪz tu _____|| kwɑrt tʌn jɑrd paʊnd

ræmz ɑr tu _____ æz bɔɪz ɑr tu gɝlz|| ʃip bʌks juz læmz

daɪət ɪz tu fæst æz _____ ɪz tu fæmɪʃt|| θɝstɪ hʌŋgrɪ fud

kɝɪdʒ ɪz tu brevɚɪ æz _____ ɪz tu kaʊɚdɪs|| rʌnɪŋ kaʊɚdz fɪr æŋgɚ

_____ ɪz tu stroks æz soz ɪz tu stɪtʃɪz|| wɑtɚ mɛnɪ simz swɪmz

33. Read and heed.

     hwɛn wi juz ə nu wɝd fɔr ðə fɝst taɪm wi fil əz stɑrtl̩d əz ɪf wi hæd dʒʌst lɪt ə faɪrkrækɚ|| wi lʊk əraʊnd hestɪlɪ tu si ɪf ɛnɪwʌn hæz notɪst|| no wʌn ɛvɚ hæz|| ðɛn wi faɪnd ðæt ə wɝd juzd θri taɪmz dɪlɪbɚətlɪ bɪkʌmz aʊrz forɛvɚ| slɪpɪŋ ɔf ðə tʌŋ nætʃɚəlɪ||

34. What is this word? gheauphtheightptough

gh	is the sound of _____	in *hiccough*
eau	is the sound of _____	in *beaux*
phth	is the sound of _____	in *phthisic*
eigh	is the sound of _____	in *eighth*
pt	is the sound of _____	in *ptomaine*
ough	is the sound of _____	in *though*

35. Is that so?

     wʌns ə feməs ɪŋglɪʃ skolɚ sɛd tu rʌdjɚd kɪplɪŋ| ðɛr ɑr onlɪ tu wɝdz ɪn ðɪ ɪŋglɪʃ læŋgwɪdʒ bɪgɪnɪŋ wɪð ðə lɛtɚz ɛs ju ænd hwɪtʃ ɑr prənaʊnst ɛs etʃ ju|| ðə wɝdz ɑr ʃugɚ ænd ʃumæk|| dɪd ju no ðæt|| hi æskt|| ʃur|| sɛd rʌdjɚd kɪplɪŋ||

ɪf ju fel tu si ðə pɔɪnt əv ðɪ ænɪkdot raɪt ɪt aʊt ɪn ɪŋglɪʃ||

36. Reading passage. How well can you articulate these?

     əmɪdst ðə mɪst ænd koldɪst frɔsts wɪθ bɛrɪst rɪsts ænd staʊtɪst bosts hi θrʌsts hɪz fɪsts əgɛnst ðə posts ænd stɪl ɪnsɪsts hi siz ðə gosts||

hɪz kraɪ muvd mi|| hɪz kraɪm muvd mi|| ðə sʌn ʃaɪnz ɑn ðə ʃɑp saɪnz||

sɪks θɪk θɪsl̩ stɪks|| ðə si sisɪθ ænd ɪt səfaɪsɪθ||

ə rurəl rulɚ trulɪ rurəl|| aɪ skrim fɔr aɪs krim||

flɛʃ əv frɛʃlɪ fraɪd flaɪɪŋ fɪʃ||

37. Here is the English alphabet written out phonetically. Cross out all of those which are not also real words.

e bi si di i ɛf dʒi etʃ aɪ dʒe ke ɛl ɛm
ɛn o pi kju ɑr ɛs ti ju vi dʌblju ɛks waɪ zi

38. What are the modern forms of these words? In the two left-hand columns are their pronunciations in England in the years:

1100 A.D.	1300 A.D.	Today	
muð	muθ	_____	hwɛr jʊr tʌŋ ɪz
toð	tuð	_____	ju baɪt wɪð ðɛm
fot	fut	_____	ɑn ðɪ ʌðɚ ɛnd
deop	dep	_____	ðɪ æntonɪm əv ʃælo
blod	blud	_____	ɪn jʊr venz

39. Fill the blank squares with consonant symbols so that the boxes are completed with meaningful words both vertically and horizontally.

40. Read each line of the following on one breath without error.

1. ɑ ɔ ɪ i e ɛ ʊ u ɔ ɑ ɜ ʌ u ɪ ʊ ɔ e ɛ ɪ æ
2. u o i ɑ ɪ ɛ ɔ ɑ u ɑ u ɑ e ɔ u ɔ ɪ æ ɜ ʌ
3. ɔɪ eɪ aɪ au ou au ɔɪ au ɛɪ aɪ ɜɪ ɔɪ ou aɪ eɪ
4. tʃaɪ ðau muŋ dʒɔp kʌθ ŋko æli oʒu luŋ bɜd gɔɪ
5. ɔntʃ taʒ vuð tʃʌŋ lɛʃ kjen æŋkʃ θrɪd switʃ ðʌθ

41. If you are still having trouble on the vowels, here are some words to transcribe.

file	_____	pail	_____	stood	_____
full	_____	hung	_____	many	_____
where	_____	stands	_____	cools	_____
seeing	_____	ideal	_____	olive	_____
lonely	_____	loons	_____	turmoil	_____
askew	_____	around	_____	honor	_____
nature	_____	mirror	_____	virtue	_____
glanced	_____	casual	_____	awful	_____
business	_____	author	_____	oozes	_____
church	_____	error	_____	fire	_____
roar	_____	hangs	_____	down	_____
air	_____	drawer	_____	lured	_____
island	_____	covet	_____	worthy	_____
park	_____	cure	_____	passion	_____
double	_____	glanced	_____	personal	_____
view	_____	tutor	_____	Indiana	_____
coiled	_____	moss	_____	hunger	_____
night	_____	rocks	_____	azure	_____
neither	_____	beneath	_____	rough	_____

observe _____   stones _____   fields _____

Indians _____   howled _____   pulpit _____

other _____   poor _____

42. Reading passages.

lʌv le ðaɪ fobɪəz tu rɛst
　　ɪnhɪbɪt ðaɪ tæbu
ænd ʃɛr wɪð mi fɔrɛvɚ blɛst
　　ə kamplɛks bɪlt fɔr tu
　　　　　　　—ənɔn

ænd ðə bɛst ænd ðə wɝst əv ðɪs ɪz
　　ðæt niðɚ ɪz most tu blem
ɪf ʃi hæz fɔrgatn̩ maɪ kɪsɪz
　　aɪ hæv fɔrgatn̩ hɚ nem
　　　　　　　—swɪnbɚn

43. Transcription passages.

[e]

Maybe Mable came to stay in Haiti. Daily play in the bay makes great aches go away.

_____

_____

[ɪ]

If his list is in his hand, will he give his people quick peeks into its mysteries?

_____

_____

[i]

We seem to keep reaping any seeds we sow. Be good, be brave, and the seeds may be sweet.

_____

_____

[o]

We hope he knows that roses grow in rows, and lilies float in pools.

_____

_____

[u]

Soon a new improved fruit will be put into food stands. Proof of its newness will be in its loose skin.

_____

_____

215

[æ]

Ask Max if his antics have made any people laugh as he dances.

_____

_____

[ʊ]

You could put your cook's best cookies in a bowl and the food will be good and plentiful.

_____

_____

[ɛ]

A telephone is necessary if a man intends to fill his empty days with entertainment.

_____

_____

COMPREHENSIVE READING

Answer True or False

lɪtl̩ draps əv wɔtɚ| lɪtl̩ grenz əv sænd|
mek ðə siʃɚ ædɪkt blɪstɚd| pild ænd tænd||

44. ðə sʌn ɪz nat ðə sol pɚpətretɚ əv ɪlz fɔr ðə swimɚ   _____

ðə kraun ænd glɔrɪ əv ə jusfəl laɪf ɪz kɛrɪktɚ|| ɪt ɪz ðə
noblɪst pəzɛʃən əv mæn|| ɪt fɔrmz ə ræŋk ɪn ɪtsɛlf| æn əstet
ɪn ðə dʒɛnɚəl gud wɪl| dɪgnɪfaɪz ɛvrɪ steʃn̩ ænd ɪgzɔlts
ɛvrɪ pəzɪʃn̩ ɪn səsaɪətɪ| ɪt ɛksɚsaɪzɪz gretɚ pauɚ ðæn wɛlθ| ænd
ɪz ə væljuəbl̩ minz əv səkjurɪŋ anɚ||

45. ju wɪl ɛnd ʌp wɪð ðə sem kɛrɪktɚ no mætɚ hwat kaɪnd
əv laɪf ju hæv lɪvd   _____

46. If ju want tu bi əklemd baɪ ðə papjələs si ðæt jur laɪf hæz
bɪn jusfəl   _____

hi wəz əpraksɪmɪtlɪ sɪks fit tɔl ænd hɪz badɪ wəz wɛl
prəpɔrʃənd|| hɪz kəmplɛkʃn̩ ɪnklaɪnd tu bi flɔrɪd|| hɪz aɪz
wɚ blu ənd rɪmarkəblɪ far əpart| ə prəfjuʒn̩ əv hɛr kʌvɚd
ðə fɔrɛd|| hi wəz skrupjələslɪ nit ɪn hɪz əpɪrəns ænd| ɔlðo
hi əbɪtʃuəlɪ lɛft hɪz tɛnt ɚlɪ| hi wəz wɛl drɛst||

47. hi wəz ənimɪk   _____

48. hi wəz ʌnkɛmpt   _____

rɪspandɪŋ tu ðɪ ɪmpʌls əv hæbɪt dʒosifəs spok æz əv old||
ðɪ ʌðɚz lɪsn̩d ətɛntɪvlɪ bʌt ɪn grɪm ənd kəntɛmptʃuəs

saɪləns|| hi spok æt leŋkθ| kəntɪnjuəslɪ|| pərsɪstəntlɪ| ænd
ɪngreʃɪentɪŋlɪ|| faɪnəlɪ ɪgzɔstɪd θru lɔs əv streŋkθ hi hezɪ-
tetɪd| æz ɔlwɪz hæpɪnz ɪn sʌtʃ ɛkszɪdʒənsɪz hi wəz lɔst||

49. ðɪ ɔdɪəns rɪspɛktɪd hɪm _____

50. hi tɔkt tu lɔŋ fɔr hɪz ɔn gʊd _____

ðɪ ətrækʃn̩ əv ðɪ əmerɪkən preriz æz wel æz əv ðɪ əluvɪəl
dɪpazɪts əv idʒɪpt hæv bɪn ovərkʌm baɪ ðɪ æʒur skaɪz əv
ɪtəlɪ ænd ðɪ æntɪkwətɪz əv romən arkɪtɛktʃər|| maɪ dɪlaɪt
ɪn ðɪ æntɪk ænd maɪ fandnɪs fɔr arkɪtɛktʃurəl ənd arkɪə-
ladʒɪkəl stʌdɪz vərdʒɪz antu ə fənætəsɪzm̩||

51. hi prɪfərz ɪtəlɪ _____

52. hi laɪks best tu stʌdɪ plænt laɪf _____

ðɪ haɪpaθəsɪs kənsərnɪŋ fɪzəkl̩ fənamənə fɔrmjuletɪd baɪ
ðɪ ərlɪ fəlasəfərz pruvd tu bi ɪnkənsɪstənt ænd ɪn dʒenərəl
nat junəvərsəlɪ æplɪkəbl̩|| bɪfɔr relətɪvlɪ ækjurət prɪnsɪplz
kʊd bi ɪstæblɪʃt fɪzɪsɪsts| mæθmətɪʃn̩z| ænd stætəstɪʃn̩z
hæd tu kəmbaɪn fɔrsɪz ænd wərk ardjuəslɪ||

53. entʃənt θɪŋkərz hæv bɪn pruvən raɪt baɪ madərn saɪəntɪsts _____

54. Transcribe completely the text of this letter.

Dear Dr. Van Riper,
    In an effort to fulfill a part of my obligation as a University professor
toward the extension of knowledge and the discovery of truth, I hereby
submit to you the following liturgy to be chanted in unison by all your
students each morning at dawn.
    "One hen
    One hen, two ducks
    One hen, two ducks, three squawking geese
    (Carry on with the following additions each time)
     Four corpulent porpoises
     Five Limerick oysters
     Six pairs of Don Alfonso's tweezers
     Seven thousand Macedonian warriors in full battle array
     Eight brass monkeys from the ancient, sacred crypts of Egypt
     Nine apathetic, sympathetic, diabetic old men on crutches, and
     Ten lyrical, spherical heliotropes from eleemosynary institutions."
If this doesn't build their characters, send them where the wild goose goes.
                                                    Sincerely, John Pruis

55. Write the following in English.

ðə stərnoklaɪdomæstɔɪdɪəs ɪz juzd ɪn kləvɪkjulər brɪðɪŋ||
ventrɪkjulər foneʃən ɪz əkamplɪʃt baɪ ðə fɔls vokəl kɔrdz||
ðə rektəs æbdamɪnəs rʌnz frʌm jur pjubɪs tu jur stərnəm||
daɪədokokɪnɪsɪs ɪz wʌn heləvə wərd fɔr niofaɪts||
lɪtərerɪ æspərənts ʃud vɪgərəslɪ estʃu palɪsɪlæbɪk vokæbjulerɪ||

56. Transcribe the following telephoned telegram which was sent to describe an accident.

"Bruises hurt. Erased afford. Analysis hurt too. Infectious dead."

_____

_____

Now see if you can translate it into a meaningful message.

_____

_____

57. [hɪr ɑr sʌm kamən freɪzɪz‖ trænskraɪb ðəm ɪn tɝmz əv gʊd kəlokwɪəl jusɪdʒ ænd əgɛn ɪn tɝmz əv sʌbstændɚd spitʃ‖] *Example:* "I don't want to." [aɪ dont wantu‖] [aɪ don wan:ə‖]

did you	good bye	good morning
you ought to	it sure is	all right
what do you know	not yet	what's that
how are you	how should I know	who's going
not yet	pleased to meet you	didn't you
aren't you	did you get your	would you

58. Read these words aloud but whisper the unstressed syllables. Then write them in English.

bruk	ɑbvɪəs	pətrol	nak	ʌnskru
ədæpt	kom	pɔd	west	salətud
ɔfɪs	bɪlif	kənve	pulɪts	notɪs
ɪgzækt	əkru	aktɪv	bulɪt	hestɪ
dɪkri	wʊmən	ɛlɪgənt	res	mərin

_____ _____ _____ _____ _____

_____ _____ _____ _____ _____

_____ _____ _____ _____ _____

_____ _____ _____ _____ _____

_____ _____ _____ _____ _____

59. Transcribe exactly as written, then read your transcription aloud.

When fishermen meet: "Hyamac." "Lobuddy." "Binearlong?" "Cuplours." "Ketchanenny?" "Goddafew." "Kindarthy?" "Bassencarp" "Ennysizetoom?" "Cuplapowns." "Hittinard?" "Sordalite." "Wahchoozin?" "Gobbawurms." "Fishanonaboddum?" "Rydonnaboddum." "Igaddago." "Tubad." "Yeahtakideezy." "Slong." "Guluck."

60. Reading Passage.

kansənənts ɑr æksɛsɚ ɹ muvmɪnts hwɪtʃ ərɛst ænd rɪlis ðə tʃɛst pʌls‖ ðə sɪləbḷ kənsɪsts əv ə sɪŋgḷ tʃɛst pʌls juʒuəlɪ med ɔdɪbḷ baɪ ə vaʊəl‖

ə sɪlæbɪk nezəl kansənənt ɪz bɛst dɪfaɪnd æz ə nezəl kansənənt fonim fʌŋkʃənɪŋ æz ðə nuklɪəs əv ə sɪləbḷ‖ ɪt kæn fɔrm sɪləbḷz əlon ɔr wɪð ʌðɚ kasənənts‖

61. Transcribe the following.

Syllabic consonants in American English occur mainly in the atonic position, immediately after another consonant, except that nasal syllabics cannot follow other nasals. If any vowel whatever, no matter how obscure or short, intervenes, it becomes the syllabic sound and the consonant is no longer syllabic.

62. Translate into English.

ə mɔrfim ɪz ðə besɪk junɪt əv minɪŋ‖ ə fonim hæz no minɪŋ‖ ɪt kənsɪsts əv ə fæməlɪ əv saundz hwɪtʃ tu ðə netɪv spikɚ saund əlaɪk‖ ðʌs [s] ɪz ə fonim ænd so ɑr [u] ænd [p] bʌt [sup] ɪz ə mɔrfim‖ sʌm wɝdz kənten mɔr ðæn wʌn mɔrfim‖ fɔr ɪgzæmpḷ prifɪksɪz ænd sʌfɪksɪz ɔlso hæv minɪŋ‖ ðʌs [kʊkt] hæz tu mɔrfimz ɪn ɪt hwaɪl [kʊk] hæz onlɪ wʌn‖

63. Fill in the spaces with the proper symbols.

	sonənt	sɝd	nezḷ
lebɪəl	_____	_____	_____
ælvɪələ	_____	_____	_____
vɪlɚ	_____	_____	_____

64. Sort out the following sounds into the indicated categories.

z   s   θ   dʒ   ʒ   k   ŋ   ð   tʃ   v   t   f   ʃ   g

affricates _____

fricatives _____

219

voiced plosives _____

unvoiced plosives _____

nasals _____

65. Reading passage.

ɪn nɔrðɚn tʃaɪniz ðə fɔr tonz juzd ɪn ʌtɚɪŋ ðə sem sɪləbl̩ wɪl krɪet fɔr dɪfɚɪnt mɪnɪŋful wɝdz‖ ɪn kæntəniz naɪn tonz kæn bi juzd tu provaɪd sɛpɚɪt mɪnɪŋz fɔr ðə sem sɛt əv saundz‖

ðə pɔzɪz ɪn aur spitʃ ɔlso hæv mɪnɪŋz‖ fɔr ɪgzæmpl̩ ɪn ðə sɛntɪns‖ ðə titʃɚ sɛd ðə pjupl̩ wʌz stupɪd‖ ju kæn baɪ pɔzɪŋ prapɚlɪ mek ɪðɚ ðə titʃɚ ɔr ðə pjupl̩ ðə stupɪd wʌn‖ traɪ ɪt‖

66. Write the following in English.

ðɪ ævɚɪdʒ tʃaɪld ʌtɚz fɪftin θauzənd wɝdz ə de ɔr faɪv mɪljən faɪv hʌndrɪd θauzənd wɝdz pɝ jɪr‖

—mɪkarθɪ

67. Some foreign words. Practice pronouncing them.

French:	swan	[siːɲ] (palatalized [n])
Arabic:	write	[kɑtɑbɑ]
Finnish:	fish	[kɑlɑ]
Gaelic:	harbor	[ɪnvær]
Eskimo:	woman's	[ɑrnɑp]
Armenian:	went	[tʃnogaɪ]
Turkish:	to love	[sev-dir-mek]
Fiji:	basket	[nɑːsu]
Arawak:	my son	[nuɑnː]
Polish:	deer	[ĩos] (velarized [l])
German:	spirit	[tʃaɪt]
Spanish:	wife	[muxeɹ] (glottal fricative)
Italian:	church	[ɛʎi]
Dutch:	mother	[muːdər]
Lithuanian:	bewitch	[ʒau jeti]
Bantu:	I	[mbɑ]
Nootka:	boy	[kweko]
Salish:	father	[mɑmɑ]
Australian aborigine:	seven	[kukokukokukoki]

68. Transcribe the following.

shrink _____	choose _____	gnash _____
book _____	ditch _____	dumb _____
nut _____	lawns _____	sauce _____
sheep _____	shout _____	toy _____
catch _____	clings _____	isle _____
law _____	shall _____	mouth _____
should _____	lisps _____	edge _____

clack	_____	shoes	_____	thine	_____
about	_____	out	_____	fetched	_____
dull	_____	buy	_____	mouse	_____
lumps	_____	mine	_____	full	_____
claws	_____	jaw	_____	hum	_____
aisle	_____	month	_____	shook	_____
nice	_____	thumb	_____	fought	_____
noise	_____	might	_____	hush	_____
flies	_____	chest	_____	hymn	_____
mouths	_____	bleach	_____	clung	_____
gem	_____	would	_____	gives	_____
thin	_____	much	_____	glove	_____
blinked	_____	sung	_____	cow	_____
foot	_____	fun	_____	oil	_____
love	_____	caught	_____	wrought	_____
taught	_____	cash	_____	my	_____
ship	_____	must	_____	thigh	_____

SHORT READING PASSAGES

ɪn ðə gardn̩ əv idn̩ ædəm sɔ ði ænəməlz lɔŋ bɪfɔr hi nemd ðɛm‖ ɪn aur trədɪʃənəl ɛdʒukeʃənəl sɪstəm aur tʃɪldrən mʌst nem ðɛm bɪfɔr ðe si ðəm‖ hau ɔfn̩ du aur tɪtʃɚz sɪn ɪn ðɪs sem we‖

—e etʃ mæzlo

ə lardʒ nʌmbɚ əv tʃɪldrɪn frəm sɪks θru et bɪliv ðæt wʌn θɪŋks θru wʌnz mauθ ɔr ðæt θɔt ɪz ə vɔɪs ɪnsaɪd wʌnz hɛd‖

—piaʒe

ðə tʃaɪld tɔks ɪnsɛsəntlɪ hwɛn əlon‖ əlaud hi vɔɪsɪz hɪz wɪʃɪz| hɪz hops| hɪz ənɔɪənsəz‖ sun hauɛvɚ səsaɪətɪ ɪn ðə fɔrm əv hɪz pɛrənts steps ɪn‖ dont tɔk əlaud hwɛn ju θɪŋk| ðe sel‖ dædɪ ænd mʌðɚ ar nat ɔlwɪz tɔkɪŋ tu ðɛmsɛlvz‖ sun ði ovɚt spitʃ daɪz daun tu hwɪspɚd spitʃ ænd ə gud lɪp ridɚ kæn ˌstɪl no hwat ðə tʃaɪld θɪŋks əv hɪmsɛlf ænd əv ðə wɚld‖

—dʒan watsən

ðə most ræpɪd ɔrəl ridɚ ɪn ðə wɚld kæn hændl̩ æt most onlɪ sɪks wɚdz pɚ sɛkənd‖ ðə most ræpɪd saɪlənt ridɚ kæn rid ɪnkrɛdɪblɪ fæstɚ‖

—tʃarlz braun

əntɪl ɪzəbɛl dɪvɛləpt spitʃ n̩ læŋgwɪdʒ ʃi hæd ɔl ðə kɛrɪktɚɪstɪks əv a fibl̩ maɪndəd tʃaɪld‖ wʌns ʃi hæd əkwaɪrd spitʃ ænd hæd lɚnd tu raɪt ʃi bɪkem æn ələt ʌndɚstændɪŋ ænd nɔrməl pɚsən‖

—mesən

saɪlənt ridɪŋ ɪz ɔlmost ɪnvɛrɪəblɪ əkʌmpənɪd baɪ ɪntɚnəl spitʃ‖ vɛrɪ fju pɚsənz kæn rid baɪ aɪ əlon‖

—tɪtʃənɚ

ɪn ðə kes əv hjumən lɚnɪŋ| ɪnsaɪt ɪz juʒuəlɪ əkʌmpənɪd baɪ ə vɚbəl fɔrmjulə hwɪtʃ pɚmɪts ðə prɪnsɪpl̩ tu bi əplaɪd tu nu prabləmz‖

—hɪlgard

221

pɚhæps wʌn rizən pɚsənælitiz wiðin ðə sem kʌltʃur rizembl̩ itʃ ʌðɚ æz mʌtʃ
æz ðe du iz ðæt ðe juz ðə sem wɝdz ænd se ðə sem θiŋz||

—ɔlpɔrt

most impɔrtənt əv ɔl iz ðæt speʃəl fɔrm əv kəmjunikeʃən in hwitʃ æn ində-
vidʒuəl kəmjunikets wið himself|| du nat θiŋk hir onli əv daiəriz bʌt kənsidɚ fɔr
igzæmpl̩ hwat teks ples in ðə prədʌkʃən əv ə wɝk əv art||

—tʃarlz mɔris

ðə prases əv memɚaiziŋ me bi simpli ðə fɔrmeʃən əv vɝbl̩ tʃʌŋks ɔr grups əv
riletəd wɝdz ðæt go tugeðɚ əntil fainəli ðer ar fju inʌf tʃʌŋks tu pɚmit ʌs tu hold
ðem||

—rabɚt braun

ai æm nat ʃur hwɛðɚ ðer kæn bi ə we əv ʌndɚstændiŋ ðə mirəkl̩ əv θiŋkiŋ||
ai du nat θiŋk ladʒikli|| əv ðæt ai æm sɝtn̩|| no riəli prədʌktiv mæn evɚ θiŋks in
sʌtʃ ə pepɚ fæʃən||

—ainstain

ai nu ðæt dʌbəlju e ti i ar ment ðə wʌndɚfuli kul sʌmθiŋ ðæt wʌz floiŋ ovɚ
mai hænd|| ðæt liviŋ wɝd əwekənd mai sol| gev it lait hop dʒɔi ænd set it fri|| ðer
wɝ beriɚz stil bʌt beriɚz hwitʃ kud in taim bi swept əwe|| ai left ðə haus igɚ tu
lɝn|| evriθiŋ hæd ə nem ænd itʃ nem gev bɝθ tu ə nu θɔt||

—heln̩ kelɚ

dɛf mjuts ʃo mɔr nɝvəs impəls rekɚdz kʌmiŋ frʌm ðer fiŋgɚ mʌsl̩z ðæn frʌm
ðer θrots in drimiŋ ɔr in prabləm salviŋ|| nɔrməl pɝsənz wið nɔrməl hiriŋ ʃo
præktikli no æktiviti in ðə fiŋgɚz in ðiz fʌŋkʃənz||

—ɛl mæks

dʒan duwi in kritəsaiziŋ hiz edʒukeʃənəl ɔfspriŋ| ðə prəgresiv skulz| sed ðis||
æz ðə tʃaildz leriŋks wʌz rilist ænd tɔkiŋ wʌz inkɝidʒd ðə nu skulz wɛnt ðə hol
distəns ænd bikem gerələs ræðɚ ðæn θɔtful||
tʃildrinz æktiviti in ðə klæsrum iz veri lardʒli kənfaind tu ðə risepʃən ɔr ivokiŋ
əv inɚ spitʃ|| it is ðə titʃɚz dʒab tu invait ænd tu gaid inɚ spitʃ ænd ðə spoken wɝd||

—gʌθri ænd pauɚz

artikjulət spitʃ iz ðə most impɔrtənt fɔrm əv simbalik ikspreʃən|| rimuv spitʃ
frəm ðə kʌltʃɚ ænd hwat wud rimen||

—lɛsli hwait

ə prəfeʃənəl liŋgwist əprotʃiŋ ðə saiəntifik ənæləsis əv ə hiðɚtu ʌnrikɔrdid
læŋgwidʒ| ænd ə lemən ətemptiŋ tu əten ə spikiŋ nalidʒ əv ə sekənd tʌŋ fes ðə sem
fʌndəmentl̩ prabləm|| nʌθiŋ mɔr ðæn krud prəliminɛri wɝk kæn bi dʌn əntil sʌm
græsp əv ðə fonimik sistəm iz əbtend||

—glisən

ɛksəlθɔlmik gɔitɚ iz ə disɔrdɚ kɔzd bai haipɚθairɔidizm| ðə prinsipl̩ simptəmz
biiŋ ə protruʒən əv ði ai bɔlz| mʌskjulɚ tenʃən| iritəbiliti ænd haipɚkinisis||

—herəmən

hwɛn ə vəraiəti əv æntisidənt stets ɔr stimjulai kənvɝdʒ əpan ə kamən sʌb-
sikwənt stet ɔr rispans| trænsfɚ iz pazətiv ænd retroæktiv ifɛkts ar fəsilətetid| ðə
digri əv fəsiləteʃn̩ veriiŋ direktli wið ðə siməlɛrəti əmʌn ði æntisidənt stets||

—ə kɝst saikɔlədʒist

222

əˈkɔrdɪŋlɪ ðə nɜˈv faɪbɚz rɪzɚvd fɔr ðə prasɪsɪz əv homɪostesɪs| ðə sɪmpəθetɪk ænd pɛrəsɪmpəθetɪk sɪstəmz ar ɔfn̩ nanmaɪəlɪnetɪd ænd ar non tu hæv ə kənsɪdɚəblɪ sloɚ ret əv trænsmɪʃn̩ ðæn ði maɪəlɪnetɪd faɪbɚz||

—winɚ

hwaɪ wɪmɪn fel: ðə kɔz ðɛrəv| æz aɪ se| ɪz nat ɛkstɜrnl̩| bʌt ɪntɜrnl̩|| ɪt laɪz ɪn ðə sem dɪskənsɜrtɪŋ æprɪhenʃən əv ðə lardʒɚ rɪælɪtɪz| ðə sem ɪmpeʃəns wɪθ ðə pɔltrɪ ænd merətrɪʃəs| ðə sem dɪskwalɪfɪkeʃən fɔr məkænɪkəl rutɪn ænd ɛmptɪ tɛknɪk hwɪtʃ wʌn faɪndz ɪn ðə haɪɚ vɚaɪətɪz əv mɛn||

—etʃ ɛl mɛnkɪn

ðoz hu tɔk əbaut ɛdʒuketɪŋ ðə hol tʃaɪld sim tu fɔrget ðæt hɪz hɛd ɪz part əv hɪm|| ɛnɪ ræʃənəl θɪərɪ mʌst bi best əpan sʌm kənvɪkʃən ðæt ðə mæn əv hum ðə tʃaɪld ɪz ðə faðɚ ɔt tu bi ɪn maɪnd| ɪn test ænd ɪn kənvɪkʃən sʌmθɪŋ mɔr ðæn hwat hi wɪl bi ɪf hi ɪz əlaud tu falo onlɪ hɪz sɪmpləst ɪnkləneʃənz ænd hwatɛvɚ hæpənz tu bi ðə kɜrənt kənvenʃənz əv hɪz grup||

—dʒe dʌbl̩ju krutʃ

ɪts ənlɔfḷ tə drɪŋk bɪr ɪn jɚ ʌndɚwɛr ɪn kuʃɪŋ| okləhomə||

ɪn ɪndiænə| motɚɪsts kn̩ bi tɛstəd fɚ ælkəhɔlɪk brɛθ əgɛnst ðɛr wɪl ʌndɚ ə lɔ ðət sɛz"æftɚ ðə brɛθ livz ðə badɪ| ɪt sisəz tə bi ðə prapɚtɪ əv ðə pɚsn̩ frm̩ hum ɪt kem"||

ju kænt tek ə frɛntʃ pudḷ tu n̩ aprə haus ɪn ʃɪkago||

frɔgz ɚ prohɪbɪtəd frm̩ krokɪŋ æftɚ ɪlɛvn̩ pi ɛm ɪn mɛmfɪs||

ɪntɚnæʃnḷ fɔlz|mɪnəsotə fɚbɪdz kæts tə tʃes dɔgz ʌp tɛləfon polz||

ɪn kɛnəlwɚθ ɪlənɔɪ| ə rustɚ məst stɛp bæk θri hʌndrəd fit frəm ɛni rɛzədɛns ɪf hi wɪʃəz tə kro||

ɪt ɪz ɪligḷ tə mɪsprənauns arkənsɔ ɪn ðæt stet||

barbɚz ɪn wɔtɚlu nəbræskə ɚ fɚbɪdn̩ baɪ lɔ tə ɪt ʌnjənz bətwin sɛvn̩ e ɛm n̩d sɛvən pi ɛm||

ɪn rʌmfɚd men ɪts əgɛnst ðə lɔ tə baɪt jɚ lændlɔrd||

ɪn siætḷ jə kænt kɛrɪ ə kənsild wɛpn̩ ðæt ɪz mɔr ðn̩ sɪks fit ɪn lɛŋkθ||

ɪn dænvḷ pɛnsəlvenjə ɔl faɪr haɪdrənts mʌst bi tʃɛkt wʌn aur bɪfɔr ɔl faɪrz||

ɪn lɛbənn̩ tɛnəsi ə hʌzbn̩d kænt kɪk ɪz waɪf aut v bɛd| ivn̩ ɪf hɚ fit ɚ kold| bət ə waɪf kn̩ kɪk ɚ hʌzbn̩d aut əv bɛd æt ɛni taɪm wɪðaut gɪvɪn ə rizn̩||

tæksɪ draɪvɚz ɪn sprɪŋfild mæsətʃusəts ar fɚbɪdn̩ tə mek lʌv ɪn ðə frʌnt sits əv tæksɪkæbz durɪŋ wɚkn̩ aurz||

ɪn vɚmant ɪts əgɛnst ðə lɔ tə hwɪsḷ ʌndɚwɔtɚ||

aur θæŋks tə dɪk haɪmənz "ðə trɛntn̩ pɪkḷ ɔrdɪnəns n̩d ʌðɚ bonhɛd lɛdʒəsleʃn̩"| stivn̩ grin prɛs| naɪntin sɛvn̩tɪ sɪks||

Index